G000153769

WILD CARD

For lovely Ella Rose — so lovely to meet you at the glorious LSMT!

HOW I LEARNED TO BE A FRIEND, HAVE A FRIEND & FINALLY LOVE MY BIRTHDAY

I hope you'll have fun reading WILD CARD!

WILD CARD

MARTIN MILNES

Thanks for a great lecture!

Best Wishes always,

Martin

Pass The Baton!

First published 2020

by Zuleika Books & Publishing

Thomas House, 84 Eccleston Square
London, SW1V 1PX

Copyright © 2020 Martin Milnes

The right of Martin Milnes to be identified
as author of this work has been asserted in
accordance with sections 77 and 78 of the
Copyright, Designs and Patents Act 1988.

All rights reserved. No part of this book may be
reprinted or reproduced or utilized in any form or by any
electronic, mechanical, or other means, now known or
hereafter invented, including photocopying and recording,
or in any information storage or retrieval system, without
permission in writing from the publishers.

British Library Cataloguing in Publication Data

A catalogue record for this book is
available from the British Library

ISBN: 978-1-9161977-2-5

Designed by Euan Monaghan
Printed in England

For my parents,
Alan and Pauline Milnes,
with love and thanks for everything

MY DREAM

The other night, from cares exempt,
I slept – and what d'you think I dreamt?
I dreamt that somehow I had come
To dwell in Topsy-Turveydom!

W.S. Gilbert, *The Bab Ballads*

For, look you, there is humour in all things, and
the truest philosophy is that which teaches us
to find it and to make the most of it.

W.S. Gilbert, *The Yeomen of the Guard*

'This the autumn of our life,
This the evening of our day'

The Yeomen of the Guard

Monday 4 August 2014

The tiny ancient lady was sitting bolt upright at a small round wooden card table. By the electric fireplace, her husband dozed content, a glass of white wine within easy reach of his grasp. In the kitchen, a Filipino lady cleared away the engraved silver cutlery – which had originally belonged to the mother of the ancient lady. Across the years, the monogramed silverware had been used at soirees attended by the famous and the infamous, for through the doors of this hostess had passed the greatest artistes and intellectuals of the modern Western world. But now decades had passed, and the only person left alive to tell the tale of those halcyon days was the hostess herself. And at that very moment she was making a highly important decision on which rested the outcome of the entire evening – what was she going to discard? The queen of hearts or the ace of diamonds?

'Aw, *shit!*'

'Take your time,' I reassured her. There were certain rules we always played by. One was that Ginny had all the time in the world to decide what she was going to discard, as she insisted this must be thought through very carefully. Another rule was that, when it was my hand, I had to discard as quickly as possible, otherwise she got irritated and impatient as hell. Finally, she was ready.

'Queen of hearts.' And with that she threw the card onto the pile in the centre of the table.

No one in the world, outside of her closest friends, had even heard of our card game. 'Posso' was the exclusive property of Ginny's inner circle. It had been brought to her years ago by Alfred, who in turn had learned it from a group of Franciscan nuns in California. One of them, Sister Ruth, had always brought a gun with her to the card table. I thanked my lucky stars that no firearms lay within Ginny's reach, for this normally demure and co-quettish maid would happily have spilt blood in the name of Posso if necessary.

'More wine!' cried her husband. 'I'm getting dehydrated!'

Lenny chose to do little these days apart from sit by the fire and drink wine. At the age of ninety-four, for his own sake, he was often encouraged to be a little more active… but persuading him to exercise was easier said than done. However, I couldn't help but think that at his grand age he'd more than earned the right to do as he pleased. He'd escaped from Dunkirk – on his own, abandoned by his commanding officer, left behind after the official evacu-ation. Four years later he returned to reclaim the French beaches on D-Day as a Squadron Leader of the Royal Air Force. He'd witnessed horrors that were still fresh in his mind more than seventy years on. So, I imagined he was entitled to a glass of wine.

However, for the good of their health, a compromise had been reached, about which both Ginny and Lenny were blissfully unaware. Tracy in the kitchen, on doctor's orders, had gradually been watering down their wine. The elderly couple now unwittingly had the best of both worlds – they weren't denied their enjoyment, but nor were they at risk either. And they'd grown accustomed to the taste.

One evening a few weeks previously I went into the kitchen to chat to Tracy, leaving behind my own glass of un-watered wine in the lounge – which Ginny picked up by accident, believing it was hers. A disgusted voice – still loud enough to reach the back of the gallery in a Broadway theatre, unamplified – rang throughout the apartment.

'Ugh! What's *this?* This isn't wine! Send it back!'

'I'm discarding the five of clubs,' I imparted slowly, 'and I'm taking a jack of diamonds.'

'Posso?'

'*Si.*'

Ginny greedily grasped my discarded card and placed it carefully in line with her others, the identity of which she was jealously guarding. All her cards were clustered in a curved wooden holder on the table in front of her. 'Bloody arthritis' made holding the cards difficult, not to mention, occasionally, painful.

Tracy came in and topped up Lenny's glass, walking past the only other occupant of the room, Marilyn Monroe. The life-sized cardboard cut-out of Lenny's ex-girlfriend had been presented to him as a birthday gift by his children, and she now lived with us just inside the doorway of the lounge. Ginny had once made a movie with Marilyn, before her co-star hit the big time. Ginny was from Broadway. Marilyn was a starlet, and not an entirely experienced one. After their first scene together, Ginny went home and reported to her then-husband, 'She can't act her way out of Grand Central station.'

Lenny's eyes always lit up, impishly, at the mention of Marilyn Monroe. He'd repeated to me his favourite stories about her many times, but when pressed for further information always drew a gentlemanly blank.

'Times long gone,' he replied as he raised the glass to his lips.

Ginny picked up a joker victoriously.

'I've got the wild card! Goody! So! Now I take another.'

As Ginny made her time-consuming decision about what to do next, out of the window of the fourth-floor flat I could see the neighbouring apartment block. A lady was lighting a candle and placing it in her window. Over the next few minutes more candles appeared in windows the entire length of the street. It was a clear dark night and the flickering orange flames dazzlingly illuminated the black summer night sky.

And then I realised… today marked the centenary of the outbreak of the Great War. A commemorative service had just taken place at Westminster Abbey, and now across Britain candles were being lit to remember the countless millions mercilessly slaughtered across front lines the world over, exactly a century ago.

Ginny didn't notice the candles. She was concentrating on winning the hand. But I was awestruck by the situation before me. The world at large was remembering the forgotten masses – faceless and nameless men without number – which had been lost for a hundred years.

The lady sitting opposite me, who was now beating me at cards and had correctly predicted the outcome of *Deal or No Deal* on television just that afternoon, pre-dated the Great War by six months. When she was born into Old Southern luxury on 17 February 1914, the cataclysmic events which would alter the course of history were yet to take place.

'I feel no pain, oh mother dear,
But oh, I am so dry.
Connect me to the brewery
And leave me there to die!'

Lenny was chanting familiar words – he recited them at least three times a day. But he probably didn't recognise the significance of the utterance that night. Great War troops had written those parody lyrics – fitting the tune of 'My Love is Like a Red, Red Rose' – to divert their attention from the horrors around them in the trenches. Lenny was born a year after the Great War had ended, but his war record and adventures between 1939 and 1945 was testament to the extraordinary achievements of a re-markable man.

There was living history in this apartment. And I had been welcomed into its world and embraced into the lives of two of the most incredible people I had ever known – or indeed, ever will. When I'd met them three and a half years previously, my life had sunk to its lowest ebb. But the unique occupants of that fourth-floor flat in London had touched my soul. Although they didn't know it, my elderly companions were the guardian angels who would ultimately give me the strength to turn my life around.

There were others too. For Ginny and Lenny were not alone in extending a guiding hand. Amongst them – the star whose heart was first to be 'blessed with the sound of music'; a pistol-wielding femme fatale; a sultry vamp who had famously and seductively 'smoked'; and a band of men to whom it was not only I who owed a debt, but the entire world – The Few.

And there were still more. All of them great, all of them blessed by humility, kindness and generosity. As they approached the ends of their lives, those who had lived and loved through the golden years of the twentieth century helped a lost young man, out of his time, find his way slowly but surely across the jungle of the modern world. And eventually he was able to repay their kindness and belief by passing on their wisdom to yet an even younger generation.

The times we shared together were filled with discovery, joy, sadness and loss – but above all love, inspiration and laughter. The following pages are filled with the names and memories of people whom, in all probability, you may never have heard of… but perhaps you might like to.

This is our story.

PART ONE

CHAPTER ONE

'Yet, if we go by birthdays…'

The Pirates of Penzance

September 2017

I'd always hated birthdays. I always thought that every-body I knew would have somewhere far more exciting to go than to head out celebrating with me. In fact, I'd actively *not* done anything for my birthday for many years to save the potential embarrassment of issuing invitations and having no one turn up.

Stiofan knew and understood my reasons. He was the best friend who knew me inside out… and was able to quote, word for word, virtually all my 'anecdotes'. It was the most bizarre but beautiful pairing of 'besties'.

Stiofan was a former catwalk model whose hair and eyebrows had once been insured, respectively, by two of the leading fashion brands in the world. He'd juggled that with becoming a go-to Gilbert and Sullivan baritone… a career avenue which, as an untrained singer, he'd stum-bled into much to his utter bemusement. Currently, he was making his reputation as one of London's top por-trait photographers. His musical world was that of Amy Winehouse and Whitney Houston, and his knowledge of film was purely contemporary.

I, meanwhile, was a Renaissance man. I'd worshipped Gilbert and Sullivan since the age of six (when I'd received, at my own request, a video of *The Gondoliers* for my birthday). And I was now forging a highly individual career path as one half of a West End musical theatre duo. My musical world was pre-1970, and I knew virtually nothing about any celebrity who'd risen to prominence during my own lifetime.

One night, during Stiofan's modelling period, a friend informed us:

'I heard that Rihanna's legs are insured.'

'So were Betty Grable's,' I added helpfully.

'So is my hair,' said Stiofan. There was an awkward pause.

'Well,' I countered, 'that's somewhat indicative of all our personalities.'

'Darling,' Stiofan said with a chuckle afterwards, 'I love you. You're so weird.'

'Thank you, darling.'

'No. You really are! But that's why I love you!'

'I love you too!' I told him. 'You see, you're the only friend I have who's under ninety!'

The last comment was an exaggeration. But not as wild as some might think.

Life had been ticketyboo for a long and happy period… but even so, because of unpleasant memories, I still harboured a horror of issuing birthday invitations. Therefore, Stiofan insisted on taking me out to dinner for my thirty-first… I much preferred a quiet intimate evening to a crazy rave.

'Come 'ere, darling,' said Stiofan, giving me a hug at the Italian restaurant. 'Happy birthday!'

Not long afterwards the phone rang.

'Oh… my *gosh!*' ballyhooed my bubbly young friend Charlie. 'That was just…'

'Brilliant?'

'Fab! *The* best show ever!'

Charlie and his friends Jay and Ben had just left the National Theatre having seen Stephen Sondheim's musical *Follies*. I'd originally met the boys when I'd lectured at their drama school on the history of musical theatre, and I was delighted that my passion for the subject seemed to inspire them. Ben had even come up to me afterwards and said:

'Before I met you, I was like: hate "legit"! Love "contemporary"! Ya know, like *Dear Evan Hansen* and stuff! But now that I've met you, I, like, wanna do *The Desert Song!*'

'Get them over here!' Stiofan instructed, and before I knew it the boys had joined us. Three more chairs were found whilst Stiofan faithfully ordered another bottle of Prosecco.

I was loving my birthday.

'Oh gosh!' gushed a sparkling Charlie. 'The lady who sang "I'm Still Here"! She was…'

'Sensational?' I offered.

'Yes! Fab!'

'That's my favourite song in the show,' I told the boys.

'Why that one?'

'Well, I've known a few people in my life who you might say somewhat personify it.'

'What do you mean?' asked Jay.

'Tell them about who you used to live with!' said Stiofan, grinning ear to ear, knowing exactly what I'd say next.

'Ohhh, they don't want to hear about *that*…'

'Hear what?' asked Ben.

'Well…'

From the corner of my eye I saw Stiofan beaming. He'd heard these stories a million times before. He could also anticipate the very moment I'd look up, mid-anecdote, and feign concern for my audience: 'Oh – tell me to shut up if I'm boring you!' But fortunately, my devoted friends wanted to hear more.

The boys had no idea that these memories had shaped the person they were talking to. And they certainly didn't realise why this night had suddenly become so very special.

Because it hadn't always been this way.

* * *

Birthdays. When anybody at school had a birthday, their friends always made a great fuss. Cards were given, gifts were brought in and the weekend before the big day there would always, of course, be a party.

Great planning would go into these parties – the timing of your friends' arrival, the smuggling of alcohol into the house, deciding who was 'sleeping over', and indeed the 'games' to be played. Spin the Bottle and Truth or Dare ensured a healthy amount of snogging took place, to be gossiped about at school. It was the early 2000s and teenagers texted constantly about their birthdays. Birthday parties were something everybody loved… so I gathered.

Unfortunately, I never really found out. Because, sadly, I was the kid who never got invited. But they'd never have guessed that I cared. Birthday parties? Oh, I was too busy to have attended anyhow – even if I'd been asked. I had so much to do, you see! Why, I was out rehearsing at least four nights a week. Oh, dear me, I had no time for birthday parties! Which is why, of course, I would never have found time to host one of my own either.

It was easier to adopt that attitude rather than let them see how I really felt. Permanent exclusion does little for one's confidence. But I'd be damned if I let them have an inkling.

It was the same with 'teacher training days'. Kids would meet up and go to the cinema, or hang out in town, or go to each other's houses whilst Mum and Dad were at work.

Those were the days I spent at home, by myself.

And exam results day – that dreaded morning in August when you went into school to discover your fate. Friendship groups would always plan a party afterwards… it was an excuse to go out and get drunk.

Everyone arrived in their nervous little huddles – trembling whilst handed their envelopes. And then a short while later everyone left – in their now joyous little huddles – clutching their precious pieces of paper and bounding down the lane, whooping.

I hadn't been scared about the exam results. I just felt crushed because nobody wanted my company. I left school quietly, by myself, got picked up by my mum (who'd been sitting in the car, waiting), and driven home.

School is an environment where everyone must 'fit in'. I'd observed many nice children submit to the expectations of more dominant kids, bending to their will. Teenage yes-men to those trendy leaders of the pack. But then they fitted in! As long as they continued to please everybody, they belonged.

I wanted to fit in alright – but I was a failure in my relationships in school. The vast majority had no interests other than getting drunk and getting laid. And through no lack of trying, I just found nothing remotely exciting about TV soaps, Z-list celebrities and contemporary pop culture. It left me completely cold – and with good reason: it paled in comparison to the world I'd discovered. But this world, I told myself, was beyond my reach. For, as one of my favourite movies so aptly described…

'Look for it only in books, for it is no more than a dream remembered.
A Civilisation gone with the wind…'

* * *

'I learned a new word today,' I told my mother.

'Oh, really?' she asked, whilst distracted by tasks. 'What was that?'

'Nymphomaniac.'

At nine years old I'd been reading the autobiography of Myrna Loy, the glamorous 'perfect wife' in 1930s MGM movies. But prior to this metamorphosis, she'd served a cinematic apprenticeship playing villainous Asian vamps. In *The Mask of Fu Manchu* (1932), Myrna Loy portrayed, in her own words, a 'sadistic nympho-maniac' who utters 'gleefully suggestive sounds' whilst having a beautiful young man tied down and whipped for her pleasure. I had no idea what a nymphomaniac was, so thanks to Myrna Loy I went and looked it up in the dictionary, before informatively reporting the results to my parents.

BBC2 and Channel 4 broadcast vintage movies as a matter of course – sheer heaven for a precocious young movie buff! I'd set the video to record and raced home from school every day to devour a new old film.

The movies were my salvation and my passion. Here was unbelievable glamour – wit – imagination! A beautiful glossy black and white or Technicolor universe in which everyone was accepted, and everything always turned out alright.

I was developing an old head on young shoulders. I wanted to be just like my friends – and my friends were the movie stars. To say this exposure at such a young age was character-defining is an understatement. At the age of six I sprinkled movie dialogue into everyday conversation. One day I proclaimed to a friend in an American accent, 'Gee, Sammy – you're a pal!'

Sammy looked at me, uncomprehending. Had I said something wrong? I couldn't have. I'd said the most natural thing in the world. After all, it's what Gene Kelly said to his pal Frank Sinatra in *Anchors Aweigh*! And didn't everyone talk like that?

I couldn't understand why I left those six-year-olds so utterly bewildered. My abiding memory of infant school is standing by myself in the bottom corner of the playground in a grey duffle coat, white balaclava and mittens. And I remember telling myself, everyone must think, *Oh, Martin must be playing with someone else.*

But at least, every night, I could lose myself in that safe, comforting world of yesteryear. The stars were there for me, no matter what.

It began in Woolworths in Sutton Coldfield, age four. I was allowed a new video as a 'treat'. Browsing the shelves, I ignored the children's films... but caught sight of something truly magical. On the cover of one particular VHS was a purple banner, adorned with the logo of a roaring lion: 'MGM MUSICALS'. The photograph depicted a man dancing on a heathered hill with a beautiful brunette: Gene Kelly and Cyd Charisse in *Brigadoon*.

Don't ask me why I wanted *that* video but, somehow, I knew I *had* to have it – so after persuading my surprised mother that I was in earnest, *Brigadoon* it was.

It was magnetising. Beautiful people sang and danced in an enchanted world; my young eyes had beheld nothing more beguiling than Kelly and Charisse roaming the highlands of Scotland. Forget children's television and contemporary cartoons – this was what I wanted to see.

Pocket money was saved to buy *Singin' in the Rain, An American in Paris, Seven Brides for Seven Brothers, The Pirate, Easter Parade*. I wanted to be just like Ann Miller performing 'Shaking the Blues Away'.

At the age of seven, in Santa's grotto, I was placed upon the knee of a man wearing a long white beard.

'Ho, ho, ho! And what would *you* like for Christmas?'

'I'd like a video called *Show Boat*.'

Other children idolised the Spice Girls, Take That and Boyzone. My heroes were Clark Gable, Jean Harlow, Katharine Hepburn, Jeanette MacDonald, Cary Grant...

My bedroom became a museum. Movie books, posters, scrapbooks, postcards, vintage fan magazines, framed cigarette cards. Much of this came from Sheringham in North Norfolk, my family's annual holiday destination, where the owners of antique shops, flea markets and second-hand bookstores knew me well.

Norfolk also provided theatre: in the annual Cromer Pier *Seaside Special* I saw the last of the great British variety acts. And at Sheringham Little Theatre an old-fashioned rep company performed those old-fashioned comforting well-made plays: *Charley's Aunt,* interchangeable Agatha Christie 'whodunnits' and Noël Coward drawing-room comedies. To me this world seemed wonderful and natural… and I couldn't understand why other children didn't thrive on it too.

The world of yesteryear was more vivid to me than the current day – but even then, I realised it was fading, and therefore something to be treasured. I was nine when Dorothy Lamour passed away. At school I told everyone, 'Sorry if I'm a bit quiet today, you see my favourite film star's just died.' And when Shirley Temple turned seventy in 1998, I stood up and announced her birthday in the school assembly.

I wanted to share my all-consuming passion with everybody – even if the kids hadn't a clue about Old Hollywood – or indeed the *Carry On* films. In creative writing classes, my teacher eventually asked me to stop using the phrases 'Cor blimey!', ''Ere, stop messin' about' and 'Oh, hello!'

One night I had to go home with two brothers who lived nearby as Mum couldn't pick me up from school. I'd told the boys about Barbara Windsor's bikini flying free in *Carry On Camping* and all the other 'boobs' flashed throughout the film. The brothers became lustily excited.

I think they expected a porno – but what they got was Terry Scott and Betty Marsden squabbling on a tandem. I had to go home before we even reached the famous bikini scene… and wasn't ever invited back.

At home, I even took to my typewriter (yes, typewriter) and wrote a screenplay called *Carry On Kids*, announcing to my Year Four classmates that we'd go to Pinewood Studios to make the film, co-starring Jim Dale. Nothing came of my ambitions, but for a brief and wonderful time, 'casting' my classmates in *Carry On Kids* ensured my wild popularity. I was soon, however, back to the bottom of the playground.

But finally, there was hope – a junior school disco! I couldn't have been more excited. I'd seen so many 'high school dances' in movie musicals and therefore knew just what to expect. Everybody would sing and dance in unison, like the kids in the Mickey Rooney and Judy Garland films! I put on my jazz shoes in preparation for the wild high kicks which were bound to occur and couldn't wait for everyone to start throwing themselves around the room doing Jerome Robbins choreography and yelling 'Mambo!' like I'd seen in *West Side Story*.

I left that night knowing the precise definition of the term 'wallflower'. I'd spent my entire evening standing alone against the wall bars. No one had approached me, and the only familiar track played by the DJ had been a medley from *Grease*… a movie I couldn't abide. It wasn't a patch on *Road to Morocco*.

* * *

I'd just turned six when I made my stage debut in an amateur production of *South Pacific*. A few months later I was enlisted as a miniature dragoon guard in *Patience* – carrying a flagpole twice my height – by the local Gilbert and Sullivan society.

I'm afraid I was rather precocious – always running centre stage to sing my heart out with something from G&S or MGM. I must have been the sort of child that adults want to either kiss or kill. I developed a fan base of little old ladies who never missed a G&S show – they looked forward to my moments as a tiny midshipman, Lord High Drummer Boy or pint-sized pirate. There must have been plenty of others who found me nauseously irritating and probably worthy of a good throttle! But I couldn't have been happier – the stage was where I was comfortable – where I belonged.

However, in all these shows, I was a child making guest appearances with adult companies. There were no like-minded kids with whom to connect, and when I tried to tell my schoolmates about my latest 'rehearsals' I was met with vacant stares. So, age eleven I joined a youth theatre in the hope that at last I might have like-minded friends. In *Sweet Charity* I was a very small Big Daddy – and 'Rhythm of Life' tore the place down.

But the social effort proved frustrating. Like Mickey and Judy, I was there to 'put on a show'... what could possibly more be more exciting? But most others were only interested in having a laugh – to them the rehearsal breaks were more fun than rehearsals themselves. During those wretched periods when they ran out on the playing fields or went to the shop across the road, I retreated to the safety of a chair and a book... aware of the sniggers and whispers which, on the surface, I ignored. Inside, I was hurting.

What I wanted was a friend. Someone who'd really understand and share my passion. And who could possibly understand me better, I thought, than someone who'd actually been there – in Old Hollywood? Maybe, I told myself, it might not be impossible to reach that world after all. I began writing letters...

Whenever movie stars appeared in London's West End, I sent fan mail. Charlton Heston and his wife Lydia Clarke posted me an autographed flyer for their play *Love Letters* at the Haymarket. From Kitty Carlisle Hart, who appeared with the Marx Brothers in *A Night at the Opera*, I received a glossy black-and-white signed photo.

And as for MGM's Howard Keel... well I knew he'd be a nice man! I wrote and asked whether he'd like to visit me at home and then come into school. Mr Keel was indeed a nice man. He sent back an autograph with his hand-written regrets that he was 'straight back to the USA for another concert'.

So for me it was back to the junior school playground... and then the senior schoolyard. At breaks and lunch, I tagged along with a group of teenagers who begrudgingly accepted me in their midst. I suppose I was a kind of 'court jester'... but I wasn't tolerated for my wit. Deep down I knew I was a figure of fun. Insignificant and unwanted.

But I used my talent to fight back. In school concerts, assemblies and shows I sang, did comedy routines and generally astounded teachers and pupils with no-holds-barred bravado performances. However good or bad they were, these performances were certainly larger than life!

Age fifteen, I decided to emulate Broadway impresario Florenz Ziegfeld with my own variety spectacular – *The Aldridge School Follies*. I went to the teachers in charge of putting on the shows. They told me they weren't interested – it couldn't be done. So, I went ahead and did it myself. After all, Mickey and Judy 'put on a show' all the time… so why couldn't I?

But in any Mickey–Judy film there's always a villain to stop the 'kids', and in this instance it was one of my teachers. He did everything conceivable to sabotage the production. I didn't let him win.

The victorious Martin Milnes that everyone saw the night of *The Aldridge School Follies* was confident, unstoppable and entirely self-assured. I gave the cast a pre-show pep talk declaring that men 'shall think themselves accursed they were not here!' Even those from the alleged friendship group who cold-shouldered me couldn't help but applaud.

But when the show was over – and it was back to the schoolyard – their opportunity emerged to reclaim superiority. Everyone received their invitations and planned their birthday parties in front of me, outlining every detail of how 'cool' it was going to be; a silent acknowledgement that I was not invited. The blatant snub hurt. And the following Monday morning the party was all they talked about.

I had enough strength of character to stand up to any blockade in my professional path. But offstage I was fragile. I did not 'belong' anywhere at school, and there were plenty of people prepared to make sure that I realised it. But I didn't have the strength to stand up and tell them to shove off – yet.

I was quirky, I was spotty, I was gawky, and – the worst of all crimes at school – different. It takes strength to be different. To survive, I decided to simply accept the fact that whilst I could dazzle the world from the stage, having real friends in real life *off* stage was probably just something that would never happen. Not to me. And for a very long time I believed that. Like Bette Davis in *Now, Voyager* I told myself 'don't let's ask for the moon...'

CHAPTER TWO

'I write letters blatant'

The Gondoliers

The snubs continued into sixth form. I tried to ignore them as best I could… but prior to my final academic year, I had a rude awakening. I was in hospital for quite a serious operation on my jaw. Although my friends knew I was undergoing treatment, I received absolutely no contact. Not even a text message.

As I lay in quite considerable physical pain, I felt rejected at first. Then I felt anger. But I channelled my emotions into inner strength. Eventually I concluded: Fuck them! I'd show them! There was a life beyond the school walls.

So, I caught the train to High Wycombe for singing lessons…

Elen Môn Wayne was the first of my mentor figures. I wouldn't have had half the career I've enjoyed if it weren't for Elen's indispensable guidance. As well as being a tutor, Elen became a great friend, confirming in my young mind that I appeared to be happiest – and most at ease – around older people.

Elen lived in nearby Walsall, but when she joined the original cast of *Jerry Springer: The Opera* at the National

Theatre, she and her husband Phil moved to High Wycombe. Elen was too good a friend and tutor to lose – so I took myself on day trips down south.

Meanwhile, *Jerry Springer: The Opera* became a seminal show in my life. A few weeks after my jaw op, Mum, Dad and I went to see Elen in the West End transfer. The hilarious and unashamed irreverence was *exactly* what I needed at that moment in time. Who, I decided, gave a 'fucking fuck' (as the show said) what the school kids thought? I'd do everything in my power to get into drama school – and then eventually end up in a West End show!

Like all teenagers who aspired to be in the West End, there was one musical which – at that time – I revered: *Les Misérables.* Therefore, when a golden opportunity unexpectedly presented itself, I couldn't have been more excited…

One Day More at Symphony Hall in Birmingham featured numbers from all the musicals by Alain Boublil and Claude-Michel Schönberg. For weeks a scratch choir of enthusiastic Midlanders rehearsed in a church in Walsall ready for a workshop with *Les Mis* composer himself, Claude-Michel Schönberg. It seemed implausible that Mr Schönberg would travel to somewhere as dingy as Walsall to put an amateur choir through its paces… but nevertheless, remarkably, there he was!

I was seventeen years old – with braces, glasses and gawky mannerisms. I was the epitome of the archetypal geek and lived up to expectations. I made sure that I arrived at the rehearsal super early to catch the maestro alone. When I saw him make his way to the gents, I hung around outside until I heard the loo flush. And as he emerged out into the corridor, I pounced.

'Mr Schönberg,' I gushed, my heart pounding. 'I was wondering if I could ask you something? I'm auditioning for performing arts establishments later this year, and one of the songs I'm auditioning with is 'Martin Guerre'!'

Poor Monsieur Schönberg couldn't escape – he said nothing, but I had his attention – and here was my chance to impress him!

'I was wondering,' I continued, 'did you have anything particular in mind when you wrote that song?' The tempo of my speech began to increase with my pulsating palpitations. 'What's going through the mind of Martin when he's singing this? Is there any particular style for it to be sung? Is there anything you specifically like to have portrayed when people are singing this song?'

Mr Schönberg looked at me blankly for a moment. Finally, he replied in a heavy French accent: 'No.'

I've never asked a pretentious question since. But Mr Schönberg took it all in good humour, and when choir members asked for a demonstration of his piano skills, he let me sing the opening of 'Bring Him Home' to his accompaniment.

And, of course, one thing in this world always leads to another...

A member of the *One Day More* creative team presented a Sunday night musical theatre radio programme. He announced a special upcoming episode dedicated to Broadway composer Richard Rodgers, featuring interviews with the composer's daughter, Mary Rodgers, and an actress named Jean Bayless, who in 1961 created the role of Maria in the original West End production of *The Sound of Music*.

I decided to write letters to both Mary Rodgers and Jean Bayless, which were duly passed on at the radio station. I asked for their advice about a career in the theatre – and to my surprise, each sent warm responses.

Mary Rodgers was not only a great champion of the Rodgers and Hammerstein legacy, but she was also an author in her own right. She composed the Broadway musical *Once Upon a Mattress* and penned the children's novel *Freaky Friday*. Her son was Adam Guettel, composer of *The Light in the Piazza*.

I received a package from New York, emblazoned with the stationery of Mary Rodgers Guettel. As well as a charming letter, she'd also sent a book stuffed with invaluable interviews – with Stephen Sondheim, Hal Prince, her father and others – about the art of auditioning.

I was overwhelmed that Mary Rodgers had taken such time and effort on my behalf. She was Broadway royalty – and even though we'd never met, her act was far kinder than any I'd received from my apparent school friends! I wrote back thanking her for the book, which proved to be a useful aid. In the years afterwards, whenever I had professional updates of note, I let Mrs Rodgers Guettel know, and she replied with very kind personal messages of congratulations.

Sadly, Mary Rodgers died in 2014, two years before my first visit to New York – and I regret missing the chance to thank her in person. But she planted a seed in my mind which continued to grow: if, one day, in years to come, I reached a position in my industry where young people wished to ask for my advice, I'd remember the generosity of Mary Rodgers – and try to be as encouraging to others as she'd been to me.

But it was the reply from Jean Bayless which was to change the course of my life…

When Jean Bayless was interviewed on the Richard Rodgers programme, I learned that by the time she auditioned for the role of Maria in *The Sound of Music* she'd achieved success both in the West End and on Broadway, where she'd taken over the lead role of Polly Browne in *The Boy Friend* from Julie Andrews.

After numerous recall auditions in London for *The Sound of Music*, a telegram arrived from New York advising the production team 'KEEP BAYLESS HOT'. Jean was then flown to America where she auditioned for Richard Rodgers himself. Listening at home in my bedroom to the broadcast, I was fascinated:

I was on the stage of the theatre on Broadway rehearsing with the pianist and I didn't realise that Richard Rodgers was actually there – in the auditorium! Then he appeared and walked down the aisle and said, 'Jean! You are *our Maria in London! So just sing the song, will you? And then we can go and have some lunch!' So, I sang 'The Sound of Music' for him like I'd never sung it before! And I thought we were going for lunch at the Waldorf Astoria – but we ended up in a hamburger joint around the corner – and I had a hamburger with Richard Rodgers! I've* never *enjoyed a hamburger more!*

Several tracks from the original London cast recording of *The Sound of Music* were played during the programme – and I was quite genuinely captivated by Jean Bayless's performance. She had a beautiful lyric soprano of great charm, with impeccable diction. Each of her songs was exquisitely characterised, and her effervescent talent shone through the recording.

And if I'd found the concept of Claude-Michel Schönberg visiting Walsall incomprehensible, it seemed even more bizarre to learn that Jean Bayless – who was by now a legend in my eyes – didn't live in a glamorous far-off city like London, New York or LA – she lived half an hour from me – in Birmingham!

I received a note in the mail, with a Birmingham postmark, in elaborately theatrical italic handwriting: *'Dear Martin – Call me. Let's meet and have a chat...'*

On the phone, I found it hard to believe that Jean Bayless herself was talking to me. In a frivolous soprano voice, she asked to meet at her son's jewellery shop on Corporation Street. After writing fan letters to stars all my life, this invitation was every dream come true!

My gran, now aged ninety-two, offered invaluable advice: 'Buy her some flowers. When visiting a lady, you must always call with flowers.' So, armed with carnations and roses, on Tuesday 19 April 2005, I wended my excited way on the bus into central Birmingham...

Roberts Jewellers was a theatrical-looking establishment, with lights around the sign above the door, not unlike bulbs around a dressing-room mirror. I nervously walked into the shop through an open archway from the street and, clutching my carnations, approached the counter.

'Oh, thank you very much!' said the shop assistant, eyeing the flowers.

'Oh! Er... good afternoon,' I stuttered. 'I have an appointment to meet Miss Jean Bayless here at 4 p.m.'

'Oh, are those for me?' asked another shop assistant, making a beeline. 'You shouldn't have!'

'He's here to see Mrs J,' said the first lady.

'Daniel!' the other cried, peering down a flight of stairs. 'Young man here with flowers to see Mrs J!' But 'Daniel' did not emerge.

'I'm Sonia,' said the first lady. 'And she's on her way, but it's not quite four yet. You can have a look round inside or there's a bench outside if you'd like it.'

I was admiring the window display when a jolly-looking man strutted down the archway.

'Are you the young man who's come to meet my mother?'

'Oh, er, yes! At 4 p.m.!'

'Come on in,' said Daniel Johnson. 'I won't have you waiting outside! Here,' he said, gesturing to an elaborate seat, 'you can have the special director's chair! And when she walks in, we all shout "We love you, Jeanie!"'

At 4 p.m. on the dot, a glamorous redhead in high heels briskly entered the shop and flitted towards the counter.

'We love you, Jeanie!' chorused the employees. But this couldn't possibly be Jean Bayless – she looked far too young! Daniel gestured towards me, and, as the lady approached, I rose to greet her.

'How do you do, Miss Bayless?'

At last I was able to hand over the flowers. 'Oh, thank you!' she cried. 'Look at my flowers, everyone! Martin got them for me!'

The shop returned to business and Jean leaned on a counter, looking me in the eye. 'Well, here we are! I could have stayed in America – but no! I was *followed* to America by a young man from Birmingham – who then wooed me and wooed me. And so, I married him! I could have stayed out there with Julie and Milly Martin… but I've never regretted it. It just shows how fate has different things in store for us!'

'Oh…' I offered quietly, not entirely sure how to reply. 'What a romantic story…'

'Oh, no!' Jean replied. 'I think it was just hormones! Those *raging* hormones of his!'

An old lady then appeared, hunched over, and started wiping down the counter with a duster. She wore a tatty, moth-eaten jumper and a Star of David diamond necklace.

'Martin,' Jean explained, 'this is Peg. She's one of our best customers. She buys lots and lots of diamonds. But she gets bored, so she comes in and cleans for us.' Jean raised her voice and leaned towards Peg's ear. 'This is Martin! He's a fan!'

'Oh,' said Peg, staring vaguely in my direction. 'What are you going to buy?'

'He doesn't have to buy *anything* here,' said Jean. 'I'm going to give him something.' Jean disappeared in the direction of a stock cabinet whilst Peg loped towards me extending her wrist, showing off a heavily laden charm bracelet.

'Do you like me bulldog?' she asked (and then asked twice again before I left two hours later). The dog's ruby eyes seemed incongruous against the rest of her shabby clothing but Peg continued cleaning as she chatted. 'Now, I don't know who you are or what you're doing here because I forget things. I came into town to buy something today. What was it? Oh, yes. A mug! Sometimes I don't come in here. But they can't sack me – because I don't work here. I just come in and clean.'The crazy set-up of madcap characters at Roberts Jewellers was like something out of a 1930s screwball comedy – and I loved it!

Jean re-emerged and presented me with a good luck charm – a little garnet elephant. She also had something else – an original black-and-white photograph of her as Maria, signed and dedicated to me – and she asked about the amateur shows I was currently rehearsing.

'Did you hear that, Peg? Martin's doing *42nd Street* at the Hippodrome!'

I was longing to ask Jean about her career – but she was asking me to sing – so I gave her an excerpt of 'Largo al factotum' from *The Barber of Seville*, right there in the shop. The customers seemed bemused. The staff seemed nonplussed. Nothing at Roberts Jewellers was out of the ordinary. Jean even joined in with the final chorus.

'I suppose I miss it really,' she sighed. 'Being there backstage and everything. And I do love singing Ivor Novello. I toured in Novello with John Hanson. Do you like Ivor Novello?'

'Yes, I do! Very much!'

'Do *you* remember Ivor Novello, Dan?' Jean asked her son as he walked by.

'Ohh,' he groaned. 'I can't forget him!'

Finally, I prised some nuggets from her past, including her training at the Italia Conti stage school: 'There were several of us there,' she remembered nostalgically. 'Me, my boyfriend Tony Newley, Nanette Newman, Milly

Martin… We did a lot of opera work. I was in the opera at Covent Garden in the children's chorus.' Then she was struck with a thought. 'The man in *Carmen!* That role would be yours!'

Gradually, sensing that I was genuinely interested, she opened up further, recalling her early courtship with her future husband, businessman David Johnson, during the 1950s.

'I have an argument with David, don't I?' she told me. 'So, I get on the phone to the War Office and ask them to send me to Korea – I want to entertain the troops. I just have to get away as I can't be anywhere near David! David phones me and says, "You can't leave! We're so in love!" But for me, that was it! We were finished! I was off! And I'm being flown over the Malaysian jungle by drunken pilots.'

Peg continued to wipe down nearby silverware, in a world of her own; Daniel was beating down the price of a watch that someone had brought in to sell.

'Then I'm in the jungle – in a truck with the comedian, his wife and an officer in the front with a long Sten gun. And there's me sitting in the back, heartbroken. The Royal Fusiliers were driving in front and behind our truck in lorries protecting us… and then suddenly, out of the blue, I hear someone yell "Ambush ahead!"'

By now, Jean was remembering the event full throttle and was back in the war zone. None of the staff batted an eye.

'The officer says, "Get on the floor of the car!" The ambush begins, shots are flying and I'm on the floor, with the comedian and his wife – and I'm weeping, "I'm never going to see David again!" The Royal Fusiliers jump out into the jungle, fight the bandits, the ambush ends and off we go to do the show! And we perform it on the back of a lorry, entertaining all these boys. The officers sat in the front, then all the sergeants…'

'Mom!' Dan suddenly interrupted, yelling across the shop, gesturing to a new customer.

'We're ridiculously short staffed at the moment,' she muttered, rolling her eyes. Breaking away from her story, Jean glided towards the counter. 'Good afternoon, sir! May I help you?'

I was speechless. Here was a *star* happily serving a customer in a jewellery shop in Birmingham! And the customer had *no* idea who was serving him – he didn't realise this lady had been shot at by bandits in the Malaysian jungle!

I learned a very valuable lesson that day – *never* take anyone at face value. You never know who they are, what they've done or what their story is.

While Jean was occupied, I wandered around the shop, admiring an ornate gold mirror on which were mounted photos of the Johnsons and their friends. I spied a signed colour film still of a face I instantly recognised from the *Carry Ons*…

'Do you know Fenella Fielding?' Jean asked me. 'Fenella comes up and sees me whenever she's at the NEC appearing at the film fair. She really is a legend, isn't she? She gets invited to all these glamorous parties. You'd like to meet Fenella, wouldn't you?'

'O-Ohh,' I stuttered. 'Yes, please!'

And at last we were able to discuss Richard Rodgers.

'He was a wonderful, *brilliant* man. I'll always be so grateful I had the chance to work with him. He held my hand at the side of the stage before I went on to sing "The Sound of Music" on opening night.' Jean's eyes glistened as she recalled it in detail. 'He walked me to the papier-mâché rock on stage and said, "Have a wonderful night, Jean. And don't pay any attention to the reviews. I haven't had a decent review since *Oklahoma!*"'

Surely enough the critics hated *The Sound of Music* – but it ran for eight years. And Jean Bayless, I later discovered, had earned personal rave reviews.

'Who came to see the show?' I asked her, my eyes pinging out on sticks.

'Well, I didn't know Noël Coward was coming,' she remembered, matter-of-factly.

This was unbelievable – how, I asked myself, could I be in a jewellery store in Birmingham hearing Jean Bayless tell a first-hand story about Noël Coward?

'After the show, I'd always take my face off and get ready again, as David and I ate out. There was a knock at the door, and my dresser answered it and said, "Miss Bayless is washing at the moment and can't see anyone," and this voice said, "I'll come back later." I asked her, "Who was that?" and she said, "Oh, I think it was Noël Coward." And I yelled, "You've turned *Noël Coward* away from my door?" So we got him back! And Gloria Swanson I was very jealous of! She was sixty then and had her ninety-year-old mother with her. She had these little gloves on and talked to David for a long time.'

This meeting was everything I'd always dreamed of my entire life. And there was more…

'One night,' Jean continued, 'David danced with Nureyev! We were in a restaurant in Soho. "I'm David," he said. "I'm Nureyev." And he took David *in his arms* and did a little waltz with him! David dined out on that for ages!'

My jaw must have been reaching the floor.

'Another night at the Grosvenor, Eartha Kitt and I were having these press photographs taken when Sammy Davis Jr forced his way in for a picture! It was terribly sad because Sammy wasn't flavour of the month. And he – Sammy Davis! – was feeling left out. I know that feeling – when you're not on top – it's a terrible business for that. It really knocks the guts out of you when someone points at you and says, "Who's that?" and then they say, "Oh, it's nobody." It's not very nice!'

Sonia rolled down the entrance shutter, whilst Daniel packed up the safe. It was time to go. As Peg continued polishing the counter, Jean asked, a little shyly, 'I wasn't too presumptuous in giving you the photograph, was I?'

'Oh no, of course not! I was going to ask for your autograph anyway, if you hadn't minded.'

Jean looked into my eyes with an expression of poignant sincerity. 'Thank you. You've really made me feel like everything was worth it. You've given me a real lift.'

As I walked back to the bus, complete with signed photograph and lucky elephant, I had a spring in my step. A star had given me her time! She'd wished me luck in my career and told me she believed in me. Jean Bayless made me more determined than ever to forget the sorrows of the schoolyard and achieve my dreams. But moreover... I had made *her* 'feel like everything was worth it'. Could it be, I suddenly wondered, that I'd made as much of a difference to Jean Bayless as she'd made to me?

CHAPTER THREE

'By a set of curious chances'

The Mikado

My singing lessons with Elen stepped up in intensity. And whilst I approached my A levels, I commenced auditions for leading UK drama schools.

I'd whittled my choices down to five institutes. My audition song was 'On the Street Where You Live', ingrained in my voice from amateur concerts; my Shakespeare monologues had been carefully rehearsed.

I was turned down by every single drama school. At three out of the five I was cut after the first-round audition. At the fourth place, I got down to the final recall – and then rejected. And at the fifth school, they gave the applicants a 'yes', 'no' or 'maybe' then and there.

'Martin!' said one of the tutors. 'We've never seen anyone like you before.'

'We're not sure what we can do with you,' added another. 'We think there's an artist in there – but we're not sure.'

'Can you come back and audition for us again?'

Well, actually, I thought, *No!* Having spent a whole day instructed in strange dramatic exercises making all kinds of weird noises, I didn't feel this was the place for me.

My parents, whilst never dictating what I should or shouldn't do, asked whether I might apply for academic university courses. Elen's husband Phil thought I should take the Oxbridge route, studying Music and joining the Footlights. My closest ally at school, Mrs Shelley, suggested the same, although she encouraged me to read English. But with an unshakeable resolve, I decided that if drama schools didn't want me, I'd simply launch myself straight into the theatrical world regardless.

It was a brave decision – although being young, I thought nothing of it. My parents supported me, and I was heartened by words in a motivational letter from a professional comedian I knew, for whom I'd made guest appearances in a couple of local shows.

The output from drama schools is appalling. They're so up themselves it's not true… While they're all in drama school learning to do something the same way, you, young man, can be out there earning money and <u>creating</u> things that they will, one day, all copy afterwards. These 'samey souls' aren't worth very much. They 'dally' and 'darling' around each other's arses and can each be put in a little box with their type and number on it.

They <u>can't</u> put you in a box, Martin; they'd need a whole bloody container for that – and they can't <u>afford</u> that. If they <u>could</u> they wouldn't know what to do with you, and, in the end, you'd be the one directing the sodding thing…

So please, <u>please</u> don't let this seeming setback worry you – actually it's a kick in the right direction in disguise… Go and celebrate keeping your identity!

I intended to follow his advice.

One day at school I had a Classics lesson with a teacher named (amusingly for a History tutor) Mr New. He and I had always got on well – when I was in Year Seven, he'd told the rest of the class to shut up and colour in maps of the Roman Empire whilst he and I chatted about Humphrey Bogart movies. Therefore, by A levels, Mr New thought nothing of me sitting in his lesson reading *The Stage* newspaper, scanning audition opportunities.

I saw a quarter-page ad for something called the Thursford *Christmas Spectacular* – billed as 'one of the largest Christmas shows in Europe'. It required a vocal ensemble of forty-four singers – and I put a star next to the advert. I knew of Thursford! Although the *Christmas Spectacular* was huge, Thursford itself was a tiny hamlet deep in rural North Norfolk, not far from Sheringham.

I had a headshot taken and put together a CV – which at this stage, of course, only listed amateur productions. I posted them with a covering letter to Thursford's artistic administrator, Colin Window. I didn't expect to hear back, assuming my CV wouldn't compare with the many professional applications. But to my surprise, I received a postal invitation to come and sing for the creative team in London...

I chose 'On the Street Where You Live' and the aria with which I'd serenaded Jean Bayless, 'Largo al factotum'. Ignorance is bliss – I am *not* a proper opera singer! But I didn't know any better at the time, so off I went to London for my first professional audition.

When I arrived at the venue, nice and early, the building appeared to be locked, so I rang the buzzer. A drag queen answered the door. A rude one.

'Yeah, whaddya want?'

'Oh! I'm here to audition for Thursford…?'

'Yeah,' she replied in a huff. 'Well, the panel are out having their lunch, and you're interrupting mine, so go away and come back in twenty minutes!' And with that she shut the door in my face. Welcome to show business!

I didn't realise at that time *why* I'd been offered the audition – it later emerged that it was through an error. When sifting applicants, Thursford's casting team had two piles of CVs on their desk – a pile of people to offer an audition and a different pile of less suitable candidates to throw into the bin. I *should* have been thrown into the bin. However, due to a lucky admin oversight, I was accidentally put on the pile of people to see.

'We didn't realise our mistake,' one of the panel told me – a long time afterwards – 'until you were standing outside, and we said, "Right, who's next?" And we looked at your CV and asked, "How the *fuck* did *this* one slip through?" Then you came in, and you opened your mouth, and we said, "Well, we don't know how he slipped through, but thank fuck he *did!*"'

Colin Window – plus Thursford's musical director Patrick Bailey and casting director Andrew Hammond – took a chance on an eighteen-year-old unknown, untried amateur. They offered me the position of Tenor Dep, which entailed covering twelve tenors, learning all their individual harmonies and movement tracks.

It was like something out of a Rooney–Garland movie. A magical show-business opportunity had fallen into my lap – and now, just like that, I was a professional! At last, I realised, I could do what I loved – and get paid for it! – with truly like-minded people. When I rang Jean Bayless, she was thrilled and asked me to send photographs whilst I was away. It had turned out to be more than just a one-off meeting at the jewellers. Jean Bayless was now my friend.

On the last day of school, with A levels completed, I left the building without regret. My salvation during sixth form had been Mrs Shelley and my A level English group. Mrs Shelley allowed me to run amok during our lessons, singing highlights from *Jerry Springer: The Opera* full blast as a light relief from Chaucer and Shakespeare.

I'd had to *make* school interesting, as it hadn't been my natural environment. But perhaps Thursford would be.

* * *

Before the Christmas contract began, I was invited to sing in Thursford's annual *Last Night of the Proms* concert. During a rehearsal break I heard a voice behind me:

'First job?'

I turned around and saw a Puck-like figure of a tenor. 'Er… Yes!'

'Oh! How did I guess?'

That night, before my professional debut, I took a moment to reflect. This was the beginning of my professional career – the turning point of my life – a moment I'd remember forever…

'Do you mind if I ask a personal question?' a young bass suddenly enquired. 'Are you gay or straight?'

I paused for a moment, taking in the young man's

startling frankness. A little nervously, I gulped and told him: 'Straight.'

'Oh, that makes four of you then!' he replied. 'Tim's straight, John's straight and Terry's straight, but I think that's all of you for Christmas this year!'

Moments later I was on stage – and my career began.

I hadn't lied when I'd said I was straight. Of course I was! Well, at least as far as I was concerned, because that's what I'd seen in the movies! But at nineteen years old I was completely devoid of any romantic or sexual experience. My first and only kiss had happened on stage in a production of the musical *Ragtime*.

Having made few friends at school – and mostly adult friends in am-dram – romantic opportunities had not presented themselves. I realised with great embarrassment that I was far behind my contemporaries.

But if there was one thing I'd learned from MGM musicals, it was that someday she'd come along – the girl I love! *On the Town* was proof that all you had to do was tap a girl on the shoulder, she'd turn around and she'd say, 'I love you!'

As I grew up, I honestly believed in this MGM dream. But on the few occasions I'd found courage to say something to a girl, my old-fashioned, self-conscious approach had been snubbed. I longed to be as masculine and virile as Rhett Butler – but was hardly Clark Gable. I thought, perhaps, I was the dapper Cary Grant or Douglas Fairbanks Jr-type. But really, I was Norman Wisdom – 'Don't laugh at me, 'cause I'm a fool.'

And as for gay men... well, I didn't really know any. There certainly hadn't been any out gay boys at school, and I'd never thought about men romantically. I just cared about my MGM sirens! I was fascinated by the *Kismet* vamp Dolores Gray and adored blonde sexpot Jean Harlow... but I really wanted to find a 'perfect wife' like Myrna Loy; or perhaps an innocent Kathryn Grayson-type; maybe even a wisecracking glamour gal like Carole Lombard. These were all my childhood celebrity crushes.

Perhaps at Thursford I'd find her. We'd snuggle down together watching Judy Garland in *Meet Me in St Louis*, and then I could introduce 'my girl' to my dearest friend, the original Maria from *The Sound of Music*...

* * *

There were a few days of music rehearsals in London before moving up to Thursford. I was so naïve that I called Colin 'Mr Window', as if I were still at school! I was the youngest singer in the cast; the average age was early to mid-thirties. I kept my head down, determined to work hard and justify the production team's faith in my appointment. Therefore, I approached each day with a solid work ethic of commitment and professionalism – something I hope I've never lost.

On site at Thursford, the fun began. I lived in a spare bedroom belonging to a farmer's family down the road from the show. On the gate they had a sign advertising horse manure for sale at 50p a bag. My landlady, Mary Lee, took good care of me, and sometimes when her horse-riding daughter Alison arrived at the front door, she asked me to hold the reins of Master Bubbles whilst she stepped inside.

One day Bubbles came through the door, poking his head into the hallway – and when Alison sharply ordered him out, I worried he'd take off at top speed, with me clinging on. John Wayne I most certainly was not!

The *Christmas Spectacular* was the brainchild of its producer and artistic director, John Cushing. He knew his audience – the show sold out twice a day, every day from mid-November to 23 December. Coachloads travelled the length and breadth of the UK to reach this tiny hamlet. It seemed that with enough imagination and drive, anything was possible. I watched and learned...

Nothing about the *Christmas Spectacular* should have worked – but somehow it did. The audience sat in a grotto with illuminated trees spread amongst the seats and hugely elaborate Christmas decorations hanging from the ceiling. The stage was 110 feet long... and attached to the stage-right side was an enormous nineteenth-century fairground ride – a Venetian Gondola Switchback (perhaps best described as a Victorian rollercoaster) which was incorporated into the show.

Everything in the *Christmas Spectacular* came out of John Cushing's head, and it ranged from the sublime – an epic Biblical staging of 'The Holy City' – to the ridiculous – dancers dressed as Little Red Monkeys running amok to Wurlitzer accompaniment. When we opened, John arranged for a canon to come backstage and bless the show, praying with the cast, and at the end of each performance, white pigeons flew from one end of the auditorium to the other as a sign of a peace.

When I asked a veteran cast member to describe the *Christmas Spectacular*, he replied, 'It's like *The Muppet*

Show, but with people.' Former production numbers had included snowmen dancing with teddy bears to the strains of 'I Know Him So Well'. In 'The Lonely Goatherd' roller-skating milkmaids had appeared with dancers dressed in goatskins. The show featured a Norfolk comedian telling jokes in his county dialect. His act usually overran by several minutes whilst the elderly audience screamed with laughter. It was the way he told 'em…

> *'Ave you seen that advert on the telly? 'Be bright, wear white at night.' Last winter, old grandfather did just that – cor, 'e looked a sight! White shoes, white socks, white trousers, white jacket. 'E'd not gone ten yards… got knocked over by a snow plough.*

National press described the *Christmas Spectacular* as 'kitsch, sentimental and deeply, deeply strange… so camp that it would have Graham Norton weeping in envy'. Long after my departure, yet another tabloid described Thursford as 'Europe's biggest – and most demented – Christmas show'.

'Demented' or not, Thursford was everything I'd seen in the movies: like being wrapped up in a real-life MGM musical. The dancing girls' costumes were every inch as glamorous as Ziegfeld's! My jaw literally dropped – it was more female flesh than I'd ever seen displayed outside of *Carry On Girls*! But I was much, much too shy to say even hello to the dancers.

To the disappointment of many, there were no young dancing boys. Most male singers were indeed gay.

'So, Martin,' one of them asked me, early in the run.

'Tell us about you. Have you got a girlfriend? Or a *boy-friend*?'

'Er, no, I haven't got a girlfriend and I definitely haven't got a boyfriend.'

'Oh! Where are you living? I'll give you a call and maybe we could go out...'

'Percy!' cried a motherly gay in a warning tone, comforting me reassuringly, 'Don't worry. I'll protect you from all these horrible homosexuals!'

Another time, one of the boys offered to help me with driving lessons.

'Oh, you can drive around the car park in my car, darling. I'm *such* a good teacher...'

'No, Tarquin!' objected my protective friend. 'He's straight... and we *know* what you do to young boys in car parks.'

* * *

Throughout the run it was invaluable experience, as dep, to perform the show from many different angles. When I wasn't on stage, I went out front and watched multiple times, observing how the production developed. I also scrutinised audience reactions – an equally important way to learn.

I always enjoyed the end of the interval, when a male singer entered with a 'beautiful assistant' to announce the winning raffle tickets. Thursford is still the only professional show I've ever known to have a raffle, and it was tradition for the MC to declare something ludicrous about his assistant: 'Jenny collects ceramic pottery, ladies and gentlemen! And it's been said she has the best jugs in Norfolk.'

When Elen came, not long before the end of the run, she said she'd seen the biggest change in me within the shortest time. I certainly felt different. And I'd learned how to deal with some tricky characters...

On 'general swing days', I had to be a different person in every single number. One tenor named Ash bamboozled me into covering him for almost everything – meaning the other boys didn't get a look-in.

'Just be aware of people taking the piss,' one of the tenors gently advised. 'I know you don't like to say no, 'cause you're a nice guy – but you *can* tell Ash no!'

The next day, Ash tried again – several times. 'Well, Ash,' I eventually retorted, 'I'd hate Colin to think you weren't earning your money by taking the *entire show* off!'

Everyone in the dressing room cheered! By December I was calling them 'a bunch of cunts' – a favourite phrase used within the cast, and one I now found the assurance to use myself.

'Oh, I love it when they fight back!' cried the Puck-like tenor who'd seen me blossom since the *Proms*.

When the run ended on 23 December it was a strange sensation. Thursford was a microcosm of every aspect of show business – and it had cocooned me in a bubble – a bubble in which everything was possible and nothing made sense. Our existence was all-consuming; quarantined, with no time off, the outside world ceased to exist. It was, to say the very least, acutely intense.

I saw cast relationships form, bloom and shatter, all within the space of a few weeks. Romantic liaisons erupted overnight – leading to high drama. Occasionally, people's worlds came crashing down about them whilst trapped inside the bubble. One of the tenors told me that a few years previously he'd broken up with his boyfriend over the phone, outside during a performance. The shingle pathway by the stage door was the only place to find phone reception, and he'd stood there shivering in the freezing December cold, amidst the chickens roaming the back yard.

'Love you!' he said, signing off. His boyfriend did not respond. Annoyed, he then asked, 'Why don't you ever say you love me too?' And then suddenly he realised. 'It's because you don't love me anymore, isn't it?' Then, late for his entrance, he ran on stage, all smiles and animated, in a ridiculous costume singing 'Snow! Snow! Snow!'

However, I couldn't have asked for a better first job – and I was extremely grateful to Colin, Patrick, and those cast members who'd truly looked out for me. I was making friends – albeit older ones – but, sadly, of course, I had not met the girl of my dreams. Despite this, Thursford proved that I could thrive in my native habitat: the theatre. I was growing as a person the whole time – and people liked me. So, I knew that someday she *would* come along, the girl I loved.

And moreover, now that I knew I wasn't eternally fated to be a complete reject, I realised it was not impossible to eventually meet a perfect friend. Someday I'd find him. A friend my own age who'd become a lifelong companion. A Morecambe to my Wise; a Laurel to my Hardy.

Until then, however, it was back to Birmingham – and the uncertainty of an actor's life. I'd had one magnificent job. But what now?

CHAPTER FOUR

'I don't think much of our profession, but, contrasted with respectability it is comparatively honest'

The Pirates of Penzance

'Red Red Wiiiiiine!' belted an out-of-tune singer, queuing in front of me. This was the first open audition I'd ever attended, and I was surrounded by a motley crew – slightly more *X Factor* than West End.

In answer to hit jukebox musicals *Mamma Mia!* (featuring the songs of ABBA) and *Jersey Boys* (featuring the songs of Frankie Valli), the Birmingham Repertory Theatre proudly announced its own jukebox spectacular: *Promises and Lies*, featuring the songs of reggae band UB40. As a publicity gimmick, the Rep advertised auditions in the local press for small roles. Star-struck Brummies arrived en masse.

I handed the casting director my headshot and CV.

'Oh,' she said, reading my latest credit. 'You've just done Thursford! You must know Wyn!'

I did indeed – Wyn Hyland, Thursford's assistant MD, had been a great supporter. I sang UB40's 'One in Ten'

– and was given a recall. In the meantime, the casting director rang Wyn, who kindly recommended me for the show. John Cushing always told his cast, 'Thursford on your CV will get you any job in the world!' Maybe he was right...

At my recall I was handed 'sides' – the theatrical term for pages of script – for a scene set in the dungeon of a dominatrix. I was reading for the role of the Adult Baby. Being familiar with *Jerry Springer: The Opera* I knew all about Adult Babies... and I remembered an interview in the book which Mary Rodgers had sent, advising actors to wholeheartedly throw themselves into cold readings, no matter how crazed the material. So, I just went for it – wailing, bawling and blubbering.

I was offered a contract to appear in *Promises and Lies*. I was the only person taken from the open audition; to my surprise, the show turned out to be quite a big deal. The cast included Olivier Award winners Clive Rowe *(Guys and Dolls)* and Paul Clarkson *(The Hired Man)* as well as David Burt, whom I'd idolised on cast albums of *Les Mis* and *Jesus Christ Superstar.*

The characters in *Promises and Lies* included a pimp, a prostitute, a junkie rent boy, a dominatrix, two nightclub bouncers, a jealous husband and a hen party. An older actor was cast as the Adult Baby, so I was assigned the roles of two younger dominatrix clients – Rope Man and Wanking Man.

As Rope Man I made my entrance suspended in mid-air strapped in a harness, wearing a gimp mask, dog collar and a pair of black rubber boxers, being whipped by the dominatrix and her apprentice, the prostitute. And whilst I was delighted to create the role of Wanking Man, I did wish to clarify a rather specific stage direction: *Wanking Man comes.* Being nineteen and frightfully innocent I asked the director, 'When it says here "Wanking Man comes"…?'

'I think he comes, mate,' he replied.

As part of the rehearsal process, we had a real dominatrix come in to show us the ropes. The cast became a little unnerved when the stage manager papered over the rehearsal-room windows to avoid prying eyes, but it was a fascinating afternoon. Mistress Karen revealed the inner workings of her industry, from genital torture to toe sucking, and gave technical advice on our onstage undertakings. A few weeks later at the press night party she rushed up to me and cried, 'Martin! You came brilliantly!'

But the critics did not enjoy *Promises and Lies*: 'After an evening in the theatre I felt like I'd been mugged.' Another concluded, 'There is zero to enjoy.' *The Daily Telegraph* judged it, 'A musical fit only for masochists… *Promises and Lies* must be the most remorselessly bleak pop-anthology musical ever staged.'

Even with a turkey that we knew would fold, the cast of twelve grew close. Clive Rowe – whom I'd long admired – was especially kind to me, and I attended rehearsals even when I wasn't called, just to watch the actors at work. Because the source material was weak, the cast had to bring far more to the piece than was on the page. I learned a helluva lot.

I almost ended up taking over the role of the junkie rent boy after the young method actor in question fell ill having slept rough several nights along Birmingham Canal. Whilst relieved that he recovered, I did miss singing the rent boy's upbeat number in the second act, just before he set off for hospital to have his arm amputated having developed a maggot-infested abscess. No musical is complete without a scene like that.

Again, I was the youngest in the cast, but my older colleagues found my quirkiness endearing.

'*What* are you reading?' asked the Adult Baby, looking at my book with surprise.

'It's the autobiography of Debbie Reynolds.'

'*Why*,' queried the junkie rent boy, 'are you reading *that?*'

'Well, because I read it before, and it was really good.'

* * *

After UB40 I managed to blag my way into an opera tour – *Tosca* and *Il Trovatore*. We rehearsed in Bradford where I was billeted in a shabby hotel, complete with drunken fistfights outside my bedroom door.

The leading man in *Trovatore* was a huge bald Russian tenor. Prior to each performance he approached me holding an old-fashioned black greasepaint stick.

'Martin!' he barked. 'You colour me in!' I used the stick like a crayon all over his scalp - which, from a distance, looked semi-passable until he started sweating profusely under the lights and the greasepaint streaked down his face.

The renowned musical director was brilliant but somewhat accident-prone. One night whilst vigorously conducting he stabbed the baton into his palm, causing it to snap and embed itself in his left hand. Continuing to conduct, he sprayed blood all over the first violins.

Another night, during the energetic aria 'Di quella pira', whilst giving an upbeat, the MD raised the baton so close to his face that it wedged itself vertically between his eye and his glasses – meaning that when he thrust his arm forward to give the next beat, the baton ripped off his spectacles. They went hurtling over the orchestra, high over the head of the Russian tenor downstage centre and landed at the feet of the Gentlemen's Chorus. He conducted the last half hour of the opera completely blind.

For a drama school reject my career was flying – but my newfound colleagues and friends were still exclusively older. And when the shows closed, I was back on my own with my parents in Birmingham. But the glamour of suddenly becoming 'a professional' did carry a certain allure for a couple of girls from my former am-dram circuit, who now finally looked my way. I took one girl to see a show at a local theatre, but when conversation ran dry, I began to struggle… that is, until I spied a signed photograph on display in the theatre bar.

'Ah!' I cried. 'Now, *this* is Olive Gilbert! *She* had multiple roles written for her by Ivor Novello in his Drury Lane musicals. *And*,' I added cockily, 'she played Sister Margaretta in *The Sound of Music* with my friend Jean Bayless, the original Maria!'

* * *

My personal development may have been out of proportion to my career progression, but I was thrilled to return to Thursford for Christmas 2006. This year I had my own solo moments, including as a schoolboy whose goldfish was stolen by devious Siamese cats. Additionally, the show featured inflatable fat ballerinas, singing sunflowers, and my all-time favourite Thursford segue: 'Time to Say Goodbye' into 'The Hokey Cokey'.

One night the residents of a retirement home came to watch. During the interval, one of the carers drank a pint of wine, and by the middle of the second half was paralytic. During the 'Act Two Processional' (a serious sequence in which we sang in the aisles wearing cassocks) she leapt onto a baritone, flinging her arms around his neck and wrapping her legs around his waist.

Later, as the cast joined together in the finale line-up singing 'Auld Lang Syne', streamer cannons went off over the audience and the paralytic woman ran up on stage, joining in. One of the dancers, dressed in a Field Mouse skin costume, grabbed the woman and managed to waltz her off into the wings. The carer was last seen drunkenly weaving an old lady in a wheelchair through the car park back to their coach.

I picked up where I left off with old friends in the cast… and now that I seemed a little more assured within myself, they spoke candidly and without reserve. One of the gays commented that he missed having an 'eighteen-inch waist, like Scarlett O'Hara'.

'Oh!' I cried. 'Have you seen the Carol Burnett spoof where she comes down the stairs wearing the curtain rail and says, "I saw it in the window and just couldn't resist it"?'

The room fell silent.

'Are you *sure* you're straight?'

Back home, between contracts, there was no escaping how isolated I felt without friends my own age. However, I knew it was only a matter of time – the perfect friend was out there, and someday he'd materialise. It was a hope to which I constantly clung... a hope which began to build in intensity.

There was nothing much to do in the Midlands except wait for London auditions. I used the time productively, broadening my knowledge and repertoire, making multiple trips into Birmingham Library. I'd study Sondheim shows with the librettos and vocal scores in front of me whilst listening along to recordings. This instilled a solid knowledge of the composer's work... and I didn't know it then, but this Sondheim expertise would eventually pay off big time.

There were other reasons to go into Birmingham too. Despite the generation gap, Jean and I had grown increasingly close, sharing in our special magical world of the theatre. Whilst others around us appreciated this world, only Jean and I fully understood what it really meant to dedicate our lives to our craft.

Amidst the madness of the jewellers, Jean transported me back to 1949 when she'd been 'the youngest starlet in the West End', working with Audrey Hepburn in the musical revues *Sauce Tartare* and *Sauce Piquante*.

'Audrey was the most *beautiful* girl. She gave me my first pair of fishnets,' said the lady who still nipped behind the counter serving customers. 'She and her mother, the Baroness, lived in South Audley Street, which was very, very expensive, and I used to go up to her flat. Although it wasn't grand, it was posh in comparison to the Tottenham council flat where I came from!'

Seeing my eyes widen into saucers, Jean then reminded me, 'But none of that – *none* of that – made any difference whatsoever, because when you're all together in a show, none of your backgrounds matter. The only thing that matters is your talent – your singing – whether you can do the job.' Jean may have retired, but greasepaint and professionalism still ran through her veins.

'We did a show called *Christmas Party* in the morning, followed that with two performances of *Sauce Tartare*, and then sang at Ciro's nightclub. I danced with Walter Pidgeon there. He asked Audrey and me to join his table! We had pink tablecloths, candlelight, romance, a beautiful little band – and a wonderful, *wonderful* cabaret.'

'So you did four shows a day?' I asked.

'Oh yes,' she replied, unfazed. 'By the time I got the twenty-nine bus from Trafalgar Square back to Tottenham, believe it or not, my father would be there, waiting for me, at two o'clock in the morning with his bicycle! I'd sit on the handlebar and he'd take me home. He had to be up again early, but it didn't mean a thing to him – I was his daughter. I look back and think he did *all* of that!'

As oblivious customers browsed the shelves, Jean launched into further fascinating memories.

'Audrey designed me an evening dress – my first ever – and it was made of green satin. I had this long red hair and we were going to the Albert Hall for some function – it must have been at New Year. We all got a £20 salary and she bought two coats with her £20 – two coats for £10 each, from Austin Reed. She bought a black and she bought a grey. And *I* bought a little plastic handbag. She did *not* approve and tried to teach me to have a little more taste. I'm afraid my money had to go a little further than coats!

'She and I shared a dressing room. Marcel LeBon, the male star of the show, was a young Maurice Chevalier-type.

He was in love with Audrey. I adored him, but he only ever said to me' – and here Jean adopted a heavy French accent – '"Jean, I love *you* as a *sister*. But *Aud-e-rey* I *love* as a *woman!*"'

Before long, this first-hand link to the glorious Golden Age had become a normal part of my life. For the first time ever, I felt I had a friend who truly understood me. And what was more, Jean knew that I understood *her*.

A few months later I invited Jean to the small family celebrations held for my twenty-first birthday – but her husband David had been growing increasingly ill, and she was hesitant to leave his bedside.

'Jean,' he eventually asked her, 'you remember your twenty-first, don't you?'

'Of course, I remember my twenty-first!' she replied. 'I was in Blackpool with Morecambe and Wise, and Harry Secombe, and Norman Evans…'

'Precisely,' said David. 'You've remembered your twenty-first all your life. Go to Martin's twenty-first so he can remember *his* all his life.'

Amongst the intimate handful of guests, my friend Jean surprised and captivated all. Everyone acknowledged the presence of a star – and, just for me, the star sang a silver soprano solo 'Happy Birthday'.

Indeed – in no small part thanks to Jean – this was my *first* happy birthday.

A short time later, not long after the Johnsons' golden wedding anniversary, Jean's beloved David peacefully passed away. And I shall remember my twenty-first all my life.

CHAPTER FIVE

'This is calculated to provoke remark'

Ruddigore

Seminal moments in life can happen unexpectedly. One of mine occurred during a tech rehearsal – for Gilbert and Sullivan's *The Pirates of Penzance*. It was Summer 2007 at Kilworth House Theatre, Leicestershire – and, as always, tech week involved lots of waiting around. One of the boys set a challenge – which of us pirates could sing the soprano cadenza from the leading lady's aria 'Poor Wand'ring One'? Two boys tried and failed. Then it was my turn… Suddenly, it became apparent that I had a rather strong and unusually high soprano falsetto range. The tech was brought to a standstill whilst everyone applauded! In the car, my housemate turned on the *Phantom* cast album and told me to sing along as Carlotta. I hit all the stratospheric notes.

Although I'd vaguely known that I had this upper register it had never occurred to me to use it. I hadn't considered it anything special. But at the end-of-run party there was a cast cabaret, so I sang 'Poor Wand'ring One'.

'Martin!' said one of the boys. 'To sing that, you've got balls! But… you've got *no* balls!'

'You should do something with this voice!' people kept telling me. But I hadn't the first idea what. And besides, I had no need of falsetto back at Thursford…

In the 2007 *Christmas Spectacular* I portrayed one of my childhood heroes, Inspector Clouseau, in a *Pink Panther* dance routine. The artistic concept had been mine, and I'd originally outlined my vision to Colin Window about how Clouseau could chase the Panthers as they jumped onto the Gondola.

'You're frightening,' Colin told me. 'You're frightening, but I think it'll work.'

This time, I escaped good-natured taunts from the gays thanks to the presence of a straight boy even less masculine than me. Spyros was a pixie-like foreigner who glided around sighing, 'What would life be without a step ball change?' But when asked if he was gay, Spyros animatedly insisted, 'I'm not! I'm not!'

I'd received flack in the dressing room for reading books about Katharine Hepburn. But Spyros poured over Nigella Lawson's *How to Be a Domestic Goddess*. One day, he told us about his early years in Spain as a ballet teacher.

'The little girls – they would come to my lessons with their hair all straggly and messy. So, I said to them, "No! Go back to your mothers! I will *not* teach you unless you put your hair up nicely in a bun!"'

'I didn't know you worked in Spain,' I said. 'You've crammed a lot into your twenty-five years, haven't you, Spyros?'

'Yes,' he replied. 'I blow where the wind takes me – like Pocahontas!' The dressing room erupted. 'I'm not! I'm not!' he cried. 'I just like *Pocahontas*!' And then he turned to the dowager gay who doubted him most. 'But if I ever decide to *be* a gay, *you* can host my coming out party.'

'No,' came the reply. 'I'll host your it's-about-time-I-realised party.'

I could sympathise with Spyros because I very much considered myself a straight man in touch with his feminine side. But like Spyros... I wasn't.

Meanwhile, 2008 became the year of Gilbert and Sullivan – commencing with a West End season of *The Mikado, Iolanthe* and *The Pirates of Penzance* at the Gielgud Theatre on Shaftesbury Avenue. The cast included two members of the original D'Oyly Carte Opera Company – Bruce Graham and Barry Clark – who inspired and reignited my passion for Gilbert and Sullivan. In the months afterwards, I absorbed myself in the Savoyard world, relishing its history and exploring all the works in detail.

And then finally, the opportunity arose to use my falsetto – I was cast in an all-male production of *The Mikado* as the leading lady, Yum-Yum. When major casting directors came to watch, my career advanced several notches. But the most important night of the run, for me, was when Jean came. It was the first time she'd ever seen me performing in a show – and she couldn't have been prouder.

Immediately after *Mikado* there was yet more G&S: I made my debut at the International Gilbert and Sullivan Festival in Buxton. This insane annual event – described as 'near as humanly possible to a G&S theme park', saw 20,000 fans from around the world, plus hundreds of performers (both professional and amateur), descend on

Derbyshire for three weeks of non-stop productions, lectures, concerts and memorabilia fayres.

The G&S anoraks were zealous. One overjoyed festivalgoer emailed the organisers stating, 'I thought I'd died and was in heaven'; perhaps more tellingly, another said, 'I have had more pleasure from the Gilbert and Sullivan Festival than from either of my husbands.' Each night in the Festival Bar, the Inner Brotherhood of Savoy Addicts joined together for communal singalongs. My first evening, I arrived mid-*Patience,* greeted by a lady playing an air cello.

In a non-falsetto capacity, I appeared in *The Gondoliers* and *Iolanthe* at the beautiful Buxton Opera House. The MD was John Owen Edwards, whom I'd revered my entire life – I'd grown up listening to his countless musical theatre recordings. John was known to friends and colleagues by his initials J.O.E., and one night in the Festival Bar he accompanied me at the piano as I sang 'Poor Wand'ring One'. ''Tis Martin!' he declared.

The audience reaction was extraordinary – and the impact, in time, would be considerable. An absent friend had asked me to get this 'Poor Wand'ring' filmed, so I posted the video on Facebook... and then, for the time being, put it to the back of my mind.

Therefore, approaching the 2008 Thursford *Christmas Spectacular,* I was on a professional high – yet still seeking that elusive perfect friend. But I had my hopes...

When auditions were advertised in *The Stage*, the wording of the casting breakdown changed. Thursford now required, specifically, 'young-looking' singers. Many regular but older and more experienced Thursfordians were sadly not asked back. They were replaced by graduates from drama school or music college. I'd recently turned twenty-two. And for the first time in my career, I was going to perform alongside people my own age.

The evening before the *Last Night of the Proms* concert in September 2008, the singers were put up at The Shrine of Our Lady of Walsingham. As if Thursford wasn't a mad enough institution already, the *Proms* singers were billeted amongst the priests and nuns who made pilgrimages to the holy site where in AD 1061 a young girl had a vision of the Virgin Mary. The Bull pub was just opposite – and boozy Thursford singers who missed the Shrine's curfew had to scale its mediaeval walls to reach their spartan bedrooms. There were no room numbers – just individual room names – such as, amusingly given the character of certain occupants, 'Virgin Most Prudent'.

As I chatted with young newbies in The Bull, I very much enjoyed being a veteran and told them anecdotes of Olde Thursford. Making conversation with a young male graduate – whose first professional gig this was – I casually asked: 'Are you a classical singer or musical theatre?'

He turned up his nose. 'Classical!'

'Lovely! Have you done any Gilbert and Sullivan?'

'Ugh! *No!*' he scoffed. 'I couldn't possibly degrade myself by singing Gilbert and Sullivan!'

A few months later I had an email from this singer, who now found himself unemployed. He asked me to send him audition details for the Buxton Gilbert and Sullivan Festival.

Turning away from this rather confident classical singer, I looked over to the doorway and saw a group enter. There was a boy about my age and height. He saw me and smiled, making his way over.

'Hi!' he said brightly. 'I'm Josh.'

In a moment I knew. This was him. My heart and gut told me that I'd found my friend.

CHAPTER SIX

'The things are few
I would not do
In Friendship's name!'

Iolanthe

'Martin! *Martin!*' hissed one of the tenors. 'Is it like looking in a mirror when you're talking to that guy?'

I'd never formed such an instant connection with someone my own age. For me, this was an entirely new experience. Josh and I chatted incessantly after his arrival at The Bull, and an immediate friendship seemed to have sparked. He asked me lots of questions about Thursford and laughed uproariously as I rattled off my anecdotes. Back in my room at The Shrine, I was buzzing. From the moment I'd seen him I just knew that Josh was going to be *the* friend. My very first thought the next morning was that I couldn't wait to see my new buddy. We sat together during the *Proms* rehearsal and proved inseparable throughout the day. I'd never been so excited!

Afterwards we spoke regularly on Facebook and met up for a drink the day before Christmas rehearsals began in London. Josh told me that he'd just split up with his girlfriend.

'Oh, I'm sorry!' I said.

'No, no, it's fine. Actually, it hadn't been working for some time.'

'Well,' I said confidently – as if I actually knew what I was talking about – 'it's probably best to start Thursford life single. One never knows when one may get a Thursford Fuck!'

'Yes!' said Josh, his eyes lighting up. 'That's what I'm hoping for, anyway!'

Josh was two years older than me and had graduated from drama school some time before. Thursford, however, was his first job. But although his professional life had progressed slowly, I soon found that his track record with women was impressive. He'd never been without female company for long – he sounded like Errol Flynn!

Josh was equally as impressed by my professional success – but eventually I admitted to him that I'd had no luck with the opposite sex. We each seemed to have been touched by good fortune in different areas… but perhaps, Josh suggested, he could lend me a helping hand with the ladies? I now not only had a friend – I had a personal mentor!

I held Josh in awe, and our blossoming friendship was a talking point amongst the company. One evening, during the last break of a twelve-hour rehearsal day, the two of us walked side by side several laps around the entire building, happily chatting away, entrusting our first secrets to one another.

Later, at my cottage, we stayed up talking into the small hours. Before I knew what was happening, I found myself pouring my heart out to Josh, revealing everything I'd ever wanted to say; everything I'd bottled up my whole life. I revealed things I'd never told anyone because I hadn't yet found the person whom I felt comfortable enough to tell. Everything from my school years and my frustrations at my lack of experience, to the stings I felt when teased about being gay.

Halfway through my cathartic release I realised I'd just made a monumental personal breakthrough. Josh helped, assured and advised. Like Bogart and Claude Rains in *Casablanca* I knew it was 'the beginning of a beautiful friendship'.

My life lessons with Josh began the night I ordered an orange juice at The Bull.

'Martin,' he declared. 'Let me buy you a pint!'

I was thrown into an absolute panic. If I'd drunk a pint of anything before in my life, it had only ever been milk!

'A-A pint?' I stuttered nervously. 'But… that's very nearly an armful!'

And true to his word, Josh helped me with women. There was a particularly attractive young soprano in the company named Tiffany. I told Josh that I really fancied her, and he encouraged me to try my luck. For a while, I seemed to be in there. She couldn't get enough of my Thursford stories, and I channelled David Niven's charm as a dashing raconteur. However, as physically stunning as Tiffany was, I was alarmed that my wit seemed to go straight over her head.

'I've got loads of family in America,' she told me. 'I've got family in Florida and family in Chicago and family in San Jose…'

'Oh!' I cried. 'Do you know the *way* to San Jose?'

She looked at me blankly. 'No.'

Another time, during a dispute with someone in the dressing room, she told them: 'You've 'ad your cake – now lie in it!'

I wasn't convinced that Tiffany and I had the greatest meeting of minds, but knowing I liked her, Josh encouraged my pursuit. However, I confided to him that even if I was successful with Tiffany, when it came down to it, I wouldn't have a clue what to do with her in the bedroom! With no practical experience, and never having had anyone to discuss things with, I was genuinely in the dark. The closest I'd come to watching porn was *Carry On Emmannuelle*. Oh yes, dear reader… no one was ever as innocent as I at the age of twenty-two!

Josh patiently explained to me all kinds of things about sex – and I freely admit that a lot of what he said was news to me. He kindly told me everything I needed to know, and then some – miraculously keeping a straight face.

But when Tiffany told me she thought that Robin Hood and his Merry Men came from Sheringham – confusing it with Sherwood ('oh yeah, like the forest!') – I have to admit that it was rather a turn-off. I told Josh that I thought it best if I left things with Tiffany. I feared that not only would she eat me alive sexually (which could prove very embarrassing as *everyone* at Thursford would know about it), I just wasn't entirely sure what we'd talk about!

Josh then admitted that he quite fancied Tiffany himself… and he wasn't quite as fussed about conversation. So, as long as I was no longer interested, if anything happened between the two of them, would I be okay with that? I told him to be my guest.

At the cast Halloween party, Tiffany arrived hammered and immediately started pawing Josh all over. Although I'd given Josh my blessing, why, oh why, did this have to happen the second I'd given the all-clear? This was too much for my inexperienced pride to take. Tiffany even screamed at me, 'GO AWAY!' They drunkenly snogged, and in despair, I decided to get sloshed myself (which wasn't hard – two glasses of wine being my inexperienced limit).

But… I was just so happy to have a friend that I could forgive him anything. What really depressed me, however, was that I'd been at Thursford *four years* now and never been snogged – and this guy had been here less than three weeks and already scored – and that with a girl whom I'd so recently fancied!

The next day we began tech rehearsals. As we repeated the opening sequence time and again, I thought, *I'm here wearing the* same *cape, walking down the* same *aisle, with the* same *silver top hat, in the* same *show, and I'm no further personally than I was at nineteen*!

I found myself in a bizarre situation, caught between two extremes. I had no lack of professional assurance… against all odds I'd managed to forge a career. I could place myself in professional situations which terrified others – for instance, hosting Thursford's raffle. The thought of having to improvise comic patter in front of an audience sent others into meltdown. But I thrived – and made the raffle my own. I continued the Thursford tradition of being creative about my 'beautiful assistant'. Audiences applauded wildly:

*Believe it or not, ladies and gentlemen, and this is ab-
solutely true – Camilla's just been cast in the new James
Bond movie! Camilla plays a beautiful temptress. Her
plan is to seduce Bond wearing a diaphanous night-
gown... but he sees through it!*

But beneath the sparkly red raffle jacket, I was emotionally vulnerable. The more I found that I didn't know about
life, the more important Josh became to me – whether he
knew it or not. He was everything I aspired to be, and I
couldn't believe that this cool, trendy and popular guy (he
now had two girls fighting over him) wanted to hang out.

'From now on you're going to have friends,' he told me.
'*Proper* friends!'

It was overwhelming. These were the words I'd wanted
to hear my whole life. I arrived home on Christmas Eve
the happiest I'd ever been. Meeting Josh had changed my
life, and I just *knew* from now on that everything was
going to be perfect.

In a strange way, though, it also brought back unpleasant memories of my school days. I'd realised at the time
that I'd been mistreated by my friends – but I'd had no
experience with which to compare it. Now that I knew
what it felt like to have an amazing friend, I started getting upset again. I hadn't thought about my school peers
in ages, but now it all came flooding back. I comforted
myself, however, with the thought that from now on it
would all be different – and I'd never be mistreated or hurt
by a friend ever again.

With three years of savings in the bank, and a wonderful buddy in the big city, I finally moved to a flat in

London. But life outside the Thursford bubble was different. Josh had an in-built social network of drama-school chums, and they were around all the time. My world, of course, consisted only of Josh.

If there was one thing Josh loved, it was going out and having a good time. But when I joined him and his cronies for nights out 'on the lash' I felt nervous and out of place. However, when Josh said we were going to the Empire Casino I was very excited. I knew exactly what to expect from a casino – I'd seen them in the movies!

There'd be men in white tuxedos and a black singer crooning at an upright piano. A bombshell like Carmen Miranda would emerge and do a floor show; glamorous women in slinky gowns would lean over the shoulder of an Orson Welles-type mogul who smoked Havana cigars playing baccarat.

What I got was fruit machines, boozy men in jeans drinking beer, trashy hen parties and piped pop music. There was no sign anywhere of Lana Turner.

'Where are the floozies?' I asked Josh.

'The what?'

'The floozies! The blonde floozies hanging round at all the tables!' (I swear I'm not making this up, dear reader.)

Lost in a crowd, I occasionally felt forgotten. But I didn't raise the issue, because I realised that the problem was me – and my inexperience. Josh, of course, was endlessly wonderful – and I wouldn't hear a word said against him.

Now that I had someone to talk to, I felt as though a weight had been lifted from my shoulders. But I also started feeling strange new things. I confessed to Josh that

I was having weird sensations about one of his gay friends. This boy was successful, glamorous and possessed a dangerous confidence that teetered into arrogance... but a very sexy, caddish kind of arrogance, like George Sanders. I felt drawn to this guy – which was odd, because I was straight. Admittedly, I didn't feel strongly enough to do anything about it. But still... how bizarre!

CHAPTER SEVEN

'Oh, marvellous illusion!
Oh, terrible surprise!'

The Sorcerer

The video of my Buxton 'Poor Wand'ring One' continued to be viewed on social media. In January 2009 I received an email from a producer who, impressed by what she'd seen online, offered to finance a one-man show entitled *The Falsetto*. I'd have complete artistic control, and we'd try it out at a small but prestigious London theatre.

It was an offer I couldn't refuse. I'd be showcasing myself as a performer, writer and director. Although the 'hook' would be soprano songs, I could also demonstrate my comedy skills and sing in my normal tenor voice. To make the most of this opportunity, though, I realised that I'd need artistic guidance. And I knew just the fellow to ask…

It's extraordinary how many contacts I can trace back to Jean Bayless. Jean had a remarkable friend named Graham Tallis, a showbiz socialite. Forever attending West End openings, Graham bought presents at the jewellers for his luminary friends, including Mary Rodgers. And he continually mentioned one name in particular:

'Oh, I've just been to see Steve Ross!'

'Steve Ross at Pizza on the Park last night was sublime!'

'I've just booked for Steve Ross!'

By the summer of 2008 I finally started asking myself – who *is* this Steve Ross? His website informed me this was 'the crown prince of New York cabaret' (as dubbed by *The New York Times*); a leading interpreter of the Great American Songbook, with an international following. Now age seventy, Steve Ross showed no signs of slowing down. He'd even acted on Broadway as Fred, the valet in Noël Coward's *Present Laughter*.

Watching videos, I was inspired by Steve Ross's showmanship. I sent him an email, introducing myself as a friend of Graham. Steve replied saying he was coming to London that September – and we arranged to meet.

Dapper, charming and sophisticated, Steve Ross at once made me feel his equal. For many years he'd been resident entertainer at the legendary Algonquin Hotel in New York. Prior to that, he'd been a fixture at a Broadway club called Ted Hook's Backstage. Theatrical and Hollywood royalty frequently attended; a spotlight illuminated the stars at their tables as fellow diners applauded.

'Ginger Rogers was there,' Steve remembered. 'I wanted her to sing "But Not for Me" and I asked her, "What is your key?" And then this long red fingernail descended onto the piano and played a B flat. She said, "Honey, that's my high note. You figure it out!"'

Steve invited me to a party the following week. Artistes, authors and aficionados gathered around a grand piano singing the greatest songs of the Golden Era. Steve called the room to order and announced a surprise. I was then presented and performed several numbers. Finally, Steve and I duetted together – Novello's 'We'll Gather Lilacs'.

Fortunately, Steve liked my work, and told me to just ask if I ever needed help or advice. The timing was fortuitous. Six months later, in March 2009, he returned to London for the two weeks leading up to my debut performance of *The Falsetto.* I asked Steve whether I could preview my show for him to get his opinion; he offered me an afternoon at Pizza on the Park in Knightsbridge where he was currently performing. There was no one in the room except my producer, Steve scribbling notes and a cleaner setting up for that night's show, lifting down chairs from the tabletops.

In the hour which followed, I received a masterclass in how to create and construct the perfect show. Steve took what I had and transformed it into something far superior – his suggestions about what to add, what to cut, how to programme the music and pace the dialogue were invaluable.

I would not forget this kindness. Steve Ross didn't have to help me, but he gave up his valuable time on a day when he himself had a performance. When I watched him that night, I observed how carefully and skilfully he'd crafted his show.

The next week was spent frantically rehearsing the re-structured *Falsetto.* But just two days before the performance I hopped on a train to Birmingham for an overnight trip… Jean Bayless had arranged something special.

We'd now grown so close that I called my friend Nanny Jean, just like her family. And at last the opportunity had arisen for Nanny Jean to introduce me to her friend

Fenella Fielding, a boon companion since their 1970s tour of *Gigi* (during which the IRA blew up their scenery truck).

Since childhood I'd revered Fenella's sultry star turn in *Carry On Screaming*. 'Do you mind if I smoke?' she purred – and then disappeared into clouds of vapour. Her sensual come-hither voice was a trademark – Sandy Wilson, who wrote Fenella's breakthrough role in the musical *Valmouth*, described it as having 'the texture of crumpled damask'. Her range was vast. She'd excelled in Shakespeare and Chekhov; Kenneth Tynan hailed Fenella's *Hedda Gabler* 'one of the experiences of a lifetime'.

As I approached Jean's flat, I spied the unmistakable features of Miss Fielding through the front window. Fenella had maintained her exact same look across half a century, as if frozen in time. She wore a wig (or sometimes two simultaneously) and never appeared in public without her signature eyelashes, from which Dusty Springfield had drawn inspiration.

'Hello, dahhhling,' she purred, almost in self-parody. For the first time in my life I was completely lost for words. Both onstage and off, Fenella had a magnetic star quality which rendered people speechless.

At Jean's request I gave Fenella a performance of 'Poor Wand'ring One' right there in the lounge. Fenella, beyond startled by my unexpected cadenzas, proceeded to erupt into a fit of the giggles but, recovering herself, told me: 'I have friends, countertenors, who do opera – but I must say your show sounds much more fun!'

Nanny Jean, Daniel and the rest of the Johnson family booked tickets for *The Falsetto*, making a special trip down to London. They gave Fenella a lift home en route, stopping off for tea at an upmarket hotel.

Here, the dowager actresses bumped into a very famous composer of contemporary British musical theatre. Having initially overlooked the ladies, the composer eventually extended his hand in greeting, but Fenella remained unimpressed. She opened her handbag and carefully put on a pair of long white gloves. Reluctantly shaking his hand, she then peeled off the gloves as if they were now contaminated and dropped them back into her bag, snapping it shut. Fenella was a true individual, but as I grew to know her better, I discovered a razor-sharp intellect beneath her veil of eccentricity: this was a lady who kept a copy of Plato beside her bed.

The Falsetto ended with Bernstein's grand soprano aria 'Glitter and Be Gay'. During the encore – Gracie Fields' 'Wish Me Luck as You Wave Me Goodbye' – I handed out Union flags to people in the front row. The show was a success! And Steve Ross gave his official approval.

Things moved fast – the Edinburgh Fringe Festival offered us a venue for three weeks in August. Flyers were ordered in bulk, and I recorded a *Falsetto* album, with beautiful photo artwork printed onto the disc. Alistair McGowan, who'd played the title role in *The Mikado* at the Gielgud, was also heading to the Festival with his stand-up comedy show and asked me to be the support act for his out-of-town Edinburgh preview.

Then we got to the Fringe – a catalogue of disaster. Our venue was a prominently located ninety-seater portacabin… which was moved without warning, a week prior to opening, to an unlit remote area behind a huge stone wall.

Apparently, this was to avoid noise from nearby building work, but festivalgoers couldn't find the new location.

My producer, an Edinburgh newbie, had been assured that 9.15 p.m. was a primetime slot. For stand-up comedy, yes. It was a graveyard shift for songs by Gracie Fields.

Somewhere along the line we had a technical fuck-up. The *Falsetto* CDs didn't play on CD players – only laptops. We had to buy blank CDs in bulk from Tesco, re-burn all the albums and tear the wrapping off the CD cases to place the Tesco-branded discs inside.

But artistically, the show was a five-star success. Critics loved it. So did audiences – when they came. I was only averaging about five people a day. And despite brilliant reviews, I couldn't even *give* tickets away. It was that bad. One night, the tiny spattering seemed entirely response-less – trilling my cadenzas, I was dying inside. But a few days later I was stopped by a man on the street.

'I just have to tell you that I've been here for the last two weeks, seeing four shows a day – and yours was my favourite show of the whole festival.'

'Thank you!' I replied very sincerely. 'Which night did you come?'

'Last Friday.' It was the night of the responseless audience. Just because a crowd is quiet doesn't mean they're not enjoying it. And no matter whether they're cheering their heads off or sitting in silence, every audience deserves the exact same commitment and exact same performance. I was also heartened by a morale-boosting text from an unknown number: 'Met u at jeans a while back. Wishing u lots of luv and every success. Fenella Eff.'

I also had other concerns. Josh had assured me that the

Edinburgh Festival was the easiest place in the world to get laid. If I couldn't pull at Edinburgh, I told myself, there must be something seriously wrong. After all – I was the star of my own show! My face was plastered on billboards all over the city (or at least briefly, until other shows pasted their posters over me). But I was not arousing female interest and found meeting girls difficult. After all, I could hardly go out partying in crowded bars and expect to chirp like Joan Sutherland the following night. But at least some nice gay men came along to my show – they were fantastically supportive and took such an interest.

Things got worse. I had to flyer my own show – in the pouring rain. No female soprano should have to stand in a downpour and then sing 'Glitter and Be Gay', let alone a male one. Back at the theatrical digs I couldn't relax. The flat overflowed with people and animals, including a magician dressed as a dragon, and his dog named Mr Piffles. During the last week of the run, the flat literally started falling apart. Door handles came off in our hands and windows started to implode. You couldn't make it up.

Everyone had predicted *The Falsetto* was a guaranteed Edinburgh goldmine. We died on our arses. At the end of the run, on the phone to Alistair McGowan, I finally cracked and bawled my eyes out.

'But, Martin,' he consoled me, 'look at your reviews. Google yourself. You're a five-star success. Back in London, no one's going to know whether you played to five people or five hundred.'

He turned out to be correct. In London I showed evidence of a glittering triumph, with no one any the wiser to audience figures. I was certainly learning my industry from the ground up. I was becoming one tough cookie – professionally speaking.

Personally, it was still another matter…

CHAPTER EIGHT

'Soho! pretty one – in my power at last, eh?'

Ruddigore

In a couple of weeks, I'd turn twenty-three. My ambitions for *The Falsetto* to launch me as the Edinburgh Festival's most eligible straight bachelor had been crushed. I returned to London as innocent and inexperienced as when I'd left – and to my alarm, I was venturing further into my twenties unfulfilled! I began to feel panic.

'Well,' Josh suggested, remembering my tentative confessions about finding his male friend attractive, 'you could always *try* it with a guy.'

I mulled it over. In Edinburgh I'd found that I could fully unleash my flamboyant personality amongst gay men – all of whom had been terribly sweet to me. And... well... maybe I could at least *try* something with a man. Just to cross it off the list. For years people had made subtle and not-so-subtle comments within earshot, saying that I didn't know I was gay. But now I'd be able to look everyone in the eye and tell them direct, once and for all, like June Whitfield in *Carry On Abroad*, 'I tried it once and didn't like it.'

So, I texted every gay man in my phone – and told him I missed him. I was surprised how many responses

I received, and none more ebullient than from a chap I'd known socially for a while named Franklin. He was a slightly older gentleman with an exuberant personality, not unlike something from a *Carry On*.

Franklin swiftly suggested that we meet in a coffee shop on Old Compton Street. I'd never heard of Old Compton Street but gathered, by asking around, that it was in Soho… a part of town where I'd never actually ventured, except to see *Mary Poppins* at the Prince Edward Theatre.

As I prepared to leave the house my heart, if not exactly pounding, was certainly beating mezzo fortissimo. I arrived at the coffee shop early and couldn't help but notice that there wasn't a female to be seen. About five minutes later Franklin arrived, strutting with confidence, wearing a pair of flamboyantly patterned trousers and a long coat.

'Oooo,' he cooed, 'there aren't many seats in 'ere, are there? Budge up – I'll share yours.' Somewhat unglamorously half-perched, I launched into polite and fluttery small talk to distract from the slight tremor in my hands. Now that I was actually here – really in Soho itself – I was nervous. And I did what I tended to do when out of my comfort zone… react just a little too overenthusiastically to everything said.

'Why don't we go and get a proper drink someplace?' Franklin declared, suggesting with a leer. 'Let's go to a bar!'

'Oh!' I cried, wide-eyed. 'Do you know of any good ones around here?'

Franklin led me down Old Compton Street… and by now I was really getting scared, feeling myself shrinking. I'd never been in a situation like this before. What was going to happen? What was expected of me?

We walked into a bar where the joint seemed to be jumping. It was dark, mysterious; men danced on poles wearing black leather harnesses (I recognised the harnesses, because I'd seen them in *Promises and Lies*). The demographic appeared to be a somewhat older crowd. Franklin gestured to a sofa and told me, 'I'll be back – make yourself comfortable!' I was anything but.

I was completely unprepared for this scenario... no nightclub in any MGM musical looked like this! Where was Xavier Cugat and His Orchestra? The only 'music' was the pounding thumps of a cheesy disco track. And there were things going on in dark corners I was sure would never be passed by the censor! I was a loose lamb in a jungle.

Franklin returned with two very large glasses of wine. A drink was the last thing I needed, but to steady my nerves I gulped it down. Franklin moved closer. I felt an arm coil its way around my shoulder.

'So...' he purred. I was terrified. 'Tell me about your boys!'

I was stumped.

'There's not much to tell, really...'

Franklin's eyes lit up as he moved in even nearer.

'So! If I take you home with me tonight... what do you like? What do you want me to *do* to you?'

I was flabbergasted. Panic set in... but even so, I was a well-brought-up young man and knew that I must say something polite.

'Well...' I began through a jittery smile... And now, dear reader, you may not believe what I said next, but I swear it's true. From somewhere in the back of my memory a quote flashed into my mind. A quote attributed to various people including Winston Churchill, George S. Kaufman and Oscar Wilde. And before I knew what had happened, I'd actually said it...

'I'll try anything once,' I declared confidently to Franklin, 'except morris dancing and incest!'

Franklin looked at me for a moment... and pensively cocked his head to one side.

'Morris dancing... hmmmm, maybe! But incest? Noooo... Noooooooo...' And then all too hurriedly, he was back to business. 'So anyway – if I take you home – what are you into? What can I *do* to you?'

And in my floundering desperation to give a non-committal answer, a second quote flashed through my mind – from Mrs Patrick Campbell, the legendary Edwardian actress.

'I don't care what people get up to,' I informed Franklin, 'as long as they don't do it in the streets and frighten the horses!'

Next thing I knew Franklin's tongue was down my throat. Maybe Mrs Patrick Campbell quotations really turned him on? Or maybe he just wanted me to shut up. Either way, this strange sensation was weird, exciting, re-pulsive, thrilling... and I wasn't entirely sure how to react. I knew that Ginger Rogers had slapped Fred Astaire's face for doing far less than this in *Top Hat*... so what to do?

'Guys! Guys!' someone yelled. 'Calm it down, eh?'

As Franklin released me from the clinch I was shaking like a leaf. He looked at me and paused.

'If I took you home with me tonight, I would *love* to have a *filthy* night with you... and *ravage* you!' I think, by this time, my eyes were out on stalks. 'But,' Franklin continued, his tone changing – 'I don't think you're ready for that, are you?'

I managed to squeak something along the lines of 'No!' And then, to Franklin's enormous credit – for which, to this day, I am extremely grateful – he called it a night and escorted me safely to Charing Cross station.

As my train departed, I was jubilant! I kissed a boy – and I didn't like it! This was *wonderful!* Here was living proof, once and for all, that at the age of nearly twenty-three I was straight! I rang Josh and told him the good news. He was pleased that I'd experimented, and understood why I hadn't enjoyed the experience... but maybe I could keep my options open? At least, I think that's what he said, because I was far too chuffed to really pay much attention. I was just so happy that if I was put through a lie detector, I could now assure the world I was every inch as straight as Gable, Bogart or Cagney.

What a great joke on the show-business industry this was going to be – that the guy known for twirling his parasol singing 'Poor Wand'ring One' was a 100% proven heterosexual! I arrived home with a skip in my step, hopped into bed, opened my DVD case and treated myself to a celebratory screening of Barbra Streisand in *Funny Girl*.

CHAPTER NINE

'The man has vanished into air!'

The Yeomen of the Guard

I headed back to Thursford without Josh – he'd been cast in a major tour lasting a whole year. On the one hand, I was thrilled for him – Josh was fulfilling a lifetime ambition – but privately I worried. In London I'd learned I could be out of sight, out of mind. Once on tour, Josh was swept up in his exciting new world… and I stopped hearing from him.

With casual friends, such 'ghosting' can be annoying. From a close friend, it's hurtful. Whilst I didn't begrudge his professional success, I couldn't understand why I'd suddenly been dropped. Josh was like a brother, and I looked up to him. Why had he forgotten me?

I was emotionally vulnerable – and in truth, insecure in the relationship. Yet I couldn't bear the thought of taking Josh off the pedestal – it was all I knew. So, I kept telling myself everything was still great. But he never answered his phone, his voicemails or his texts – and I wondered if he realised the effect all this had on my well-being. A nasty voice at the back of my head – which I hadn't heard since my school days – began telling me that, clearly, I wasn't worthy of his attention.

After radio silence of several months, at last I saw that he'd finally messaged! But the text was disappointing. He just wanted my local knowledge for the next tour venue – casually asking how far it was from Birmingham New Street station to the Birmingham Hippodrome.

I let him know. And I then continued to hear nothing.

At least I had work – but Thursford without Josh was lonely. The 2009 singers were nice enough, but there was no one to whom I felt close. The girls still didn't get my humour, as demonstrated one day in Thursford's Fantasy Land – where to reach our rehearsal stage we had to walk down to Santa's House and turn right. Fantasy Land was often chilly, and a young soprano arrived wearing a jacket of synthetic fur.

'Oh, I love that top!' I told her. 'That's mammoth fur, isn't it?'

'What do you mean?' she asked.

'Well, I passed the shop on Oxford Street which sells those jackets. They had a sign in the window – "Mammoth Fur Sale!"'

She stared at me, bemused. 'But mammoths are extinct.'

I was, however, very close to one of Thursford's sound engineers, Ian Savage, known by the nickname 'Min'. He ran a tight ship backstage – his down-to-earth realism was hugely welcomed. And I had a hoot with the Norfolk residents working front of house: Lesley the raffle lady and Katherine on the café tills shared my keen sense of the ridiculous – an asset when working at Thursford!

But in 2009, more than any year thus far, I grew close to a remarkable veteran couple. George Fay had trained animals for TV, circus, theatre and film for over fifty years, and since 1987, George and his wife Betty had provided

Thursford's white pigeons. They had various 'teams' of birds – some of the pigeons had done the show before, but they trained up others new each year, flying them around the empty auditorium every day at 8 a.m. Throughout the run, George and Betty (now approaching their eighties) lived in a caravan on the staff car park, where I often visited between matinee and evening shows.

I'd spent the run pottering along, minding my own business, when, during the last two weeks, suddenly, out of nowhere: 'You've changed your hair!'

I turned around and saw a very attractive front-of-house girl. She told me her name was Jess, and that she really enjoyed my raffles. Next thing I knew, she'd invited herself out for a drink with me. Wow! Josh's training was paying off! I knew he'd be so proud... as and when I heard back from him.

I couldn't believe it – Jess was genuinely into me! We arranged a night to meet again later in the week... and this time, she asked if she could stay over at mine...

It was going to happen. I was 100% proven heterosexual, and finally it was going to happen! I now knew everything I needed to know about what I needed to know. All I had to do was put it into practice...

The day arrived. I could hardly wait for the two performances to be over. During the first act I was one of the four Jersey Boys singing 'Oh, What a Night'. That afternoon I had a glint in my eye singing the very meaningful lyrics... and I keenly anticipated singing them again the next day!

At 5 p.m. I bumped into John Cushing. It was particularly cold outside, but the skies were clear. Crossing his fingers, he told me, 'We've just got to hope it doesn't snow!'

By 5.45 p.m., without warning, five inches of snow had dumped itself on Thursford. The entire village lost its power supply – and we became reliant on the show's emergency generator. The evening performance went up twenty minutes late due to traffic carnage. Then during the middle of Act One, the generator broke down and the building continually plunged itself in and out of darkness. On stage, Pongo the Skunk tried to maintain order as 1500 pensioners started screaming.

Finally, during the 'Act Two Processional', someone from management stumbled out on stage soaked to the skin. She announced that the police had advised closing down the show as otherwise we'd all get trapped – Thursford was, apparently, about to get cut off. Run!

Cast, staff and pensioners simultaneously abandoned ship, battling through the pelting snow towards the car park – where all vehicles required digging out. George Fay waded outside carrying the birds in their baskets. When he reached the birdhouse, George opened the basket lids, but the pigeons refused to budge. They were so well trained that they knew they hadn't yet performed – and obstinately declined to go home!

I couldn't believe what was happening… after a lifetime's build-up, this was meant to be the Night of my Nights! I'd no idea what had happened to Jess. I couldn't find her through the chaos and had no mobile signal. Then I heard from my next-door neighbour – who rang Colin Window's office – that not only was the road to my cottage blocked by a fallen tree, but the cottage itself was uninhabitable, devoid of electricity and hot water.

My first ever Thursford Fuck was being snowed off!

This could *only* happen to me.

Min came to my rescue, sheltering me at his place in Fulmodeston… but when we finally got out of Thursford, the normal fifteen-minute journey took over two hours, driving through five-foot snow drifts. We stopped en route to rescue marooned drivers, eventually arriving back at three in the morning.

I had only the clothes in which I was standing. I now had phone signal, but just 5% battery and no charger. However, I'd kept hold of my dressing-room book… so instead of going to bed with Jess, I went to bed with gap-toothed comedian Terry-Thomas.

The next day, for the first time ever, both performances were cancelled. Miraculously there'd been no accidents, but thirty stranded pensioners had slept in the auditorium overnight. Those in the company who possessed it rallied their Dunkirk spirit and picked up a shovel – we had a show to get back on the road.

The last few days of the run went ahead, but country roads were treacherous and inaccessible. Many front-of-house staff were unable to travel into work, including Lesley, Katherine… and Jess. My night of passion failed to materialise – I arrived home on Christmas Eve as innocent as ever – and 2009 was the last year Jess worked at Thursford!

* * *

I booked a ticket for Josh's show. I was so happy to see him that I chose to believe everything was still perfect. 'Oh, you know I'm rubbish with my phone,' he told me when gently quizzed about his silence. I didn't wish to rock the boat.

A few weeks later in London, the night before a gig, I walked up a side road to Clapham Junction station carrying a suitcase of *Falsetto* props. Suddenly I felt a tugging at the case from behind – and turned around to see a teenage boy, his face obscured by a hoody, trying to wrestle the case from my grasp. Next thing I knew, another hooded lad pushed me against a wall with a nine-inch knife at my throat.

'Empty your pockets! Empty your fucking pockets!' They took my phone, iPod and cash. Then they threw me to the ground. 'Open the case! Open the fucking case!' Even with a knife at my throat I found myself telling them, 'You're not going to *believe* what's in here!'

I opened it to reveal the multi-coloured silk scarfs I used in 'Glitter and Be Gay', plus a green satin pillow and bunches of fake flowers. The muggers, rendered speechless, rifled their way through my props, utterly bewildered. Finally, they kicked the case away and ran off into the night.

The policemen were brilliant – and I told them if they came across two hooded teenagers with an iPod singing along with Jean Bayless, they'd found my attackers. I was unhurt and the show went ahead – but it took a few days for the shock to register, at which point I had an emotional meltdown.

The timing coincided with Josh's birthday, for which he returned to London. He told me that everyone was gathering in Leicester Square at 9 p.m. But when I got there, it turned out that he'd joined his closest friends for a meal beforehand… a meal I knew nothing about, and to which I hadn't been invited. Coming just a few days after my mugging, this hit me very hard. Like a surprise slap in the face, hurtling out of the past I felt the familiar and humiliating sting of rejection on a birthday. There were clearly cracks in what I considered this perfect friendship. But I buried my head in the sand. And afterwards, once again, my messages remained unanswered.

But I found sanctity in a brand-new outlet – Nanny Jean had introduced me to her friends Group Captain Patrick Tootal and his wife Janet. Patrick was Honorary Secretary of the Battle of Britain Memorial Trust, the charity charged with caring for the National Memorial to the Few on the clifftops of Capel-le-Ferne in Folkestone. The surviving veterans from the Battle of Britain – of whom Winston Churchill had said, 'Never in the field of human conflict was so much owed by so many to so few' – were actively involved with the Trust, and I was delighted when Patrick and Janet asked me to sing at the seventieth anniversary memorial celebrations.

They invited me for tea at the Royal Air Force Club on Piccadilly, where I met 97-year-old veteran Flight Lieutenant William Walker. I was in awe. I'd met many remarkable people in my life, but The Few were different. They were ordinary men who'd found themselves in extraordinary circumstances – and changed history. I was now twenty-three years old, but in the summer of 1940 the majority of The Few had been younger than me when they took to the skies, outnumbered by the German Luftwaffe. Had we lost the Battle of Britain, the Nazis would have invaded, and in all probability won World War Two. The Few saved our civilisation.

William told me that on 26 August 1940, his Spitfire was attacked by Messerschmitts. He received a bullet in the ankle, and the controls of his plane were shot away. He bailed out at 20,000 feet and took refuge on a sandbank, suffering from hypothermia. Picked up by a fishing boat, crowds cheered his arrival at Ramsgate, but the local hospital couldn't deal with his wound. He was transferred to an RAF hospital, where a .303 bullet was removed from his ankle. William kept it as a souvenir.

In the Cowdray Lounge of the RAF Club, William was youthful in outlook and chirpy in manner.

'How do you keep so young?' I asked him.

'Honey!' he cried. 'A tablespoon of honey every day.' He asked what I was up to in my career, and I told him I was about to embark on a UK tour of *The Pirates of Penzance* (I seem destined to repeat the show often!). William told me that he loved Gilbert and Sullivan and had seen multiple D'Oyly Carte productions as a child. As Janet and I resumed planning Memorial Day, William suddenly declared: 'I wasn't there!' I wondered what he was talking about, and then realised he was quoting the character of Pooh-Bah from *The Mikado*.

Over the next few years, the Battle of Britain Memorial Trust began to play an increasingly important role in my life. Gradually, my duties developed from singing to actively helping the veterans. I grew to know the Few. It was humbling to hear them say 'Hello, Martin!' and listen, first-hand, to their tales of heroism and bravery. They realised it was important to pass on their story, especially to younger generations – but they were never boastful or presumptuous. And privately, in each other's company, they just enjoyed a quiet chat over a pint of Spitfire beer.

It also put career matters into perspective. Many young performers I'd met had no concept of the real world outside the West End. They blew their own trumpets and maintained high opinions of themselves. However gifted or talented, their accomplishments did not compare with those of The Few.

CHAPTER TEN

'The *rôle* you're prepared to endow With such delicate touches'

The Grand Duke

The *Pirates* tour was one of the most enjoyable jobs I'd ever had. Paul Nicholas – The Pirate King – was greeted at stage doors everywhere by swooning middle-aged female fans. Paul took an active interest in the cast, with no sense of hierarchy. The same couldn't be said for another of the leads – who, being closely related to an established opera star, had automatically been offered principal roles throughout her career.

'So!' she asked a group of us, in a very bubbly manner. 'What's it *like* being in the *chorus*?'

By contrast, it was a joy to work again with Barry Clark and Bruce Graham. One night in a pub, Bruce told me that after performing as an amateur, his first professional job had been with the D'Oyly Carte in 1978.

'I was desperately nervous on my first day and knew nobody. But Kenneth Sandford made a point of coming over to welcome me to the company and shook my hand. He put me at ease right away, and I said to myself, "If I ever become a principal, I'll remember that – and do the same for someone else starting out."'

Kenneth Sandford had been one of the D'Oyly Carte's best-loved stars. Bruce now excelled in the roles he'd learned under Sandford – and when Bruce and I had originally met at rehearsals for the Gielgud West End season, he'd welcomed me as Sanford had once welcomed him. I decided that I too, given the opportunity later in my career, would look out for youngsters – and pass to them the baton passed to me by Bruce, passed to him by Sandford.

* * *

The *Pirates* cast agreed to help me with an exciting new project. Over the last few years, my dad and I had been writing the script for a sitcom – and Min from Thursford, who was expert in TV, agreed to film the pilot episode.

To attract the attention of commissioning editors, I cast ambitiously. In addition to Paul Nicholas, I also had Fenella! A few months earlier we'd been reunited at Nanny Jean's during her annual visit…

Before she became a star, Fenella had appeared in a West End revue for impresario Cecil Landau – the same producer who, a few years previously, had employed Nanny Jean and Audrey Hepburn.

'Twelve pounds a week!' Fenella dramatically lamented. 'To think that Cecil paid us only *twelve pounds* a *week*!'

'Well, Audrey and I,' Nanny Jean brightly informed her, 'were on *twenty* pounds a week!'

Fenella paused.

'Oh… *were* you, *dahling?*'

Fenella was accompanied by actress Janet Hargreaves. Nanny Jean and Janet had worked together on cult TV soap *Crossroads*. Jean was motel chef Mrs Cunningham (and, defending the series, declared, 'The scenery *never* shook!'). Janet played the notorious Rosemary Hunter, who shot her ex-husband. Over dinner, Janet reminded Fenella about their 1950s touring days.

'The night before we caught the train, you stayed over,' Janet recalled. 'My father was a military man, and you sat at his feet, gazing up at him. You said, "Ohhhhh, *Cooooolonel* Hargreaves. I've never met a *reeeeeeeal Cooooolonel* before!"'

'Did I?' Fenella asked vaguely.

'Yes,' continued Janet. 'And on the train, we sat in a bumpy carriage. You tried applying your lipstick and it went all over your face. But you just carried on, sighing, "Ohhhhh *fuuuuuuuuuuck!*"'

Bravely, I decided to broach a subject about which Fenella had never publicly spoken.

'I found a photograph online – you were singing around a piano with Noël Coward and Cicely Courtneidge!'

'Really, dahling?' Fenella smiled – but she did not elaborate.

'Wasn't that *High Spirits*?' asked Janet.

'Yes. Not a happy time.' And then, looking at me, Fenella confided, 'You see, I got the boot.'

High Spirits was a musical version of Coward's play *Blithe Spirit*. Coward directed, and Fenella was cast as the ghost, Elvira. Fenella and Coward did not get on. Fenella had apparently refused to take direction and been very opinionated, answering back to 'The Master'. Theatrical rumour had it that Coward snapped, 'Madam! You walk like a camel and have a mouth like a cunt on a bicycle!' Fenella found herself unceremoniously sacked – but, by all accounts, learned from the experience. Certainly, by the time I knew her, she was generous to all she encountered.

That night at Nanny Jean's, Fenella retired early, but Jean had forgotten to place Fenella's carmen rollers in her room. She asked me to knock on Fenella's door and take them in – but being a gentleman, I declined. I feared that Fenella may have taken off her wig.

It was one of life's great mysteries – what lay beneath Fenella Fielding's wig? Although I was curious to know the answer, I couldn't dream of walking into her room. I'd been told that Fenella once stayed overnight with a friend who'd been aching to know what the wig concealed. Therefore, he crept out of bed at 5.30 a.m., hoping to catch sight of Fenella in her night-things, but found her lying in wait – fully clothed and immaculately wigged.

'Bastard!' she allegedly declared. 'I know your game!'

When planning the sitcom pilot, I invited Fenella to lunch at Joe Allen's Restaurant. Many of the staff were 'resting' performers. Years before, according to popular legend, Fenella had required the assistance of a waiter and boomed across the room *'Actoooooooooor!'*

Fenella never touched alcohol, content with peppermint tea. She accidentally knocked her cutlery to the floor, and after I'd retrieved the knife and fork, she caressed them up close, whispering, 'Now, listen. *Behave yourselves! I shan't* tell you again!'

I pitched the sitcom to Fenella, and her eyes lit up, asking, 'Is it a good part?' I explained how The Biscuit Lady made a glamorous entrance, expressing utmost distress at her lack of Belgian biscuits. This tickled her and she purred, 'Well, dahling, let me know the date.'

I found an elaborate yellow coat in a Putney charity shop with a camp brown fur collar. I also bought a large supply of colourful hats and let Fenella know, by text, that her costume was sorted. She texted back: 'I can't get over you!'

Fenella's scenes were shot at the Churchill Theatre in Bromley. When she arrived – dolled up to the nines – filming ground to a halt whilst I welcomed the Great Star, introduced her to the crew and escorted her personally to the dressing room. I'd read enough about MGM to know how to greet a star… and afterwards Fenella was kind enough to say it was the best she'd ever been treated on a film set.

The fur-trimmed coat swamped Fenella's miniature frame – but she liked it so much that she took it home and often wore it parading up and down Chiswick High Road. But both her wigs (still worn simultaneously) were so large that the hats just slid off Fenella's head.

'You know, dahling,' she told her assistant (whom I'd provided for her exclusive pampering), 'I think these are all just a little too small.'

On set she was wonderfully individual. Whilst preparing a shot, Fenella turned to me and imparted reflectively, 'Dahling, I was watching a silent film the other night, and I thought to myself – haven't things improved?'

Yet when it came to her cameo, she was on it – any attempt by others to upstage her was dazzlingly trumped. Fenella knew every trick in the book. She didn't suffer fools gladly. And onscreen, she shimmered.

'Terrible!' she wailed. '*Terrible* about the biscuits!'

The pilot aroused the interest of several TV executives,

one of whom told us, 'Don't underestimate how well you've done to get this far.' Eventually it reached the Head of Comedy at one of the UK's largest networks. He sent a charming email of congratulations, saying that he liked it, but for him it was a no because, 'It's not like anything else out there at the moment.' Dad and I rather thought *that* was the point.

A good idea doesn't date. One day, dear reader, who knows? You may watch something which originated years ago thanks to the generosity of my veteran friends – including Janet Hargreaves, who abandoned glamour to play a dowdy tea lady.

All this kept me nicely busy – but when trying to share my updates with Josh, I continually hit a wall of silence. His absence made his acceptance – and that of his crowd – all the more important. I'd tasted inclusion. Now I craved it. I felt as though I was failing as a young straight man. In my head, it became an obsession – I *had* to be in the youthful cliquey set. Nothing else mattered. The pressure mounted, my emotions heightened by twelve months of repressed worry and stress.

Josh's tour ended in time for Thursford 2010. I always booked my cottage months in advance and eagerly anticipated that Josh might share with me. And indeed… he did! Josh, wrapped up in the tour, had forgotten to book digs, so it worked out very conveniently that I'd kept him a room. Now we'd see each other every day, making up for lost time. Things would be just like before. The perfect friendship could resume…

CHAPTER ELEVEN

'My rock had turned to sand!'

Princess Ida

The 2010 *Christmas Spectacular* included a number of very entertaining musical items which always brought the house down. My solo was 'I Got It From Agnes', the Tom Lehrer comedy song about a group of close friends who 'share' whatever they have, and give 'it' to one another – although we never find out what 'it' actually is.

My 'friends' (in 1920s costume) passed around a large red box, which I opened to reveal a balloon pump, onto the end of which was attached a long uninflated pink balloon (which I spun around madly, holding on to the end of the pump). Whilst singing, my next task was to inflate the long pink rocket-shaped balloon – which then deflated, on the end of the pump, into the face of a young lady, who fainted. Finally, I pulled out of the box a large red crab, and everyone ran offstage scratching themselves whilst the orchestra played 'Old MacDonald Had a Farm'. (Yes, dear reader... believe it or not, we got paid to do all this!)

At first, I was blissfully happy at the cottage and Josh told me he was proud of my newfound confidence. But at rehearsals, Josh was growing close to a group of boisterous lads: jocular, full of banter, beer-swilling types.

I saw all this – and ached to belong. After all, if Josh belonged, why couldn't I? But, try as I might, I just couldn't relate to 'the lads'. Their behaviour and conversation were completely alien. When I attempted to fit in, my attempts were beyond awkward. There were sniggers and strange looks – which brought back very unpleasant memories of days in the schoolyard – memories I'd been trying to suppress. Even so, I was determined to be accepted. After all, I was straight too, wasn't I?

The more I attempted, the more I failed. This made me feel desperate – and I was scared because Josh spent more and more time with his cronies. It was getting cliquey... and I was being left out. After a year of near silence from Josh, this, to me, was very painful. In addition, the lads were scoring with the dancing girls. And once again, I was a failure.

So I decided to do something about it.

There was a straight boy in the cast who didn't belong to the clique either. His name was Mark, and we got on extremely well. As well as being a singer he was also a qualified personal trainer and, prior to morning rehearsals, led circuit sessions in Fantasy Land.

I had scrawny arms and no muscles to speak of... and surely to get attention from the dancers I'd need to have arms like Marlon Brando in *A Streetcar Named Desire*. So, to the surprise of many, I threw myself into these circuit sessions wholeheartedly... and even more surprisingly, enjoyed it!

I really took to Mark. He wasn't like the other lads and accepted me when I feared rejection. We started hanging out – and I loved it! I could equate our friendship to being like Gene Kelly (him) and Donald O'Connor (me) in *Singin' in the Rain*. Or better yet – we were Bing Crosby and Bob Hope on the *Road to Thursford*. Moreover, I think Mark could see what was happening to me with regards to Josh and the lads – and he was there to support me. I was there for him too, when he himself needed a friend.

An intense theatrical run can bring out the best in people, as well as the worst. I'd found a wonderful new buddy – but I was terrified of losing my old one. Because of that, against my better judgement, all I wanted was for the lads to accept me – so I kept trying. And trying. And in the end, I proved to be very trying indeed. I shared a cottage with Josh, but he seemed more distant to me than ever. I was scared that I was losing someone I'd considered my best friend.

Josh indulged in boozy pub nights. When I went too, I didn't enjoy it. But when I stayed home, I felt left out. Living together wasn't easy. However, when I needed to escape completely, I knew of a haven where I could guarantee no one would find me…

George and Betty Fay continued to live in their tiny caravan – and I found myself spending increased amounts of time there. With the cast growing ever younger, many paid no attention to George and Betty. There was never a smile, or a hello, and certainly no attempts to engage them in conversation. It was like they weren't even there. But George and Betty had been in the business decades before every single cast member was born, and they were still in the business after many young cast members gave up the theatre after just a few years.

My visits to the caravan were a total release from the pressures I felt piling up. George and Betty had cakes at the ready whenever they knew I was visiting, and the heating was always turned up full blast as they shared with me photographs from their lives and careers.

'There was a time in the eighties when we had the birds in three different West End shows, all at the same time,' George remembered. 'We opened the first act of *Magic Flute* at the Coliseum, and then got into a taxi to the Savoy for *Sugar Babies*, and then on to the Palladium for the finale of *Ziegfeld* with Topol.'

Sugar Babies was a burlesque revue featuring Mickey Rooney and Ann Miller. The birds had to fly to Ann Miller and perch on hooks sticking out on her costume – one on each breast, and another down below. To rehearse the birds, the producers sent Betty a copy of the skimpy dancing outfit and, to the astonishment of their neighbours, Betty cavorted around the back garden whilst George trained the birds to fly to the appropriate places!

George and Betty encouraged my dreams and ambitions. They believed in me and were giving with their time and generosity. Having nothing to prove, they were two of the most worthwhile people you could hope to meet.

And just before the evening show, I had to leave them to go back to a dressing room full of stagey and cockily assured banter, of which I was not a part.

I also spent time with Min, who continued to be a rock of reliability, both professionally and personally. Because he was on the go all day, our only chance to talk was at the end of the night as he packed up the sound gear. By this time the cast had dashed to the pub, but the backstage staff remained at their posts to ensure that everything was reset properly for the two upcoming performances the next day.

The building at this time was completely deserted, and it was a privilege to see first-hand all the work that went on behind the scenes to make the show happen – work which nobody else in the cast ever saw, or sometimes even realised happened.

I'd stay and chat to Min and his colleague Steve. People who, again, had nothing to prove. At the end of his twelve-hour day, Min drove me back to the cottage – which I often found empty as Josh was out.

* * *

We'd now spent about ten weeks on site in Thursford – but because of the self-inflicted pressure it felt like a lifetime. I couldn't stop worrying about how much I needed recognition from Josh and his cronies – whose company appeared preferable to mine.

I was locked away in a fiercely febrile environment, in which all emotions were severely magnified. The outside world appeared not to exist, and I felt as though I were being crushed in a battle I couldn't win. I was being rejected all over again. Just when I thought I'd been getting somewhere in my personal life, now I was forgotten; ignored by those whose acknowledgement I blindly craved.

The most important friendship of my life was slipping away. I desperately needed a last-ditch attempt to show Josh how much he meant to me: so, I decided to do something wonderful, just for us. I'd create the perfect Christmas party! Seasonal music; coloured lights; *White Christmas* in the background; wine, mince pies and goodies. An evening planned with love for my friend.

I told Josh about my Big Idea – my Christmas treat – and suggested a night later in the week.

'Yeah,' he said. 'Yeah, that should be fine. But remind me on the day, 'cuz you know what I'm like!'

I did know what he was like. That's what worried me. But I tried not to think about it. I made all the preparations… and made sure that I reminded him on the morning of our special day.

'Oh yeah, that's tonight, isn't it? Yeah! That should still be okay.'

I was unnerved by the word 'should'. Alarm bells began to ring. I chose to ignore them.

Later, during the evening show, Josh came up and said, 'Oh, the lads are going to the pub for one tonight, so I'll be back a bit late.'

It was the moment I dreaded.

'But tonight was going to be our evening…'

'Yeah, I know, sorry! But they said just now that the pub was happening – and it's only for one. I'll see you when I get back. Won't be long.'

Since when, I asked myself, did 'the lads' only ever go 'for one'?

The lads dropped me off at the cottage and then continued down the road to the pub.

I convinced myself it was helpful to have extra time to prepare. I'd pulled out all the stops and was really proud of myself.

An hour went by.

Then, so did another.

It was now after 1 a.m. The party preparations were perfect. But there was one thing missing – the guest.

The truth slowly began to dawn. He'd taken the better offer. In pursuit of a short-term good time, I'd been overlooked. But surely after all those nights with the lads, he could have skipped the pub this once, knowing how much the evening meant to me? Couldn't he?

This friendship was clearly not what I'd built it up to be. I'd been living, and clinging to, an illusion. But that illusion had been the rock upon which my precarious personal progress had been built. My head began to spin, and I stuttered words over which I had no control.

'You put on a party – and nobody comes! You put on a party – and nobody comes!'

I was right back in the corner of the infant school playground. Worthless, humiliated and entirely disposable. Nobody could see me. No one knew I was there.

I felt betrayed. But moreover, I was angry and ashamed of myself for not having acknowledged the truth earlier. They must all be laughing at me. Wherever they were, out having a good time, they must all have been laughing at me waiting here, by myself. Or maybe even worse… perhaps I hadn't even been spared a single thought?

Anything positive I'd built up over the last two years suddenly unravelled before me. If I'd been stronger, I might have been able to cope. But I wasn't. The missing party guest had tipped the balance. My self-esteem completely collapsed.

And for the first time in my life, I lost control.

I felt as though my life had shattered into a thousand piercing fragments. Everything I'd been ever so gently and cautiously building towards had been whisked away; the work completely undone; the carpet pulled right out from under me.

I couldn't lie to myself anymore. I was alone. I thought I'd kissed goodbye to that haunting spectre, but on this unbearable night it hurtled back into my life with a screaming vengeance. Slumped against a wall, in a corner of the cottage, I broke down and sobbed. My cries were visceral, and I didn't know where to turn. Or indeed, now, to whom.

For more than an hour I released the repressed torrent of emotion which I'd kept locked deep inside. I could yell as loud as I wanted – there was no one there to hear. I was completely degraded. And nobody wanted me.

That's when I got the kitchen knife.

I stared at in my hand. I walked around the cottage holding it. Only a few moments previously I'd felt helpless – but now I felt empowered.

And I was also having an out-of-body experience. I didn't seem to know what I was doing.

'You put on a party – and nobody comes!' I repeated. Over and over. 'You put on a party – and nobody comes! You put on a party – and nobody comes!'

With the knife in my hand I took out my rage – on a colander, of all things, striking it again and again. It was an entirely stupid thing to do – but I was far from being in a reasonable frame of mind. The knife in my hand represented power; the power over things which, up to now, I'd felt completely lacking. The knife was something to cling to, both physically and emotionally.

After a considerable time, I put the knife down. I hadn't harmed myself. But I kept it close, where I could see it.

It was now well past 2 a.m. And finally, I rang Josh. It went to voicemail.

'Where *are* you?' pleaded a pathetic little voice – a voice which I realised had once resembled mine. 'Where *are* you?'

Eventually I got through to him. I didn't even try to hide what had been happening. I was a mess. But in a weird, twisted way, I finally got what I wanted: his attention.

When Josh walked in and found me, he completely freaked out.

'Martin, you need proper help,' he said.

'I can do this by myself!'

'No, Martin. You can't.'

I was aching to cry out and say that all I needed was a friend. But I didn't.

Josh left. He said he didn't feel comfortable staying. He went back and spent the night with the lads. Now I was alone again – with that knife. I'd never needed a friend more than at this moment – and no one was there.

I slumped back into the corner and cried more tears than I'd ever cried before.

'I hate my life! I… hate… my life!'

Worthless. Utterly degraded.

But, thank God, I did not pick up the knife again.

Eventually, after what seemed like an eternity, I staggered to my feet and trudged about in an aimless wander. I stumbled into the bathroom, and there, for the first time, I caught sight of myself in the mirror and realised that I'd hit the nadir.

And at that point – as I examined my bloated reflection – I heard a voice inside my head.

'No, Martin. You're better than this. This isn't you.'

Call it my subconscious. Call it something otherworldly. All I know is that I heard it – loud and clear.

'You've got to do *something*.'

I stared at my pitiful reflection for a long time. My mind had been torturing me all night, but now, at that moment, everything was infinitely calm and crystal clear.

I knew at this point I could either crumble or I could fight.

And I intended to fight.

I went and put the knife away.

It must have been about 4 a.m. I sat on my bed and thought everything through, long and hard. I was emotionally drained – but ironically things seemed clearer to me now, more than ever.

This 'perfect friendship', as I had once liked to call it, was nothing of the kind. I'd been clinging to something which didn't exist. What the friendship *had* been, historically speaking, was my first proper friendship with someone my own age. But first doesn't necessarily mean best. I'd staked all my emotional stability on a relationship to which each of us attached very different levels of importance.

The truth suddenly stared me in the face: Josh thought of me as an option and not as a priority. But to me, ever since we'd met, Josh *had* been my be-all-and-end-all priority. I'd always dropped everything, and everyone, to be there whenever he called. And sometimes he did call, but more often, he didn't. The friendship was completely imbalanced.

But I was to blame too. Because although Josh had often acted thoughtlessly, I was equally sure that I must have been insufferably stifling in my affections; my desperate need for his attention, and my pursuit of the laddish approval I craved, had pushed him even further away. I'd been blindly adamant that this friendship was *the* most important thing in the world – because I didn't know anything else – and therefore in my attempts to save it, I'd ruined it. Moreover, I was worn out and emotionally exhausted by pretending I was something I wasn't and never would be.

I began to feel angry – with myself. How *dare* I have been such an idiot for letting myself be treated – and treating myself – in this way? But not anymore. I'd cried all the tears I was going to cry.

However – was what Josh said true? Did I need help? Professional help? On the surface, it probably appeared that I did. But as I sat on my bed, I decided something: now that I knew what the problem was, I was going to do something about it and change my life around – myself.

I fell asleep, exhausted but in a strange way, beginning to feel at peace.

The next day I was scheduled to do all my solos in both the matinee and evening performances. I hosted the raffle with aplomb. Moments later I twirled that pink balloon around on the pump as if I hadn't a care in the world. No matter what kind of a mess I might have been personally, I would never let anyone say that I wasn't a professional.

'*Why* didn't you call me?' asked Mark when I told him. 'I'd have come over immediately.' And I knew that he meant it. But in the utter depths of despair, my judgement clouded, I'd genuinely thought I had no one to turn to. Also – although I couldn't admit it – I'd been far too ashamed of myself and my actions to let Mark, Min or anyone else I truly cared about see what had happened.

However, thanks to them, I now knew that I would never be in this position again. Why, I asked myself, had I craved the approval of people with whom I had nothing in common, when truly remarkable people like George and Betty accepted me as I was?

So *this* was what a real friendship was supposed to feel like! I might have hit rock bottom, but I was not, in reality, alone. In my head I suddenly heard the voice of Debbie Reynolds in *The Unsinkable Molly Brown*: 'I ain't down yet!'

In an ideal world, of course, this would have coincided with the end of the Thursford run; I'd have been able to go home to lick my wounds in private. But we still had about ten days to go before the show closed – performing twice a day, seven days a week. In the words of Irving Berlin, I had to 'go on with the show'.

When you work in the theatre you have a responsibility to your audience. 'Show people' have to 'smile when they are low'. Your life may be falling apart, but you carry on and do your job. It is not a profession for the faint-hearted.

And then, to cap this entirely surreal experience, the world's paparazzi descended on Thursford. On 18 December, Prince William and his fiancée Catherine Middleton attended a Charity Gala performance of the Thursford *Christmas Spectacular* in aid of the Teenage Cancer Trust. It was their first public appearance since their engagement a few weeks earlier, and our tiny hamlet was invaded by the press – all of whom drove straight past our cottage. The cast lined up in Fantasy Land to meet the Prince and his fiancée outside Santa's House. His Royal Highness stopped to chat with George and Betty, quizzing them about training the birds.

'How do you do it? Do you tempt them with sweets and bread?'

'Ohhhhh.' George smiled, before adding a simple, 'No.' And that was that.

The last evenings in the cottage were strained; we ended the run with a hug but had no communication for a while afterwards. In time, relations with Josh recovered – we even worked together again – though naturally it was never the same. But that was fine.

I accepted that we'd grown apart. There was no point in making life miserable, trying to cling on. We were both very different people with different outlooks, and our friendship circles each suited our own personalities. I finally stopped trying to be somebody I wasn't in order to try to fit in.

And my God, did life get better after that!

I owe a lot to the early days of our friendship – Josh taught me a great deal. But more recent events had booted me, however painfully, very much in the right direction. I'd learned what was both good and bad about myself; what was admirable and not so admirable.

And I learned about friendship: how it needs to be nurtured, but balanced, with each party making an equal effort. I learned what I valued most in a friend; also, in turn, what kind of a friend I should be to others.

But all of this was to sort itself out with Josh in the months and years that followed. Over Christmas itself,

I was in a very delicate place. The shock that I'd hit rock bottom was a massive wake-up call, and I realised just how far I'd fallen. It scared me – I honestly didn't know what would happen next. I'd proven expert in steering my professional destiny but never my personal life. However, changes were going to be made.

Firstly – no longer would I prioritise anyone for whom I was clearly only an option. That's how I'd ended up in this mess. It was a life lesson painfully learned.

Secondly – I would say yes to everything that came my way. I'd grab each opportunity with both hands and meet as many people as I could; I'd find out what worked for me and see where life took me. I'd only go where I was wanted, and most importantly, I would only spend time with people who genuinely wanted to spend time with me in return. As the song from *Paint Your Wagon* stated – I didn't know where I was going; I wasn't certain when I'd get there; all I knew was, I was on my way.

And I knew that I had one friend above all whom I could guarantee would be there every time, no matter what. Someone whose world I understood, and who understood mine… I spent New Year's Eve with Nanny Jean.

To see her again after the emotional turbulence of the last few months meant everything – I was welcome, wanted and where I belonged. And as an ultra-special treat, I'd be celebrating with not just one glamorous star but two. Her appearance couldn't have been better timed.

Jean had a houseguest staying from LA – her lifelong friend, actress Ann Wakefield. Annie and Jean met in 1955 when Jean joined the Broadway cast of *The Boy Friend*. Annie played the role of Madcap Maisie, who asks the toe-tapping question 'Won't You Charleston with Me?' After Broadway, Annie and Jean toured the States for a year, after which Jean returned to London. Annie stayed in America, marrying Hollywood character actor John Crawford.

John had passed away just four months previously. So, although neither Jean nor Annie had the first idea about recent events in my own life, we were all finding comfort in each other's company. Annie had been hearing about me from Jean for years, so already she felt as though she knew me.

'I tell you, Jeanie – Martin's going to be a great writer!'

'Oh no, dear! Martin's going to be a great *performer*!'

'No, no, dear. Of *course* he's a beautiful performer, but so few people can write…'

'Darling – I'm telling you – Martin's a *performer*!'

The evening was madcap, eccentric and incredibly, incredibly special. I was enveloped, without hesitation, into the stability of a friendship which had lasted over half a century; sharing in the warmth and love of two dear friends who, after all they'd been through together, welcomed me as an equal. As the clock ticked closer to midnight, we caroused with songs from *The Boy Friend*, and Annie danced the Charleston in Nanny Jean's living room.

Jean and Annie's stimulating presence was safe and reassuring; their strength and resilience inspiring. They'd lived through pain and hardship – but as the Sondheim song said, they were 'still here'. As a child, Annie had escaped the Nazis, fleeing Guernsey on the last boat just thirty minutes before the Germans arrived. And having just lost her lifelong love, here was Annie at 80 still dancing the Charleston.

I was observing survivors in action. They adapted, overcame their problems and moved on. Annie's stories about her escape from Guernsey started me thinking in more depth about others from this remarkable generation. Not just the stars of stage and screen, but also the *real* heroes: the Battle of Britain veterans.

Spitfire pilot Geoffrey Wellum was 18 years old when he was given a few hours' training time (having never flown in his life), before fighting the enemy with only fifteen seconds of ammunition. Geoffrey suffered a breakdown during his service – but returned to his post at the first opportunity. Seventy years on, he was living life to the full.

I acknowledged that I clearly had issues to overcome – but they were not anything *like* the issues which my older friends had experienced. If they could get through all that – and tell the tale with humility and good humour a lifetime later – then I could do *anything*. The older generation was there for me, guiding the way. And I was very, very lucky to know them.

Annie signed a photograph for me – one of her publicity stills from *The Boy Friend*: 'Martin, my dear, talented friend. A great 2011 to you…' I silently promised Annie that it would be.

As Big Ben ushered in the new year, it seemed fitting to share the moment with Nanny Jean – because in 2011 I knew I had to act on the advice given to Maria by the Mother Abbess: I couldn't shut out my problems. I had to face them – and find the life I was born to live.

It was time to 'follow ev'ry rainbow'…

CHAPTER TWELVE

'I'm going to take lessons'

The Mikado

'Right, Mr Milnes,' said Mark. 'You're my project for the
new year. Let's get you sorted.'

We had a blast and kept productive, looking at songs
and monologues together, seeing shows and keeping artistically busy. But I made sure that I wasn't reliant on him.
I wasn't going to make the same mistakes I had with Josh
– although knowing Mark was there, and that he believed
in me, boosted my confidence to try new things.

Whenever singers were required for one-off shows
or concerts, I always signed up, just to get out and meet
people. It worked. A new friendship circle began to open.
Sometimes I'd meet girls – but I had no idea how to talk
to them. Mark was an excellent role model, and under his
subtle guidance I avoided all faux pas (like using chat-up
lines from *Carry Ons*).

However, during these early days it wasn't romance I
needed to find. I was learning to be comfortable within
myself, rebuilding what personal confidence and esteem
I had lost.

I was able to pop into town very easily from Chiswick,

my latest London abode. And it was thanks to Nanny Jean that I'd found my new housemate…

She'd introduced me to actor Alan Curtis when he came to visit her in Birmingham. Knowing that I needed new digs in London, Alan kindly suggested that I stay awhile in his spare room. It turned out to be a great arrangement, providing me with a super base, and Alan with someone to keep him in the loop about theatrical goings-on. Over twenty years previously, whilst still in his sixties, Alan had suffered a stroke which left him unable to continue his acting career… but his memorabilia crowded all corners of the house.

Proudly on display, commemorating his West End pantomimes, were the engraved brass plaques from his Palladium dressing-room door. Alan had been one of the great pantomime villains of his generation; by all accounts the definitive Abanazar. Posters of his five Palladium pantos were mounted on the wall, as well as a photograph depicting a career highlight: Alan playing King Philip of Spain in *Queen Elizabeth* opposite Dame Flora Robson… ably supported by Eric Morecambe playing William Shakespeare and Ernie Wise as Sir Walter Raleigh!

Alan had known 'the boys' (as Morecambe and Wise had fondly been called) before they hit the big time, first working with them in 1953 at the Sheffield Lyceum in *Babes in the Wood*. Alan was the Sheriff of Nottingham, with Eric and Ernie as The Robbers, although back then Stan Stennett was the bigger audience draw. When Eric and Ernie secured their own TV series, they remained loyal to their old friend, inviting Alan to appear several times.

'I did a sketch for the boys with Fenella,' Alan remembered. 'She kept me inside her cupboard, and I had to pop out at the end to say just one line!'

His links to Morecambe and Wise were still strong. One day I answered the phone and found I was speaking to Stan Stennett; holiday postcards would fall through the letterbox from Ernie's widow, Doreen Wise.

I'd sit and absorb all I could from Alan, whose recall for names, dates and production credits was phenomenal. Alan had learned his craft as an amateur actor whilst, from the age of thirteen, digging graves and making coffins for a living. At sixteen he helped make puppet films for J. Arthur Rank; his first brush with professional theatre arrived in 1949 – painting scenery for Frinton's summer season and working backstage at the Penge Empire. By 1952 Alan was in weekly rep, acting in seventy-two different plays in seventy-six weeks, including Shakespeare twice nightly (either *Macbeth* or *The Merchant of Venice*), with two additional matinees each day on both Tuesdays and Wednesdays.

'And the cast thought they had their work cut out doing two shows a day at Thursford!' I told Mark, remembering those who moaned they were exhausted.

My chats with Alan reinforced that I didn't need to worry about fitting in with the young partying types. I wanted to spend time with Alan and felt privileged that he wanted to spend time with me. I also got quite a kick from the fact that I was living with the Spanish Chief of Police from *Carry On Abroad*. As a child, one of the many lines I'd mimicked from that film had been Alan's: 'Madame Fifi is *my sister!*'

My aspirations in life were to emulate pros such as

Alan – also Jean, Annie and Fenella. They *loved* to work, no matter how demanding their commitments. When Jean and Audrey Hepburn were chorus girls, they did four shows a day.

'Tired?' Jean laughed. 'We weren't tired! We *loved* it!'

I found this work ethic far more admirable than that of certain contemporaries, whom I knew would phone in sick because they had a cold and 'couldn't sing'. 'We *all* sang on colds,' Nanny Jean told me – which I'd once pointed out to a young performer, telling him that Jean never missed a show during her two-year run as Maria, her voice filling the Palace Theatre unamplified. 'I'd *never* let my understudy on!' Nanny Jean hissed. '*Not* while there was a breath left in me!'

In that same vein, Fenella had gone to extreme lengths to avoid missing a performance. One morning she over-slept and realised she'd missed the last train from Victoria which could get her to Chichester in time for her matinee. So, Fenella simply opened the Yellow Pages and char-tered a helicopter – she flew from London to Chichester, touching down on the lawns outside the theatre, playing the matinee as if nothing had happened.

The influence of veteran performers during this deli-cate period continued. When I played The Pheasantry in Chelsea with a new version of *The Falsetto*, I was touched that Fenella came to support me, arriving stag.

'Dahling,' she cooed afterwards, clasping my hands. 'Do you know what I'd like to hear you sing?' Then she rolled her eyes, seductively raised her arms, swirled her hands and sang (at half its usual tempo), *'How would you like to spend a weekend in Havanaaaaaaaaaaaa?'*

But beneath her idiosyncrasies, Fenella's expertise in holding an audience was unparalleled. 'Dahling,' she advised, 'always remember to ensure that they listen, never be afraid to *take...*' And then she paused... and paused... and paused... at which point I was now on tenterhooks. Then finally, she slowly smiled, and eventually purred, '*Your time.*'

In February, Steve Ross returned to The Pheasantry. On stage, Steve wore a green velvet smoking jacket which had once belonged to Noël Coward – which after that night's show, he let me try on.

Ever since he'd taken me under his artistic wing, Steve had been sure to give me his time whenever he came to London. On his last trip twelve months previously, he'd invited me to join him at the Garrick Club. It was my first visit to the legendary private members establishment – a home from home for Charles Dickens, J.M. Barrie, Coward, Olivier and Gielgud. Gilbert and Sullivan had both held membership – albeit, as Garrick Club member Bruce Graham informed me, at different times. Gilbert's writing desk, on which he wrote all his later works, was one of the many theatrical treasures on display. Across the room was a beautiful grand piano, on which Steve played and sang.

'I feel so at home here,' I told my host. 'I've always felt like I was born in the wrong era.'

Steve looked at me and paused. 'No, my dear,' he replied. 'You were born in the *right* era to maintain the *old* standards.'

Twelve months on, I invited Steve to join me for a matinee of Fenella's new show on Thursday 17 February.

The day before, I asked Steve what time and where he'd like to meet prior to the performance.

But I had no idea that his email response would change my life.

'What might be nice is for you to join me in Chelsea at the lovely flat of that charming 97-year-old coquette, Ginny Campbell, for lunch beforehand. If you'd like to, that is? I know you have particular appreciation for what has gone before, and she's really something. She loves meeting new young men, especially attractive and talented ones (well who doesn't?). If this idea appeals, we'd fore-gather on the King's Road to get a couple of things for the lunch I'm bringing to her and her husband, at about 1 p.m. And then we could make our way together to the theatre for the matinee. If not, I'll probably see you there.'

An invitation from Steve Ross, I knew, was worth ac-cepting. But who was Ginny Campbell? I put the name into Google, and found an encouraging lead on IMDb:

Virginia Campbell is an actress, known for Uncon-quered *(1947),* That Lady in Ermine *(1948) and* Home Town Story *(1951).*

I asked Steve – and he confirmed that Virginia and Ginny were one and the same.

As I clicked on the web links, my childhood fantasies of Old Hollywood were fulfilled! Virginia Campbell appeared to be living film history, having worked with two of cinema's most important early directors – Cecil B. DeMille *(Unconquered)* and Ernst Lubitsch *(That Lady in Ermine)*.

DeMille was the founding father of Hollywood. It was a California dust town in 1913 when he discovered the place by accident – he'd wanted to film outdoors in Arizona, but the natural light was better in Hollywood. When DeMille turned a decaying barn into the first Californian film studio, the movie capital of the world was born.

Lubitsch's subtle and sophisticated sex comedies were amongst my favourite movies. And Virginia Campbell's co-stars included names which, to me, were immortal: Gary Cooper, Paulette Goddard, Boris Karloff, Betty Grable, Douglas Fairbanks Jr, and a starlet who in 1951 was on the brink of a great career – Marilyn Monroe.

IMDb stated that Virginia Campbell's birthday was 17 February 1914 – meaning that when we met, the next day, it would be on her ninety-seventh birthday! I'd be lunching with the last link to the titans who'd shaped cinematic history… and therefore, indirectly, through my love of classic film as a child, my own life.

CHAPTER THIRTEEN

'Take a pair of sparkling eyes'

The Gondoliers

I felt a pair of arms coil their way around my shoulders. This was odd because there was nothing behind me except iron railings guarding the courtyard of The Pheasantry. Then I heard a familiar voice: 'You know what used to happen to young men lurking on King's Road?'

Steve and I strolled to Waitrose. 'She'll love meeting you,' he assured me, whilst gathering his contribution to lunch. 'And we'll make sure you sing something for her birthday!'

'I'll get her some flowers!' I decided.

'What a gentleman,' Steve commented. But there was no way I could *not* go bearing flowers. After all, my gran had ingrained this in me years previously – the first time I'd met Jean Bayless. I chose a bunch of yellow roses.

We crossed the road and began walking in the direction of Virginia Campbell's apartment.

'Who else will be there?' I asked.

'Oh, her husband. I'm not sure who else. He was in the war, I think. But she's had several. Husbands, that is.'

I couldn't help but smile – Virginia Campbell was already living up to my image of a quintessential Hollywood star.

We arrived at the doorway to a grand apartment block. Steve pressed the bell for number fifteen.

'Hell-oooo?' came a voice on the intercom. It was pixie-like, sparkling, and to coin Steve's own word 'coquettish'.

'Hello, my dear! It's Steve!'

'He-*llo!* He-*llo!* Come on up!'

We were buzzed inside and walked towards an ancient-looking lift. The doors opened to reveal an old-fashioned heavy iron gate, which we had to pull across with a clang to enter the car. The lift itself was tiny – space for no more than two people. As we ascended, it was truly taking us up towards a world of yesteryear.

We reached the top floor and Steve pulled aside the iron gate. There, standing in an open doorway, at the top of a short flight of stairs, was a tiny figure bursting with vitality. She had short white hair, an impish smile and eyes which sparkled with excitement. She was wearing a white blouse with a stylish red scarf, perfectly offset by a multi-coloured feminine waistcoat of red, purple, yellow and green. Her left arm was extended outwards in greeting, gesturing towards us with each cry of:

'He-*llo!* He-*llo!*'

I was captivated – and I hadn't even yet stepped out of the lift.

'I've brought you a present,' Steve said, gesturing to me. 'This is Martin. And you're going to love him!'

'Well!' Ginny replied, drinking me in with an elfin flirtatious manner. 'He-*llo!*' She extended her hand and looked me straight in the eye. My devotion was instant.

'How do you do, Miss Campbell?' I asked as we stepped inside. 'And happy birthday! I brought these for you…'

'Ohhh!' she cried, clasping her hands together. The gesture was theatrical but the sentiment entirely genuine. As she cradled the roses, she exclaimed her gratitude with a beguiling Southern American lilt: 'How *wonderful!* Thank you! *Thank* you!'

The apartment was sparsely furnished – but it was the sort of place in which every item told a story. Lampshades were adorned with miniature feminine rococo figures; the childlike paintings decorating the walls were sophisticatedly abstract.

Sitting in an ornate chair by the fireplace was an elderly Englishman. He was more casually dressed than his wife, in a light blue woollen top with an open zip at the neck.

'And this,' Ginny said proudly, 'is Lenny.'

Lenny took my hand with a firm masculine grip.

'Hello, my friend,' he said and smiled. From that point on he said little. But words were clearly unnecessary: Ginny and Lenny's adoring looks to each other were more like those of love-struck newly-weds than a couple of nearly forty years. And their humour was enchanting. When Ginny flashed her coquettish smiles my way Lenny warned me: 'Pistols at dawn on Hampstead Heath!'

'Please!' said Ginny, gesturing to an ancient wooden dining table. 'Let's sit here!'

Ginny and Lenny sat opposite Steve and me. A Filipino lady emerged from the kitchen and placed my flowers in the centre of the table.

'This is Virgie!' Ginny explained as the smiling lady proceeded to serve lunch, but not before Ginny had suitably praised my roses once again.

'We'll be flying out soon to Sperlonga,' Ginny told

Steve, before turning to me. 'This, my dear, is where we live in Italy. Steve has been there!' Then she turned back to Steve. 'I wish I could make your show tonight!' And then her face crumpled as if she were about to cry. 'But I *can't* do those *stairs!*'

The Pheasantry, Steve sadly reiterated, did not have a lift, and the music room was several flights down. Then she turned to me, as if to justify herself. 'I *can* walk! But I just can't do stairs. It's this bloody arthritis!'

Lenny sat with his arms proudly folded, gazing rapturously at his wife. I was equally as transfixed. I'd met veteran stars before – a great many – but Ginny wasn't just of another era – she was of another world, lit from within by a delicate refinement. Her style set her apart from anyone I'd ever met. I was reminded of the scene from *A Star is Born* in which James Mason defines 'star quality' as 'that little something extra'. Ginny Campbell had it in spades.

After I felt a polite period had passed, I posed the question I'd been longing to ask.

'I understand you worked with Cecil B. DeMille…'

'Oh! My *dear*!' she exclaimed. An anecdote was clearly about to commence. Both Ginny's head and her spoon – temporarily suspended in mid-air – were poised at theatrical angles. 'I was a *stage* actress,' she began. 'I didn't know who he was!' This hilariously flippant nugget about the giant of cinema delighted me – and there was more to come. 'They'd given the part to Jessica Tandy – but she couldn't do it – so Jessie gave my name to Mr DeMille, who sent for me from New York.' I was hooked. Steve was smiling. He'd anticipated this meeting would be a success, and he wasn't wrong.

'We had a meeting at Paramount,' Ginny continued, 'and he said, "Well, Miss Campbell, I'm perfectly satisfied. The part is yours." And I said, "But, Mr DeMille! You haven't given me a screen test! How do you know I'm going to photograph well?" And he replied, "I'm quite satisfied, Miss Campbell. A screen test will be unnecessary." But I said, "Mr DeMille! This is *your* picture – and I want you to be sure. You *must* give me a screen test!" And he laughed – because no actress had ever insisted on that, having already been offered the part! But I was from New York – I didn't know how it worked in Hollywood. I didn't know who he was!'

I laughed out loud. I hadn't been this happy in months!

'But you know, later in the picture we were shooting this crowd scene. There were extras everywhere. Mr DeMille came over and said, "Now, Paulette, you're doing this…" and, "Ginny, you're doing that…" And then he got onto one of those big cranes and disappeared up into the roof to get the overhead shot. But *I* said…' And then she tilted her head upwards as if addressing her director in the rafters, '"Mr DeMille! Come down here! You haven't told these extras what to do! How can they act properly if they don't know what you want?" Well – *my dear* – the place fell silent! And Mr DeMille said, "I'm so sorry, Miss Campbell." And he came all the way down and gave the extras their direction. Everyone was astounded, but *I* didn't know you didn't speak to Mr DeMille like that!'

Ginny, like so many of her generation, was a storyteller par excellence.

'After I finished my scenes, I went home to New York… but they discovered that they hadn't worked out how, at the end of the picture, Gary finds out that Paulette is trapped in the barn. So I had to come back! They flew me back to Hollywood just to shoot a few lines of me telling him where to find her!'

I wanted to listen to Ginny all day – but Steve insisted I perform before we left. Virgie turned Ginny's chair around to face the piano. It was a small white upright situated in a cubbyhole beneath a flight of stairs. And when Steve began playing, it soon became evident that the piano was hardly ever used. But nevertheless, I gave my all for Virginia Campbell's spontaneous ninety-seventh birthday concert, singing 'On the Street Where You Live', followed by, at Steve's suggestion, 'The Sun Whose Rays' in falsetto. There can't be many 97-year-old film stars given a 24-year-old falsettist for their birthday (serenading them with Gilbert and Sullivan), but Ginny was applauding with her hands over her head. Steve then performed Ginny's all-time favourite, Cole Porter's 'Night and Day'.

Just being in her presence made me feel better. Virginia Campbell radiated happiness, gaiety, wisdom. She represented all the Hollywood dreams of my childhood – and as strange as it seemed after just one meeting, I felt a connection.

'I hope you don't think me too forward,' I asked, 'but might I call on you again?'

'Of course! You must come over for dinner!'

Lenny shook our hands, and as Steve and I departed in the lift, Ginny waved us off. But as we hurried into the West End, I felt as though a piece of my heart had been left behind in that Chelsea apartment.

* * *

Fenella, as always, was enchanting – and I was the youngest person at Jermyn Street Theatre by quite a number of decades! At the end of the show an adoring crowd awaited the emergence of La Fielding. I had an audition that evening but several hours to kill in the meantime.

'Would you like to come for tea at BAFTA?' Fenella purred.

As we turned to walk up Church Place towards Piccadilly, the star and her entourage (consisting, I noted, entirely of men) passed a fierce-looking chain-smoking East End lady, far more butch than anyone in Fenella's immediate vicinity. Tattoos covered both her arms and she was deeply ensconced in a colourful argument on her mobile when suddenly she yelled at the top of her voice:

'Oh my *Gawd!* It's that woman out the *Carry On* films!' Literally chasing after Fenella, the lady dropped her phone and started kissing Fenella's hand. 'I just got to tell you – I think you're amazing! I love you!' Fenella looked surprised – and most gracious – she was a lady who knew exactly how to deal with her public.

My audition was for a fringe production of *Little Shop of Horrors*. The auditions took place in an abandoned office block – there clearly wasn't much of a production budget here! In a rather undignified manner, all aspiring applicants had to wait in a descending queue on the stairs outside the audition room.

But I was still thinking about Virginia Campbell. I was beating back the urge to grab some of the loud 'stagey' kids in my vicinity – who appeared rather sure of themselves

– and shake some sense into them: 'Don't you know what a STAR is? I've just had lunch with a *real star*!'

Ginny had shared a good deal with me that afternoon – but I wanted to know more. Lenny said hardly a word, but surely someone as remarkable as Ginny couldn't be married to anyone other than a man equally as fascinating as she.

And then I realised – I'd been the unexpected guest at a birthday party. The surprise guest whose presence was welcomed, celebrated and embraced. Virginia Campbell radiated joy on her birthday. Sharing it with her had made me feel special, so much in harmony with myself. And what's more – I'd been invited back.

Yet again the generosity of my elders was securing my pathway. Steve Ross didn't realise it, but he'd unwittingly brought Ginny and Lenny into my life at the precise moment that I needed two guiding stars.

CHAPTER FOURTEEN

'And you couldn't have desired
A more reciprocating couple'

The Gondoliers

'She was in *Unconquered*!' Alan cried, his face a picture of delighted surprise. 'I remember it playing in Leicester Square, with huge billboards over the cinema: Gary Cooper! Paulette Goddard! Boris Karloff! Virginia Campbell!'

My younger friends were not quite so familiar with her work.

'*And,*' I gushed to Mark, 'she was in one of the first ever American television broadcasts! In 1939! With Montgomery Clift!'

'Great, Martin,' he said, smiling with interest and patience. He'd been hearing a lot about my remarkable new friends. But right now, we were clothes shopping – for me. Mark's idea was that a new wardrobe would help establish a new Martin. I came out of the changing room to ask for Mark's opinion and was stopped by an animated young lady.

'Oh wow!' she said. 'You look great – that really works on you! Looks amazing!' I was chuffed to bits and bought the items immediately. Later, I asked Mark who she was.

'Don't know,' he replied. 'But I asked if she could do me a favour. I told her your girlfriend had just dumped you and you'd lost all your confidence!'

Normally I only wore contact lenses for shows, but now I decided to wear them full-time. Mark also encouraged me to grow my hair longer. I was 'Thoroughly Modern Martin', and felt just like Dorothy Malone in *The Big Sleep*, who, when she takes off her glasses and lets down her hair, goes from being the prim and mousey bookstore keeper to an object of desire, worthy of Bogart.

This was confirmed by my new Facebook profile photo – a triumph of aesthetic transfiguration. Even my body language was different. Not long afterwards I bumped into a Thursford boy, who made a point of telling me, 'Omigod, so I was on Facebook, and I saw this photo come up and I thought "Who *is* that smoking hot guy?" And then I realised, omigod, it's *you*!'

* * *

Rehearsing *Little Shop of Horrors* with new people offered a fresh slate. Socially the experience was an absolute blast. The show, however, was in trouble. Fringe productions can often be weird and wacky – and this one had weirdness in spades.

The artistic concept was to have the three Ronettes (traditionally played by female soul singers) played by boys in drag (of whom I was one); but halfway through the first act, the Ronettes would vanish in order to reappear playing the plant. The man-eating plant is normally a large puppet, voiced by an off-stage actor, but here the plant was played by the former Ronettes (without explaining the metamorphoses), wearing skimpy leafy outfits, with wild hair. The concept on paper sounded intriguing… in practice it didn't work at all.

However, as a certain patina of camp was involved, it allowed me to experiment letting fly with my personality. I'd told Mark about the Franklin Experience, which had, of course, proved I wasn't gay, but I did confess that prior to that, I'd occasionally found guys attractive.

'So what?' asked Mark. 'Doesn't matter. And if you find guys attractive again then who cares? It's just whatever you want.'

Mark's casual tone helped me realise that it wasn't an issue. And if anyone found out, no prying columnists like Hedda Hopper or Louella Parsons would scandalise the scoop. It wasn't a big deal. That was nice!

I went about my business keeping an open mind. For private one-on-one friendship and guidance, I had Mark. For fun, excitement and a group my own age, I had the *Little Shop* cast. For a comfortable and calm home environment, I had Alan. And once every week I entered a world all its own: upstairs on the fourth floor of that Chelsea apartment block.

'I had tuberculosis,' Ginny told me, 'and no one came near me. They were terrified – it was contagious! I was so lonely. But Boris Karloff walked straight into my room – and, my dear, he took me in his arms and planted this big kiss straight on my lips. You see, he wanted me to know that I wasn't alone. And I was always grateful to him for that.'

Her story resonated. I, too, knew how it felt having someone there when others turned away.

Ginny sat on the antique sofa which had been in her family for generations, adorned with the crest of her Southern lineage. Lenny sat opposite in his usual chair next to the electric fire. I perched in another antique chair between the two of them, leaning forward to catch the next golden anecdote.

'Do you *like stories*?' Ginny asked during our first dinner, with a leading smile and twinkle in her eye. But she already knew the answer.

We'd established a ritual: I'd arrive at 7 p.m. bearing flowers – yellow roses again. They always lasted until my next visit the following week, and apparently Ginny liked showing them off to visitors in the meantime, all of whom she told about 'our young man'.

Virgie served dinner at 8 p.m. In the meantime, the lovely Filipino lady, devoted to her friends and employers, supplied each of us with a glass of white wine, and often caviar canapés too.

'More wine!' Lenny cried at the earliest sign of an empty glass. 'I'm dying of thirst!' Wine was Lenny's priority: 'I'm not colour conscious.' Ginny inevitably did more of the talking, so Lenny would have to remind her, 'Drink your wine, Ginny! It's good for girls!'

In turn, Virgie reminded Lenny to take his pills – but Lenny had a sense of humour and was nothing if not stubborn.

'Ohhh, Mr Lambert!' Virgie announced. 'It's time for your pill. Now, come. Drink!' She handed Lenny a glass of water (which, being a non-alcoholic substance, he abhorred) and he put the pill in his mouth. 'Very good, Mr Lambert!' But then Lenny opened his mouth and cheekily stuck out his tongue, revealing that the pill was still there.

'Ohhhhh, Mr Lambert!' Virgie wailed, throwing her arms in the air as Lenny looked up innocently. 'You *must* take your pill!' He continued to sit with his tongue out, playing up to Ginny who, unhelpfully, just giggled, tickled by the childish prank. Being the new kid on the block, I decided to keep quiet; Lenny seemed to enjoy my tactful neutrality.

The flat was filled with just enough family heirlooms to make it feel like the Italian villa in Sperlonga which Ginny and Lenny called home. She'd owned the coastal hideaway since the early 1950s, living there with her second husband, the writer John Becker. One treasured item was now resident in London…

'John gave me that when I was ill,' Ginny said, pointing to a large ornate wooden music box next to the sofa, with a wind-up handle. 'He found it in the waiting room of a railway station in Paris – they were going to throw it out, but John knew I'd just love it. I wasn't allowed to move. I couldn't get out of bed for months. So, he had them take it out of the station and they brought it to me in my room.'

I wound the handle gently. The ancient clockwork inside achingly spluttered into life – and then suddenly there was music – the mechanical music of a past century. The interior of the box lit up, and the tiny figurines of six long-haired dancing girls began to jump, spinning round and round. Lenny smiled nostalgically, his arms folded. Ginny's silver giggle accompanied the music.

It was a magical moment: the room was lit minimally by atmospheric lamplight, and as the girls danced in their now dirty and aged dresses, we listened to the same refrain which a lifetime ago had distracted bored railway passengers at that old Parisian station.

The music stopped, and Ginny applauded the clockwork dancing girls: 'Bravo! Bravo!'

'Well, I certainly wouldn't mind receiving *that* as a present if I was ill!' I said, laughing.

'John knew I'd love it. I was in that Paris hotel room all alone – and no one came to see me. Not even Gene.'

'Gene?'

'Gene Kelly.' Not for the first time, my jaw dropped. 'We'd been great friends in New York in the thirties – on Broadway. I was in *Family Portrait* and he was playing the theatre opposite, in some revue. We met between shows and danced together – just because we loved to!' Ginny was sparkling once again, her voice and mannerisms ignited by happy memories. 'When people found out, they asked us to dance together in a big Broadway benefit!' Then her tone of voice changed. 'But years later, when John saw him in Paris, Gene asked "How's Ginny?"… and when he told Gene I was ill and couldn't get out of bed, Gene said he didn't want to see me. He thought he might catch it – tuberculosis. He just walked away. That's why I loved Boris so much. He *did* come to see me. He made me feel much better.'

Yes indeed. I could absolutely relate to all that.

Dinner was served. I'd always offer Ginny my arm as she ascended from the sofa, with Lenny following behind. As before, they sat opposite me, my yellow roses placed in the middle of the ancient wooden table. I absorbed how Ginny glistened as a hostess – investing every moment in making her guests feel welcome and at ease. She brimmed with Old Southern charm, the likes of which I'd only ever witnessed from the silver screen: *Gone with the Wind, Jezebel, The Little Foxes, Show Boat.* But this was no make-believe or game of 'just supposing'. Ginny was a genuine Southern belle…

The Hortenstine family was amongst Louisiana's most distinguished; Ginny was an heiress born into luxury. In this world, when a gentleman was insulted, he desired satisfaction the traditional way: when Ginny's grandmother had an affair with a local doctor, her husband shot him. It was her grandmother who mainly raised Ginny, as her mother died at the age of thirty-two, when Ginny was only an infant. Her father, twelve years older than his wife and frequently absent, was an engineer who helped construct the Panama Canal.

'When I grew up in Plaquemine,' Ginny told me, 'I used to ride my pony, Black Beauty, along the levee to the sugar plantation and back. Someone said to my father, "You must do something about your daughter, because when she goes out on her pony all you see is a cloud of dust and a touch of black!"'

'They always knew it was her!' Lenny chipped in.

'No roads,' she continued, 'but later, when the boys bought their first Fords, they'd drive them side by side, fast as they could. And us girls would ride on the running boards, screaming and jumping between the two cars! This was our idea of fun!' And with that she giggled and crinkled her face into a picture of coquettish delight.

This was far more interesting than any dinner conversation I'd had with the laddish types… and I was learning from someone who really knew how to tell a story.

'What's your earliest memory?' I asked.

'One of them,' she began, 'was sitting on my father's knee at my mother's funeral – I was seven. And I saw that he had tears rolling down his cheeks. So, I took his tie,' she explained, re-enacting the gestures, 'and held it in my hand – and gently wiped away his tears.'

She then looked down at her plate and concentrated on her meal, carefully gathering the meat on the silver fork – part of her late mother's engraved cutlery set. I couldn't help but wonder who else, over the last hundred years, had dined with the same implements.

Ginny didn't seem to think her life had been anything particularly special. Maybe that's because she knew no other existence. But the era of which Ginny spoke was now an age long extinct – except for its sole survivor. There was a pause as I didn't want to bombard her with questions. That's when Lenny took over.

'Adolf Galland,' he announced, 'was one of Germany's top fighter pilots. In 1944 we fought each other twice on the same day, over Antwerp. I couldn't get him – he couldn't get me. In the end,' he said, raising his hand to his forehead, 'we saluted each other and flew off in different directions.'

Lenny hadn't automatically offered anecdotes the way Ginny had. But over the last few visits, he'd begun to reveal more. I'd discovered that during World War Two, Lenny Lambert had been a very highly regarded fighter pilot in the Royal Air Force.

'Years later,' he carried on, 'Willie Messerschmitt introduced us to each other at a party in Munich. He sat
between us, and he said to me, "Do you recognise this
man?" – and I said no. And he said to Galland, "Do you
recognise *this* man?" – and *he* said no. "Well, you should.
You fought each other twice, for thirty minutes – and it
was inconclusive!"' Lenny took on the character of Adolf
Galland as he leaned forward. 'He said to me, "You were
impossible!" And I said to him – "So were *you*."' Ginny's
proud gaze was fixed on Lenny as he continued. 'He came
round here several times.' Meaning the apartment. 'We
became good friends.' And then in a serious tone, he
added, 'War is entirely the making of politicians. We had
no personal argument, him and I.'

It was humbling. Over the years, this apartment had
hosted other great figures – among them legendary dramatic duo (and Ginny's lifelong friends), Hume Cronyn
and Jessica Tandy. American silent-movie star Bessie
Love – Oscar nominee of 1928 – had lived nearby. Now
they were all gone – but as the Lamberts' latest guest, I
was being treated as their equal. And it dawned on me
that I mustn't be all that undesirable company if Ginny
and Lenny wanted me around...

I gently enquired further into Lenny's war record. And
again, he began by talking initially about someone else.

'Jock Colville was Winston Churchill's private secretary. He was in the Volunteer Reserve and wanted to fly
missions – but they wouldn't let him. Too dangerous. But
he kept bombarding Churchill until finally he gave in. I
didn't even know Jock Colville's name. But a huge convoy
of cars arrived, and I thought "What the hell is all this?"

And then from the second car, Churchill emerged – absolutely furious!'

And then Lenny took on the voice of our wartime premier.

' "Are you Squadron Leader?" he asked very quietly. And I said, "Yes." ' Then again as Churchill: ' "This gentleman is going to come and fly with you for ten missions. Ten missions *only!* And if *he* doesn't come back alive, then don't *you* bother coming back alive!" Well, I didn't like that. I didn't care *who* he was. So, I said to him: "And *fuck you!*" '

I was stunned. 'To Churchill?'

In a throwaway voice Lenny continued, 'We got on fine after that. And Jock Colville *roared* with laughter! He got to fly the aeroplane. He was a very good pilot – not a good fighter pilot, but a good pilot. He had a cyanide capsule. So did I, for that matter. But Jock didn't know for every mission they also gave me a Colt .36. And if we got shot down, it was my duty to kill him. If we'd been captured, the Gestapo would have tortured him. He knew all the secrets for D-Day.'

'Were you involved with D-Day?'

'Reconnaissance sorties. Low level. We photographed miles of beach so they wouldn't know where we'd attack. I led a Mustang squadron on the day.'

Taking in what he'd said, I quietly asked, 'Which beach?'

'Omaha.'

'Virgie!' cried Ginny.

'Yeeees, Mrs Lambert?'

'More wine!'

'Goody!'

* * *

I started visiting my elderly – but seemingly ageless – friends more and more. Ginny continued to be inspiringly sparky. She sang me a ditty she'd written as a thank you to her dentist. And there were always more stories.

'After *Unconquered* Mr DeMille wrote a letter to Lubitsch recommending me, and he cast me as the maid in *That Lady in Ermine*. Betty Grable and I had a scene where we opened a window and there was a disturbance. I wanted to know if we opened the window and then saw the disturbance or opened the window *because* of the disturbance. So, I asked Betty Grable what we should do… and she looked at me and said…' – and here Ginny went into a perfect imitation of a bored and indifferent Miss Grable, primping her hair – 'honey, you do *your* thing and I'll do *mine!*'

'She was coarse, Betty Grable,' added Lenny. 'When I met her, I found her very coarse.'

Lenny, it turned out, had spent time in California after the war on an exchange appointment with the USAF. Howard Hughes offered him a job, but Lenny wasn't keen.

'He was an absolute eccentric,' Lenny explained. 'He kept palatial offices – and he would never wear shoes. He'd run up and down the corridors in stocking feet, with one of his ladies following behind, dealing with his every whim.'

'He was quite deaf, wasn't he?'

'Hmmm?' Lenny asked – ironically not quite hearing the question.

'He was *quite deaf?*'

'In ordinary conversation he was perfectly alright, but in a crowd he wouldn't hear. He wanted me to leave the Air Force and join his company. He offered a *huge* salary. And a flat – "Anywhere you like in Hollywood! Bring your family over!"' Lenny leaned forward and looked me in the eye. 'Temptation! He was making a new movie with lots of war scenes. And he wanted it to be "authentic". Well – I'd been there, done that. So, he asked me to put the "authenticity" into war films! But I didn't do it.'

'Was this when he was running RKO Studios?' I asked.

'Yes. I really had nothing to do with movies but somehow got adopted by the movie world. Very exciting!'

For a while Lenny was fairly involved with Patti Page – who sang ('How Much Is) That Doggie in the Window?' – as well as one of Ginny's recent colleagues – Marilyn Monroe.

'She was my girlfriend for a time,' he remembered, with a glint in his eye. 'A shapely wench. She had her points – and her curves! She invited me to her ranch. But the night before, I ate something rotten – and I doubled over – food poisoning! I couldn't go!'

'Wow!' I cried, genuinely agog.

'She was a very intelligent lady, very well read. Except that she was very pedantic. You'd talk about a book and she'd say, "Oh yes – on page twenty-six dadadadada…" Well, *I* couldn't remember what happened on page twenty-six, and I'd read the book! But she had that sort of memory. Quite a gal! But I didn't want to be taken over. She was a great taker-over of men. She took me to dinner. So, I said, "Next time, my turn!" And she cried, "No, no, no, no, no!" And I said, "Well, I'm not coming!"

'Like all people in her position,' he continued, 'she had two faces. One was to the public and the press, and the other was in her private life. I saw a cheerful, happy, jolly soul. But to the press she was a different person altogether. I wouldn't have recognised her.' He paused. 'Anyway,' he announced, raising the glass to his lips. 'Times long gone!'

Although he and Ginny were in Hollywood at the same time, their paths never crossed. Lenny even worked out, years later, that he would have walked past Ginny's house several times, as he stayed close by. The pair finally met in London in 1974, when Ginny was sixty and he was fifty-five. Lenny had just moved into a rented house, which one night was broken into by a burglar. Lenny successfully chased the thief out into the street through his front door, which then slammed shut behind him, locking him out in his pyjamas. Seeking assistance, Lenny rang the bell of his next-door neighbour, whom he hadn't yet met. Ginny answered… and their destiny was fulfilled.

I'd leave the flat every night at about 10 p.m. – sometimes rather squiffy! The ritual was always the same. We'd arrange the date of our next meeting and Lenny would declare, 'I'll have the wine on ice!' I'd open the door and wave back at Ginny, sitting on the sofa, with Lenny in his chair opposite.

'Ciao!' Ginny always waved. 'Ciao!'

With Ginny and Lenny, I always had an absolute ball. Their acceptance and friendship seemed to be restoring my esteem in record time. And now, everywhere I went, I was relaxed in myself. I liked who I was.

CHAPTER FIFTEEN

'But stay!
What is this fairy form I see before me?'

The Sorcerer

'I think I've got a crush,' I told Mark.

'On who?'

'On Seymour!'

I was referring to the young man playing the lead character in *Little Shop of Horrors*. It wasn't anything too serious; certainly not enough to act upon… but when suddenly Seymour was standing beside me but flirting with Chiffon instead (one of the other male Ronettes), I did feel a pang of disappointment.

But at least I got to manhandle Ted, my blonde Dentist, at the end of Act One when the plant ate him. Ted was a Thursford friend and a jolly good egg, and I must confess it was rather exciting getting to paw him all over.

'But I still like girls,' I assured Mark, with complete assurance. 'I think I'm just liking getting tactile with people.'

'Fine,' said Mark.

I was *really* enjoying myself. It was still only four months since Thursford had ended but I felt like a new man. By not pressurising myself, I was able to accept and enjoy having these different feelings, with which I could experiment.

I loved the free flamboyancy of being the plant, although I didn't enjoy the drag (literally) of being a Ronette. The other two boys had quite a flair for doing elaborate make-up, which I most certainly didn't. And shaving my legs and armpits in Alan's bathroom was such a faff!

We performed the show in Kennington – at the back end of a pub. The bar was frequented by middle-aged boozers glued to the football, oblivious to the astonishing campery inside Mr Mushnik's Plant Shop just yards away. Despite its obvious flaws, young audiences whooped for this (as it was billed) 'gender-bending' production. The show was bats, but everyone my age knew what to expect from fringe productions. Although I did have two other friends for whom it might all have seemed a little more unusual…

'It's quite off the wall,' I warned Ginny.

She looked at me and smiled. 'We *like* off the wall.' And then examining the pink flyer in her hand she read out slowly, '*Little… Shop… of Horrors!*' Ginny and Lenny would not be talked out of it. 'We want to see our boy!'

I was, however, slightly concerned that the first time they'd ever see me on stage would be as Crystal in drag. This bizarre sight was probably not something Mr Churchill would have expected his Squadron Leader to see. But nevertheless, Ginny and Lenny booked tickets, attending with Ginny's son, Cam (from her first marriage), who lived in Rome but was visiting at the time.

I arranged for Mum and Dad to attend that same evening and act as an extra pair of helping hands – they were, by now, more than used to me befriending elderly legends. Afterwards they told me how a cab had drawn up outside the pub, from which alighted two ancient people. Ginny was in a chic black outfit, offset by a string of pearls, white scarf and a little white skull cap. Lenny was in a suit and tie. With Cam, they guided them through the boozy pub – and they seemed to be having a whale of a time.

'Let's have a drink!' Ginny exclaimed.

'More wine!' cried Lenny.

They sat in the front row. As I made my entrance, I wondered *what* the hell they must have been thinking… but as the opening burst into life, Ginny was mad with excitement and started squeezing Mum's hand, saying, 'There's our boy!'

As I saw them safely off in the taxi, I was beaming. I was inspired that at ninety-seven and ninety-one they still embraced anything they thought might be fun.

Afterwards the cast appeared in costume at something unbelievably stagey called Kinky Kabaret at Freedom Bar in Soho. I even ended up hosting the show as Crystal!

The whole *Little Shop* experience contributed magnificently to my personal development. By throwing myself into whatever came my way, I'd made the right choice – and over the last few months Mark, Alan, Ginny and Lenny had each played a pivotal role in helping me start afresh.

But soon I was departing once again for the Leicestershire countryside – and Kilworth House Theatre's revival of *The Pirates of Penzance*. Those with whom I'd previously worked noticed the distinct change in my personality.

And then, in the truest of clichés, when I wasn't looking for it, something happened…

During a lunch break in London rehearsals, the *Pirates* company arrived in the rehearsal studio café to discover a gaggle of dancing girls. I got chatting to a rather good-looking young lady – a bubbly Essex lass – and to my utter astonishment she seemed to reciprocate my mild flirtation. She even gave me her phone number! She wanted to meet up... and although I was departing imminently for tech week in Leicestershire, I decided that she was worth the effort. I announced that I'd come back down to London on my day off and we'd go on a date!

But there was just one problem... I hadn't the slightest idea what to suggest.

'London Zoo!' said one of the *Pirates* boys. 'That'd be different. She'll love it!'

'And,' advised another, 'take a picnic. Strawberries and cream. I did that on my first date with my girlfriend and she was made up with it!'

I was all set to channel my inner Gene Kelly – the charming cheeky chappy with a twinkle in his eye. Surely, she'd be swept off her feet, and I anticipated that, as the sun set, I'd be twirling my dancing girl around Regent's Park to the strains of 'Dancing in the Dark' (like Fred Astaire and Cyd Charisse in *The Band Wagon*).

Alas, I returned to Kilworth unfulfilled. Conversation did not flow easily, and there was no moment of MGM magic. As for the picnic, the strawberries and cream received no comment. Even worse, although I'd picked up the tab for the entire day (because I'd learned from Debbie Reynolds in *I Love Melvin* that girls 'adore the subtle phrase that it's the man who pays') not once did I receive a 'thank you' – which rankled. From her rather disinterested parting embrace, I did not anticipate a follow-up meeting. But actually… that suited me fine.

However, I'd had a date – so I was making progress. But Mark had advised me that on dates with girls perhaps I ought to resist chatting about glamorous old movie stars.

But then again, I pondered on the train back to Kilworth, in doing this I felt like I'd withheld an important aspect of my personality. Throughout all those tiresome laps of the zoo I'd felt like I was putting on a character, always monitoring what I was saying – and being careful about how I said it. Having 'been myself' for the last few months, I suddenly found, traipsing around Regent's Park, that I'd been pretending to be someone I wasn't. I chalked it up to experience, polished off the remaining sorry strawberries and threw myself wholeheartedly into the Kilworth Experience.

And what an experience… my adventurous landlady installed a hot tub in her garden for the exclusive use of the cast. Sometimes in the cold light of day, numerous pairs of pants and swimming trunks were found flung into the bushes – returned to their owners at the half-hour call. Hot-tub shenanigans also caused mild domestic drama. Until recently the old adage for itinerant actors that 'What Happens on Tour Stays on Tour' had squashed a multitude of indiscretions. But now with social media it was a case of 'What Happens on Tour Goes on Facebook'! Carelessly posted candid photos began to raise alarm with partners back home.

One night, after I'd turned in, I was awoken by a banging on my door: 'Martin! Martin!' I answered to find a refugee from the hot tub – a dripping-wet chorus boy, stark naked and paralytically drunk. 'Martin!' he cried. 'I want to sleep with you!' And with that he collapsed onto my bed and passed out. As I surveyed this site before me, I must confess I found it all… strangely titillating… and I actually felt rather insulted that he was out cold!

However, my mind was focused on work, and there it remained – until one day during the final week of the run. Whilst making my way backstage, I heard a voice calling: 'Oh, Martin! Martin!'

I turned around and saw a middle-aged front of house volunteer running briskly towards me. I'd seen this chap hovering around throughout the run, selling ice creams and programmes.

'You're Martin, aren't you?' he panted as he approached. 'Now, I hope you don't mind my talking to you, but I read in the programme that you've done Thursford!' Very excited and animated, he continued, 'Now, I've got a young friend, and he lives round here locally, and he's coming to see the show on Friday – and he's just graduated from drama school – and he's just got Thursford as his first job! So, I was wondering, if I introduce you to him after the show, would you have a word with him about Thursford?'

'Well, yes, of course,' I said, thinking nothing of it. After all, I enjoyed advising 'newbies' about the ins and outs of what to expect. The front-of-house man thanked me, ran off, and I continued my journey backstage.

* * *

Friday 1 July was going to be a special show: we had a guest conductor – the wonderful John Owen Edwards.

Our usual musical director was away for the night, so J.O.E. had been called in as a G&S stalwart who could reliably conduct *Pirates* without any prior rehearsal.

It was a warm summer evening – perfect for glorious outdoor theatre. During the Act One finale, everyone froze for the big lead-up to Sullivan's ravishing hymn-like anthem 'Hail Poetry'. As we posed with our fists clenched over our hearts, The Pirate King soliloquised:

'Although our dark career
Sometimes involves the crime of stealing…'

Right, I thought, surveying the audience. *Who's out there tonight?* I spied a familiar face. *Oh… there's that front-of-house man. And I suppose the guy sitting next to him is the boy who's doing Thurs-*<u>FORD</u>*!*

If this was a Disney cartoon my eyes would have pinged out of their sockets and back again. The young boy sitting next to the front-of-house man was, I could not deny, *extremely attractive.* The Pirate King continued:

'We rather think that we're
Not altogether void of feeling…'

Martin, I thought, shocked, as I drifted in line to my next position. *What the…? What* are *you thinking?* And then, two different voices in my head began to compete: 'You're not gay – he's really hot – but you like girls – but he's so damn cute…!'

'*Although we live by strife,*
We're always sorry to begin it…'

My mind was in a blur. What was happening? I'd never been so attracted to someone in my entire life…

'*For what, we ask, is life*
Without a touch of Poetry in it?'

I turned to face J.O.E., all the while thinking about that boy on row J: *He's* really *hot*!

'*Haaaaaaaaaaaaaail Poetry!*'

And at that very moment – as I sang 'Hail Poetry', conducted by John Owen Edwards, on stage during the Act One finale of *The Pirates of Penzance* – I realised once and for all: I was gay!

PART TWO

CHAPTER SIXTEEN

'Welcome, gentry,
For your entry'

Ruddigore

I didn't feel like I'd been struck by lightning. It was just a gentle, calm moment of realisation, and I continued the performance as normal, saying nothing to anyone.

After the show, I sped my way to the bar in Kilworth's log cabin, where I saw the young gentleman from row J.

'Martin,' said the front-of-house man, 'this is Rob.'

Conversation flowed easily. There was never a lull, and Rob responded brilliantly as I rattled off my best anecdotes about the madness and merriment of Christmas in Norfolk. Rob and I swapped numbers, started texting each other and didn't stop. The messages were constant. And I was flirting!

I liked this guy. He was extremely attractive. And it all felt so natural! I wasn't putting up a pretence, like I had at London Zoo. When I got back to my digs I sat in my room and contemplated – this was a milestone. Instinct told me there'd be no turning back now.

But although I somehow knew for sure, at last, that I was gay, I still couldn't quite bring myself to say those words out loud. When I got back to London, I just told Mark about 'this guy' I'd met who I really liked. To his enormous credit, he treated me just the same as he had when I'd been talking about girls.

'Alright,' he said, logging into Facebook. 'Let's have a look at your boyfriend.'

'He's not my boyfriend!' I blushed – but I was smiling.

As natural as all this felt, however, there was something bothering me. All my life, so much about me had always been unconventional: my tastes, behaviour, even my performing style. I wasn't ashamed of that, but there was still a part of me that wished I could be 'normal'... meaning, I suppose, straight.

But I couldn't deny my feelings. They were getting stronger every day.

I was churning all this over when I took Mark to Folkestone as my guest for Battle of Britain Memorial Weekend. Nanny Jean was there too – her madcap frivolity a tonic of familiarity amidst my sea of inner change. Rob was texting all the time, and throughout the parades and Spitfire displays I took every opportunity to reply, telling him about my 'glamorous' weekend. I confess, I was shamelessly aiming to impress!

And then – at the Sunday Memorial Day celebration on the clifftops of Capel-le-Ferne – I had a brief, but significant, encounter with Sir Donald Sinden. As a child I'd been star-struck by Donald Sinden because he was in MGM's *Mogambo* with Clark Gable and Ava Gardner, playing the husband of Grace Kelly. When I was twelve, I'd seen Sir Donald on stage in *Quartet*, and in my youthful innocence I couldn't believe that I was actually watching – live – someone who'd appeared in an MGM movie! And now, during this seminal weekend of my life, we stood face-to-face!

Sir Donald, of course, was oblivious to all this. He poked his way gingerly around rows of white plastic seats to find his designated chair, with five medals pinned to his jacket and an unlit cigarette dangling from his mouth. Seeing me stare, he looked up and barked in those kindly and ever-so-distinctive tones, 'Could you hold this?' He thrust a walking stick at me and then patted his torso, theatrically searching his pockets, eventually fishing out a lighter. As he lit the cigarette – with all the drawing-room-comedy technique of a bygone age – he noticed that I was looking down at the stick, on which was printed the letters 'N.C.'

'Know who that belonged to, my boy?' he asked knowingly and, leaning forward, declared in a theatrical stage whisper, 'Noël Coward!'

This was just too much! I wanted to text Rob immediately and tell him all about this magical moment. And then, with great joy – and my hand still resting on Noël Coward's walking stick – I suddenly realised that *I could…*

This wouldn't be like my texts to the London Zoo dancing girl. I could now tell the object of my affection about this interaction with a glorious old star and not worry about a thing! I could *be myself* with someone I fancied! It was like someone had just flicked a switch in my head. The seemingly insignificant moment was actually, in its way, pivotal. And Sir Donald never knew just how much he'd unwittingly helped me.

'Oh, Sir Donald!' I managed to pipe up, beaming. 'What

was it like working with John Ford?' (The hard-drinking, rough and rugged director of *Mogambo*, who revered the Irish and despised the English.)

Sir Donald paused, looked up slowly and then with great theatrical relish declared: 'He was an abso-lute *bastard!*' And then he immediately looked horrified, clapped a hand over his mouth and peered out cheekily from side to side, fearing his booming indiscretion may have been overheard.

Later that night, back at Mark's place, I silently reviewed the events of the last few weeks. And then – in Mark's kitchen – I quietly said: 'Mark… I'm gay.'

My acceptance within myself was complete.

I felt as though a weight had been lifted from my shoulders which I hadn't even acknowledged was there. Over the next few weeks I went about my business as normal – but the difference within me was tremendous: I was happy!

And the great thing was that I didn't feel that I had to change anything about myself. I was just becoming more comfortable *within* myself. Free from inhibitions, free from fear of what others might say.

'I couldn't have done this without you,' I told Mark.

'Yes, you could,' he replied.

'No,' I said, 'I couldn't. But even if what you say *is* the case – I've been able to do this because I know that you, and others, have been there to support me.'

I had friends. Little Martin in the corner of the infant-school playground, all on his own, would have been proud. I'd come a long way in the seven months since Christmas.

But while I was happy for people to know my 'news', my personal revelation was not, I felt, cause for general publicity. No soul-baring Facebook status for me! I was happy for word to seep out quietly and organically, without fanfare – because the simple truth was that despite all the parasol twirling, idolatry of Jean Bayless and lack of experience with women, I just hadn't known my sexuality for certain until that moment on the Kilworth stage.

It should always have been obvious to me, but it wasn't. I'd been rather backward, astonishingly naïve and a very late developer! There'd been no childhood friends with whom I could chat, experiment or discover. Having been turned down by drama schools, I missed out on those vital student years in which later-developers start to bloom. Professionally speaking, it had been wonderful to work with almost exclusively older casts, but no one could guide me in the way my contemporaries could. That coupled with a lack of physical confidence, plus an outlook on the world moulded by MGM musicals, meant that I was several years behind where I should have been!

It might have taken a while – and there may have been a few false starts and wrong turns along the way – but once I recognised I was gay, that, quite simply, was that. With a smile I thought of MGM and the advice given to young Leslie Caron in *Gigi*: 'Instead of getting married at once, it sometimes happens we get married at last.' In my case, I thought: *Instead of realising our sexuality at once, it sometimes happens we realise our sexuality at last.*

It is a phrase I have passed on to others since.

* * *

About a week later I went to Tunbridge Wells to sing in a charity show for a friend. A whole load of us stayed at her parents' house, including her brother and his boyfriend. Whilst I didn't know them well, I did feel I knew them well enough to share my news. They gave me a huge hug and the warmest of welcomes into a new world.

And it *was* a new world. They made me comprehend that I was now part of a kind of brotherhood. A brotherhood where I felt total acceptance and never had to explain or justify anything. I'd entered a community into which I was unhesitatingly welcomed. And after a childhood background of personal rejection, this was life-changing.

I also came to terms with something else… in recent weeks, despite the excitement of meeting Rob, I'd wanted my sexuality to be 'normal'. But both my sexuality and I *were* completely normal. There was nothing wrong or unusual or shameful or embarrassing about it. Recognising this, my life began to change for the better.

I told my parents. 'My God, you're brave,' someone said to me. But I didn't think of it that way. I knew my mum and dad well enough to know that there wouldn't be a problem – and I valued and appreciated this, because I was well aware that there were others in my position not so lucky.

I certainly had no intention of leaving my parents in the dark. I'd soon be off to Thursford and considered it ridiculous and unfair to think that an entire theatrical company – many of whom I'd never see again afterwards – would know that I was gay if those closest to me did not.

At home my news was received just as I knew it would be.

Funnily enough, the person I was most nervous about telling was Nanny Jean – which was ludicrous – she'd spent her entire life in the theatre surrounded by gay men! She was the original Maria from *The Sound of Music* – that made her a gay icon! Nevertheless, friendship aside, she was my greatest inspiration in the theatre. I looked up to her and cared deeply.

Safe to say, I needn't have worried.

And during this time, I had one wonderful constant – Ginny and Lenny. Whilst I'd been away, I'd received phone calls and voicemails from Ginny: 'We miss you!' I'd been wondering what to say about my epiphany. How to tell them? And then, as we sat eating dinner one night around that historic wooden table, I understood something – I didn't need to tell them anything. Not because my news would have been shocking or rejected, but because it wasn't necessary. I'd been accepted into Ginny and Lenny's world just as I was. Nothing mattered apart from their love for those around them. They were carefree and lived life as they chose – and with *whom* they chose. No explanation for anything was necessary.

The older generation which had always, through the movies, been there to comfort me as a child was now doing so again in my young adult life – but this time in person, and in a way I could never have imagined.

And in the meantime – what of Rob? Our texts continued to flow, and things looked set to take an interesting turn. For the rest of 2011 I had two contracts which would take me out of London – the Buxton G&S Festival in August, and then Thursford. There was no point in paying rent for a new flat, so I floated itinerantly between friends. Rob said that I could stay with him.

Now! Now was the time, I told myself!

But I was way too nervous to do anything. Being completely inexperienced, I was terrified I'd make a fool of myself. An embarrassing move now had the potential of making our three months together at Thursford extremely awkward.

'Go home, walk in and kiss him,' said Mark.

'Oh, I couldn't possibly do that!' I protested.

'Just go in and do it!'

But I didn't. And I'm very glad that I didn't. Because, over the years, Rob has become one of my dearest and most treasured friends. And for years afterwards – longing to tell him but afraid and shy – I never mentioned the significance of that enchanted evening when I saw a stranger across a crowded auditorium.

In the gay world, it can be all too easy to find a lover, but it is a much rarer thing to find a friend. And that, I am so happy to say, is what Rob truly is to me.

CHAPTER SEVENTEEN

'I heard the minx remark,
She'd meet him after dark'

Iolanthe

If there was ever a place for a geeky gay to pull it was at the G&S Festival in Buxton. The 'bubble-like' atmosphere fostered jolly jinks for both gays and straights; after the communal G&S singalongs had ceased, any number of choristers enjoyed their *dolce far niente* in the Festival Bar, the Pavilion Gardens or back at the student digs where members of the G&S Opera Company were billeted by the management (if they were lucky).

A few years previously, a liaison had formed between a chorus girl and a tenor, which for various reasons had to be kept discreet (meaning that everyone in Buxton was in on it). One night in the Festival Bar, this girl sang 'I Dreamt I Dwelt in Marble Halls'. Later, as the room cleared, a sloshed Northern mezzo challenged the chorine's lover.

'Oi!' she yelled. 'You goin' back to 'er place, then?'

'Er… whose?' the tenor blushed, innocently.

'Y'know!' the mezzo cried. ''Er what dwells in fookin' marble 'alls!'

One of the shows I did at Buxton that year – just to be different – was *The Pirates of Penzance*. At London rehearsals, a certain young pirate caught my eye. His name was Freddie, and although we hadn't previously met, we did know of one another through our mutual friend Bobby. Freddie and I were soon gossiping incessantly.

Rehearsals were intense – the entire production was staged in just five days. By the time we arrived in Buxton, Freddie and I had grown close. As our first night drew to a close, I offered to see him home from the Festival Bar. After all, it was late, and Freddie shouldn't have walked through the Pavilion Gardens unfriended, unprotected and alone.

As we climbed the hill, I knew the moment was looming when we'd have to say goodnight. I summoned all my courage, grabbed him and kissed him! Freddie seemed pleased – if a little startled.

'But… I thought you were straight!'

'What?'

'Well, Bobby said you were straight…'

'Ahhhh,' I replied, realising that I hadn't seen Bobby for a while, and therefore had not yet filled him in with my 'news'…

The next afternoon, Freddie and I met on the fire escape of the Opera House, dressed as pirates.

'Well, there's a perfectly simple explanation,' I offered. 'I *was* "straight" last time I saw Bobby – but I've just been doing *Pirates* at Kilworth, you see, and, about a month ago, during "Hail Poetry"…'

We were now on the same page. It was all so romantic – after all, there we were in Buxton, singing G&S, and holding hands every night as the moon shone down on the Pavilion Gardens.

It was my first experience of romance – our stolen meetings on the fire escape were just like everything I'd seen in *West Side Story*. My confidence began to soar!

I was entirely prepared to give Freddie my heart – but Freddie, unfortunately, was recently out of a relationship which had ended badly. He was also aware (which I was not) that a newly 'out' boy of just one month would certainly not be ready to venture into anything serious… let alone with someone healing after a long-term relationship.

Being innocent and naïve, I blindly protested – like Scarlett O'Hara with Ashley Wilkes – that we could be happy. But eventually, and reluctantly, I understood Freddie's reasons. Besides, logistically, I saw that my suit was hopeless. I was returning to London to do an Ivor Novello musical, and from there straight on to Thursford; Freddie had just been cast in a tour.

I convinced myself that Freddie and I had met each other at the wrong time. But in reality, the timing was fortuitous – each of us had needed someone special to help us through this delicate period. It was a very special Buxton season.

On the final day we found a quiet corner in a coffee shop. It was rather like the end of *Brief Encounter*: he was going away – and there, in that moment, I found it hard to believe there would be a time in the future when I shouldn't mind about this anymore.

'You're young – and you're just out,' Freddie whispered, holding my hand. 'You should go and have some fun!'

I wanted to remember every moment with Freddie always, always, to the end of my days. But... oh, dear reader. Alas! How fickle a creature is the New Gay? It took Scarlett O'Hara ten years and three loveless marriages to forget Ashley Wilkes. But I blush to say that once back in London – and with Freddie now out of the picture – it didn't take me quite as long as Scarlett to start exploring other options.

You see, Freddie *did* give a damn and had been the perfect gentleman. He was aware that by taking certain steps it could only have increased my emotional attachment. So in Buxton, goaded by maddening inaction, I remained chaste, but never caught.

However – could I head to Thursford once more unfulfilled? Not again! So I started texting people. And this time I was determined to conquer Soho! After all, I was now 'out', confident and knew exactly what I was doing... didn't I?

I decided not to text Franklin. But I did make a point of texting someone else...

The previous year I'd performed in a musical evening of Noël Coward. I gave my falsetto 'Zigeuner', and a strapping young black gentleman named Nicholas sang 'Poor Little Rich Girl'. Even in my naïvety I knew that Nicholas had a crush on me. As I didn't have a great opinion of my physical appearance, I could only imagine that he'd been dazzled by my high notes.

And now Nicholas said that he wanted to meet. It was to be my first proper gay date.

The location was Ku Bar on Lisle Street. There'd be no mistakes this time. No strawberries and cream, and definitely no Mrs Patrick Campbell. But there could certainly be a few glasses of wine – including one before Nicholas arrived, to steady my nerves. That first drink, though, is where I went wrong… for I ended up making a mistake, after all. The same mistake I made at London Zoo: I wasn't myself.

But this time I didn't channel macho Gene Kelly. I channelled Fanny Skeffington…

In 1944, Bette Davis earned her seventh Oscar nomination playing the most beautiful and desirable girl in New York. Fawning lovesick suitors fell at Fanny's feet. The role of a great beauty had, however, terrified the aesthetically insecure Davis. Nevertheless, she completely beguiled her audience – raising the pitch of her voice and batting her widened eyes.

I knew from Nicholas's texts that he was *very* excited to see me – but, like Bette, I was physically insecure. So, I decided, from within, to transform myself into Fanny Skeffington in Ku Bar.

When Nicholas walked in, he bounded over to my table. I looked up at him, extended my hand, batted my widened Bette Davis Eyes and greeted him in a voice a tone higher than normal: 'Nicholas! How *luffly* to see you!'

I was completely 'fascinating'. Nicholas hung on every word. Bizarrely, this Fanny Skeffington lark really seemed to be working…

'Oh my God,' he said after about twenty minutes. 'You're gorgeous!' And next thing I knew – like a replay of Franklin – his tongue was down my throat. But unlike that experience, this was most welcome – most pleasant – most exciting…

But, of course, I'd never been on a date like this before, so I wasn't entirely sure of the protocol. After making out for a good quarter of an hour, I thought it might be terribly impolite not to make the next move. Perhaps it was the done thing to invite him back to my place…?

'Have you *[kiss]* ever *[kiss]* seen the sights of *[kiss]* Hither Green? *[kiss]*?'

'No,' replied Nicholas.

'Would *[kiss]* you like to *[kiss]*?'

'I would!'

And all of a sudden, panic hit me. Oh. My. GOD! It really *was* going to happen – *tonight!* Fanny Skeffington had done the trick… but now I was too scared! I needed time to think! Stall… stall… I needed to stall!

'Aha-ha-haaaa,' I giggled with tinkling laughter. 'Would you excuse me just one moment?' And I wafted towards the gents in the manner of Fanny. Once out of sight I ran down the stairs, texting Mark, his girlfriend and Ted the Dentist from *Little Shop*: 'He wants to come back to my place! What should I do?'

Fortunately, they all texted straight back. Unfortunately, they all contradicted each other.

TED: Go for it! Once you've had black, you'll never go back!

MARK'S GIRLFRIEND: Well, if you're comfortable have a good time but don't feel you have to if you don't want.

MARK: Whoa, Mr Milnes. You're not ready for this. Don't do it.

There weren't any scenes in *Mr Skeffington* to prepare me for this. I was too scared to go any further. But surely it would be rude and impolite to stop now?

I wafted back à la Fanny. Nicholas picked up his coat.

'Well then? Shall we?' But I stayed rooted to the spot.

'Aha-ha-ha-ha-ha…' I tinkled coquettishly. 'Aha-ha-ha-ha-ha… Aha-ha-ha-haaaaaa!'

'Oh,' said Nicholas, seeing I wasn't moving. 'Well… we could go for another drink first if you want?'

The last thing I needed was another drink. But I *did* need to stall!

'Oh, how lovely!' I sighed. 'Where shall we go?'

He took me to the same bar as Franklin had two years earlier. And we even ended up on the same sofa… I kid you not, dear reader! Eventually I could stall no longer.

'Shall we?' Nicholas pointedly asked again.

'Right,' I said, taking a final swig for luck, the wine having gone to my head. 'Let's go!'

Walking to Charing Cross station my legs were physically shaking.

'The train now standing at Platform 2 is the 2148 service to Dartford…'

'Err…' I hesitated. 'Er…'

'Calling at London Waterloo East, London Bridge…'

'Are you alright?'

'Hither Green, Lee, Mottingham…'

'Would you… *hate me*… if I asked if we could make it another time?'

'New Eltham, Sidcup…'

I had the good fortune to be with a gentleman – albeit a clearly very frustrated one. I took the train home alone. It was the last time I would ever *not* be myself on a date.

* * *

I was now into rehearsals for a rare revival of Ivor Novello's musical *Perchance to Dream*. I'd long been captivated by Novello's enchanting melodies. This show included perhaps the loveliest of all – 'We'll Gather Lilacs'.

But it was a difficult rehearsal period. Each morning, a very experienced West End cast was asked by a very inexperienced production team to 'walk around the room, getting into character'. Cast members subsequently ate members of the production team for breakfast. One cast member came and went. So did a member of the production team.

I had a short but lovely solo in the first act – a pastiche of a Regency parlour song.

'So, Martin,' I was asked. 'What do you think your character motivation is here? Do you think your character would sing this number quietly? Or would he sing it out big?'

'He wouldn't sing it quietly. He'd definitely sing it big.'

'Ah! Interesting character decision. Why would your character do that?'

'Because it's my only solo in the show.'

Out of necessity I discreetly leapt in when friends in the cast, knowing I was familiar with Novello's style, asked me to help with their scenes.

'Not being funny,' one of them said, 'but *you* could direct this show, couldn't you?'

'Maybe I could…' I thought to myself. And then I thought seriously – well, why *couldn't* I direct a show? A seed had been planted…

A young man came to watch *Perchance to Dream* – a recent drama-school graduate. In the bar we started

17 February 2014 – Ginny's
100th Birthday

Virginia Campbell on
Broadway in 1939

Squadron Leader Leonard Lambert

Ginny and Lenny, with Ginny's son Cam, at *Little Shop of Horrors*, 2011. I played one third of the plant.

"It's like *The Muppet Show*, but with people": Thursford *Christmas Spectacular* 2012, giving my Christmas Turkey against the backdrop of the Gondola. (*Eastern Daily Press*)

George Fay rehearses the birds at Thursford, 2011

Nanny Jean and Martin
on Battle of Britain
Memorial Day, 2016

Jean Bayless and Audrey Hepburn
at Ciro's nightclub, 1949

Ginny in Sperlonga, 2012, age 98

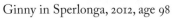

Lenny plays his harmonica, 2013

Stiofan and Martin

Fenella Fielding's 88th
birthday tea party, 2015

Backstage at *Gay's the Word*
with Elizabeth Seal, 2013.
Elizabeth's stage debut was in
the original production of Ivor
Novello's musical, age 17, in 1950.

Hazel Ascot (left) was Britain's top child star of
1930s film musicals. Peggy Cummins (right) secured
Hollywood immortality in noir classic *Gun Crazy*.

Ginny playing Posso, age 101, 2015

Ferris & Milnes premiere '33 Sondheim Numbers in 5 Minutes' at Theatre Royal, Drury Lane in Stephen Sondheim's 85th Birthday Gala, 2015 (*Darren Bell Photography*)

Ferris & Milnes with friend and mentor Steve Ross, New York, 2017

To my Martin
I'm so happy that you are in my life
Dont ever leave
Maggie the old Bag

Maggie Rennie – last of the original Windmill Theatre girls – preserved her kiss in the lipstick shade 'Gay Geranium'. "This mouth 'as seen some action, darlin'!"

Eileen Page, 92, visits Martin's cast of graduating students from the Musical Theatre course at ArtsEd Schools, London, 2018

Stiofan's portrait of Harry and Martin remembering Peggy, 2019 (*Samuel Black Photography*)

chatting, and he appeared to be taking more than just a professional interest.

I felt very comfortable. Texts began to flow. We decided to meet up. I acted naturally – emulating neither Gene Kelly nor Fanny Skeffington. Mrs Patrick Campbell remained unquoted. I was just myself.

And... well, dear reader... shall we just say that, later in the day, We Gathered Lilacs?

CHAPTER EIGHTEEN

'Life is one closely complicated tangle'

The Gondoliers

'The show takes place in Norfolk,' I told Ginny and Lenny. Lenny scowled.

'They sent a missionary there once – they ate him!'

The ghosts of the former year were behind me. I greeted my first Thursford contract as an out gay man with eager anticipation...

On the first day of rehearsals people often window-shop new colleagues – especially when they know they're going to be locked away in a remote part of the country for months on end! But a guy named Ryan, who'd previously embroiled himself in backstage romantic entanglements, arrived firmly declaring: 'No drama this year! I'm not getting myself involved in any drama!' To this statement, those who knew better just rolled their eyes...

Cast lists, with headshots, were distributed. One new singer set my heart aflutter. His name was Max – but when I showed Mark his photo, he recognised the boy from drama school... and alarm bells rang immediately.

'Don't sleep with him!' he warned. 'He's trouble. Bad news.'

'Ahhhh,' I mooned innocently. 'Well, we'll seeeeee....'

Sadly for me, Mark was in a different show which clashed with Thursford. However, I did have a rather wonderful housemate in the form of Guy Mott. We lived in my usual cottage – and this time the experience of sharing really was perfect.

I found myself placed in the dressing room between Max and Ryan. Ryan, despite his vow of 'no drama', had already raised eyebrows with his instant devotion to a new singer... and the boy in question appeared to be actively responding to Ryan's attention.

As usual, upon arrival at Thursford many newbies seemed rather shell-shocked, especially by the lack of mobile signal. Max asked me where to find some, so I directed him behind the Gondola. Then I looked down at Max's screensaver...

'That's Bette Davis in *Now, Voyager*!'

Max snapped his head round. 'Omigod, you're right!' I soon established that Bette Davis was one of Max's heroines. 'We've got to have a *Dark Victory* DVD night!' he declared. This, coming from an attractive young gay boy, was music to my ears! He loved other old movies too, and his idol was Julie Andrews, whose autobiography *Home* he was currently rereading.

'Oh,' I said casually, 'there's a photo of my friend Annie Wakefield in that!' His reaction to this little nugget was most agreeable.

This, I told myself, could be very, very exciting...

This year, I was, however, apprehensive about just one thing: indelicate reactions when people discovered I was now openly gay. I steeled myself for comments such as,

'Ah well, everyone always knew except you!' But I was thrilled this never happened. The news merely trickled out gradually, received without spectacular reaction.

A Thursford old-timer just put his arm round my shoulder and mentioned quietly: 'I've heard something on the grapevine about some news you might have. Can I just ask…?'

'Yes, it's true!'

'Ahhhh, that's so great! I'm really happy for you!'

But perhaps my favourite reaction came not from the cast but a figure from management – an unwitting master of the malapropism. One day in the café, this Thursford veteran seized upon some 'Thursford Virgins' (as first-timers were called), telling them what to expect from their Christmas experience.

'Anything can happen at Thursford!' he proudly exclaimed.

'Yes!' I said, walking past. 'And it usually does!'

'Yes!' the veteran cried. '*He* should know! *He* changed sex!'

* * *

My comedy number was 'Two Ladies'. I appeared from behind a bed sheet – poking extended pointy things outwards at groin level – wearing a red onesie and nightcap, flanked by two busty fräuleins. And on the raffle, audiences swallowed my fabrications whole. In Max's honour one day I declared:

'The fourth prize is a Van Cleef tablecloth! So-called, ladies and gentlemen, because it's an exact replica of the

*tablecloth famously used by Bette Davis, who played Mrs
Van Cleef in the 1942 film* They'll Believe Anything...'

You see, at that point – during the middle of the run – I
was doing everything in my power to keep Max's attention focused on me... because for the first time in my
life I'd found myself ensnared in a tangled web of highly
emotional romantic melodrama.

But it started out like a song...

'Ugh,' Max complained during the first week of rehearsals. 'Why can't people just be honest? I'm *always* honest!'

It appeared the boy Max had been dating in London
was now 'dicking' him around: not replying to texts and
never letting Max know where he stood, leading him
up the garden path. Naturally, I was outraged on behalf
of poor Max! This swine was a cad! A bounder! I sym-
pathised completely and told Max that I was there if he
ever wanted to talk...

We spent increasing amounts of time together. Placing
great trust in him, I confided about my inexperience. Soon
after, things broke up between Max and his paramour. He
was now a single man – and our frequent chats about Bette
Davis had formed a bond. Max was bowled over by the
scale of my knowledge about Hollywood's Golden Era; he
sat and listened with what observers described to me as awe.

But then I clocked something – something which
should have set alarm bells ringing – but I was too far
gone by then to want to realise. Max mentioned that a
few months earlier he'd been on tour in a musical playing
opposite his ex-boyfriend: 'Oh, it was *so* awkward!'

The penny dropped – the ex to whom Max referred was

Seymour! My darling Seymour from *Little Shop of Horrors*. This tour had commenced immediately after *Little Shop* closed, when Seymour had told me, horrified: 'I've got to seduce my ex on stage! And our relationship ended really badly!' He'd also told me that this ex was not a particularly gallant fellow. But the memory of Seymour's words came too late... for now I only had eyes for Max!

He invited himself over to watch *Dark Victory*. I was ecstatic! Guy arranged to go over to our friend Ed's place for the evening. I sprayed myself thoroughly with sexy aftershave and put on my tightest fitting T-shirt and jeans. We talked incessantly, and Max listened with rapt attention to my stories about Nanny Jean, Annie Wakefield, Fenella, Ginny and Lenny.

'If you asked me,' he said, 'who I'd be, if I could be anyone in history, at any point in their lives, I'd be Julie Andrews when she was starring as Eliza Doolittle in *My Fair Lady*.' To Max, *My Fair Lady* was the pinnacle of Julie Andrews' achievement – he played her Drury Lane cast recording constantly.

'We have *so* many films you're going to have to introduce me to,' he said. 'We're going to need at *least* one movie night a week!'

After he left, I was floating on air. This amazing boy seemed perfect! I never thought I'd meet anyone like this... and I'd only been out three months!

Next time, as the evening wore on, we watched Katharine Hepburn's documentary exploration of her life, *All About Me*. I looked at Max more than the screen. He was transfixed. It was the most attractive sight I'd ever seen. When Hepburn spoke about Spencer Tracy's death,

I saw tears trickle down his cheek. This was a boy I could fall for... and I was. Fast.

I confessed my feelings to Max. He then promised, and alluded to, all kinds of things... that we should play the long-term game rather than jumping into a short-term fling, making it special. The fact that he seemed serious, already looking to a future outside the Thursford bubble, made me like him even more. I was captivated, completely and utterly. Encouragement continued – and at work, our obvious bond became a talking point.

'I think Max *really* likes you,' said Paddy, a trusted confidant. 'What you two have is so special. It's a real connection, and it's beautiful to watch. You have so much in common.'

However, matters were about to take a dramatic turn...

Ryan and the boy to whom he'd attached himself had similarly aroused attention backstage – with many people assuming they were an item. But suddenly, without warning – just after his girlfriend came up to visit – the other guy abruptly distanced himself from Ryan – who now found himself without companionship.

And then – out of nowhere – Ryan developed an overnight fascination with Max. He made all kinds of attempts to ingratiate himself, which, at first, I thought quite comical. But then I became alarmed. This was my first potential Thursford romance – and it looked like Ryan might swoop down like a chicken hawk and ruin it!

But Max took my hand and looked straight into my eyes: 'It's really important to me that you know that you have *nothing* to worry about with Ryan! Ugh! He's disgusting! He makes my skin crawl!'

The dressing-room vibe began to change. Sitting in-between Max and Ryan, I enjoyed protecting my Golden Boy. But after a while, Max began to respond to Ryan's flirtation. This, Max told me, was because he enjoyed the power he held over Ryan, making him *think* he liked him (this should have been a warning sign – but I was besotted). And whenever I engaged Max in old-movie talk – which Ryan didn't understand – it drove Ryan mental!

Ryan had sworn that he wouldn't get involved in 'any drama'… but drama now there was. Encouraged by Max – who loved my witty put-downs – I responded to Ryan's barbed asides with snide retorts. Max sat there loving it, egging me on.

On Max's day off (when Ryan and I were both at work), things came to a head as he'd left Ryan in charge of his cuddly toy dog. Ryan started parading around backstage with the dog under his arm, proudly boasting he was 'under instructions from Max' to look after it. Max then texted me instructions to secretly 'kidnap' the dog and send Ryan into a blind panic – which I successfully achieved, hiding the dog somewhere Ryan would never find it (being friends with the backstage crew came in handy!).

Suspecting my handiwork, Ryan pinned posters all over backstage: a photograph of the missing stuffed Westie under the blazing banner 'DOGKNAPPED!'. Ed went around with a pen, correcting the spelling. In our isolated world, it all felt like a matter of life and death!

When Max's parents came to see the show, he invited me to meet them. I met his best friend too. But now Max was also going around to Ryan's house for 'movie nights'. I asked Max to be honest and tell me if anything was happening. He laughed, promising me he was just 'playing a game… I'm going to make Ryan squeal! He's going to be *completely* under my control!' Even I found this rather harsh. Later, Max promised to cook for me at his place… but then said he had a 'headache'. Later, I found out, he'd let Ryan take him out on a date. Ed and Guy warned me to put up my guard…

However, these disturbing character traits were contrasted by glimpses of the Max for whom I'd originally fallen. He made friends with George and Betty Fay and came with me to visit them in the caravan, multiple times! I was no longer alone when George told stories about his earliest days in variety. Max listened with veneration as George remembered appearing on the same bill as a singing act – Ted and Barbara Andrews – whose little daughter Julie had a remarkable singing voice. Young Julie would sit and watch her parents in the wings before coming out (supposedly impromptu) to sing a number with them.

Here, Max was charming, reverential and adorable – everything I wanted him to be. But then we'd leave the caravan and go back inside, and in the dressing room he reverted to the character I was growing to dislike.

What the hell was going on?

CHAPTER NINETEEN

'A shocking young
scamp of a rover'

Trial by Jury

A friend told me that he'd caught Max and Ryan kissing.

'That… That's not true!' Max protested. 'I was fighting Ryan off! *That's* why he was close to me.'

'You did say that if anything was going on, you would tell me.'

'Of *course* I'd tell you! I mean – ugh – if I was ever *stupid* enough to let anything happen with Ryan I'd be like, "Ugh! I drunkenly kissed Ryan! What a mistake! Not gonna happen again!"'

'So, if anything was going on – or had gone on – you *would* tell me?'

'Of course I'd tell you!'

Two days later – on my day off – one of Ryan's housemates, who could see I was in distress, confirmed what I already knew: Max and Ryan had been an item the entire time. And throughout all this, Max had continued to encourage my own feelings towards him.

At first, I took a cavalier attitude. But throughout the day I became angry and very upset. What really hurt was that I'd been blatantly lied to by someone for whom I had feelings, and who I thought had feelings for me.

Then I started thinking of all the sniping between Ryan and me in the dressing room... this petty unattractive behaviour had been encouraged by Max! He'd fanned the flames of discord and jealousy – playing us off against one another! I'd been manipulated and used. *That* hurt.

I told Guy to fasten his seatbelt – it was going to be a bumpy night. I could now see why Bette Davis's more conniving movie characters so appealed to Max! In *Whatever Happened to Baby Jane?* Davis sang the song 'I've Written a Letter to Daddy'. So, to articulate my feelings, I took the liberty of rewriting the lyrics:

> '*I've written a letter to Maxie saying,*
> *"Max – Fuck – You!"*''

But I was in a much better place than the year previously when my world came crashing down. Twelve months on I was much stronger. I might have been experiencing my first romantic heartache – but now I knew I could get through anything.

The next day, prior to the matinee, Max had arranged to come over for a movie. I asked outright.

'Have you got anything to tell me?'

'Er... Well...'

'Because – I know.'

Max launched into a remarkable monologue about how Ryan had unexpectedly swept him off his feet – but I wasn't to worry, because it hadn't gone very far – and they'd 'only kissed'.

'That's bollocks,' Ryan's housemate told me later. 'He's been staying over. Loads.'

I felt extremely guilty for saying so many unkind things about Ryan. Yes, I'd been encouraged to do so by misinformation from Max, but nevertheless I was appalled at these unattractive sides to my nature. My friendship with Ryan had suffered serious blows – but if I told Ryan that Max had painted a terrible false impression of him, I knew that Max would deny the whole thing… and mud would fly.

'All I'm going to say, Ryan, is – be careful. I know you really like Max, and that's great. But I've been *really hurt* very recently…'

'Really?' He seemed genuinely surprised.

'Yes,' I said, taking his hand. 'And I know *you've* been hurt a lot yourself in the past, so just *be careful.*' And I left it at that.

My heart was mauled, battered and bruised. I'd been hurt before, but this was different: I'd never been hurt romantically. But, my God, was I stronger! And as I told Guy, although what I'd experienced had been nasty, I didn't regret or wish to take back a single moment.

I'd learned some very valuable lessons: listen to alarm bells and look beyond the rose-tinted spectacles. I was also proud that I'd stood up for myself and not been afraid to challenge someone treating me badly. That was certainly a development since last year! And I was maturing emotionally. A helluva lot had changed between Thursford 2010 and 2011.

There was something on my mind… Christmas presents. Should I get Max a Christmas present? By rights he didn't deserve anything – and Max's housemate told me, 'You owe Max nothing.' But I had an idea. I wanted to show Max precisely what he'd thrown away. In my heightened emotional state, I considered that when all this was ancient history, perhaps Max might look back on the presents – and reflect. As Bogart said in *Casablanca*: 'Maybe not today, maybe not tomorrow, but soon, and for the rest of [his] life…'

I decided to give Max a Thursford goody bag crammed with exciting items relevant to him and me – his favourite sweets, a DVD, a novel I'd recommended… and then two bonanza items, including one linked to *Now, Voyager*. It amused me to think I had a few things in common with Charlotte Vale, the heroine of *Now, Voyager*: a terrified ugly duckling who suddenly, with guidance and belief, blossomed into a confident being – but did not get her man. As Bette Davis famously says to Paul Henreid at the end of the film: 'Oh, Jerry, don't let's ask for the moon. We have the stars.'

* * *

It was the morning of 23 December. At the end of the day the bubble would quiver and burst. I told Max to meet me in the dressing room at 10 a.m.

'Right,' I said, authoritatively, snapping my fingers. 'Follow me!'

I led him out through the pass doors to the back of the Gondola – our first meeting place – revealing the Thursford goody bag.

'Omigod, Martin…!'

'Don't take it,' I ordered, as he reached out. '*I'm* going to show you what's inside.' He giggled at the gummy bears and loved the DVD and novel.

'Oh, Martin! That's so…'

'We haven't finished yet.' He looked surprised. 'Before I give you this, you should know that *this* is an original.' I gave him a 1958 theatre programme of *My Fair Lady* from Drury Lane.

'Omi*god!*' He flicked through the pages and gasped when he saw Julie Andrews in her famous white ball gown. 'Martin! So… so… this is an original?'

'Yes.'

'So this would have been in the auditorium when she was up on stage doing it?'

'Yes.'

'This would have been on a programme seller's stand at Drury Lane?'

'Yes.'

'Oh… Omigod! Martin! This is the most *amazing* present I've ever had in my life…'

'We haven't finished yet!' Now he was almost speechless. 'This,' I said, 'is *also* an original.' I handed him a piece of sheet music from 1942 with Bette Davis on the front: 'It Can't Be Wrong', the theme from *Now, Voyager*. That did it. He couldn't talk.

'Ugh… Ah! Martin! But…!'

'Follow me!' I instructed, clicking my fingers and striding back towards the pass doors. Max froze but then scuttled to catch up.

'But… Martin… How? Where… Where did you find all these things?'

I barged straight into the MD's office (which I knew would be empty) and turned on the lights.

'Stand there!' I told Max, pointing to the desk. He did as he was told. I took the sheet music, placed it on the piano and swivelled round to face him.

'I'm not a very good pianist,' I told him. 'But I want you to know – this comes from the heart – from a real-life Charlotte Vale.'

I paused, and then began to play that famous chorus with my very best Steve Ross flourish: *'Daaaaa… da da da da! Da daaaaaaa…!'* I heard a gasp from behind me, with a sharp intake of breath. I'm *not* a very good pianist usually, but on this occasion, I played flawlessly, from the soul… and wondered if he'd remember this moment in years to come whenever he heard that tune. I slowly turned back round. Max's hands were clasped over his mouth.

'Oh my God, Martin,' he whispered. 'You're *perfect*!'

I looked him in the eye. 'I wish things could have been different between us, Max, I really do. But I won't ask for the moon… I have the stars.'

We walked silently back to the dressing room, where he caressed each page of the *My Fair Lady* programme. Eventually he said: 'You were right. All this *does* come from the heart.'

And then one of the other tenors arrived. I chatted away to him, not looking at Max, until he put his hand on my shoulder and said: 'I've gotta go… back to the cottage… but… I'll be right back… Don't go away!' And out he dashed.

An hour later, his housemate pulled me aside.

'I was in the kitchen when Max arrived at the front door

– and he *could not speak*. I sat him down and had to *beat* the story out of him… and then it all came tumbling out: the Gondola, the goody bag, the programme, the music – and what you'd said. He was completely stunned by the romance of it all, and the generosity. And I looked down at him with my arms folded and said, "Well, that blows any Christmas present from Ryan out of the water, doesn't it?" And he said, "Yes." And then I said, "Ryan might have won the battle, but Martin Milnes has won the war!" And he replied, "Yes. He has."'

And what, I hear you ask, dear reader, did Max get *me* for Christmas…? Bugger all!

Not even a Christmas card.

But no matter what I'd been through, this year I decided to leave the building on a high…

My 'beautiful assistant' Sarah had been a real trouper, and we'd become such good friends that whilst out partying in Fakenham she'd asked me to snog her with abandon. This was to deter the pervy locals who'd been hitting on her at the bar. As our lips locked and she twined her arms around me, I thought, This *never happened to me when I was straight*!

With managerial permission, during the final raffle I told the audience that Sarah was not only my 'beautiful assistant', but she was also 'my long-term girlfriend. We met here at Thursford, and I have to tell you, Sarah, that these have been the best few years of my life. So, I just wanted to ask you…' And then I dropped to one knee and cried, 'Will you marry me?'

The audience erupted into a wild ovation as I yelled, 'She said yes!' Sarah played the part to perfection, leaping into my arms… and as we made our exit, and Act Two began, the crowd was still cheering. In the audience that night was a celebrated bishop… who kindly asked the front-of-house staff to pass on to us his message of congratulations.

I'd made my exit from Thursford with dignity, but in my heart, I was still stuck on Max. Considering the glittering theatrical backdrop against which my heartbreak had played, I felt as though I'd lived Sondheim's musical *Follies* for real. It was like a movie in my head that played and played. And when I got home, I literally dimmed the lights and thought about Max.

I needed to get back to London – because despite everything, I felt compelled to be near him. My heart was overruling my head. I accepted the first job which came my way, despite grave doubts about the quality of the show. And on my first night back in town I knew where to head to find peace of mind. I was going back to that Chelsea apartment block…

CHAPTER TWENTY

'It certainly entertained the gapers'

Ruddigore

I knew I should never have accepted this ghastly play.

I was an American falsetto-singing drag queen. She was the best friend of a gay man – who ended up being shot by a straight man after the straight man drunkenly asked the gay man to give him a blow job; that was the entire plot.

It packed out a small London theatre with a ninety-eight per cent male audience, all of whom shrieked with laughter at what was intended to be a highly artistic and moving dramatic scene.

'Suck it,' the tipsy straight man instructed, with his hands on the gay man's head.

'Are you sure?' asked the excited gay man. The straight man nodded his assent, and the lights dimmed as the gay man (on his knees with his back to the audience) disappeared into the straight man's crotch. Meanwhile, I came on in a spotlight stage right and sang an emotive chorus of 'Zing! Went the Strings of My Heart' – which lasted the entire length of the blow job (still just about visible centre stage).

There wasn't a dry eye in the house, but not for the reasons the creative team had hoped. Nevertheless, I made it a point of personal honour – keeping poker-faced and ignoring the catcalls – to get the auditorium of howling queens to belt up by the last eight bars.

I did *not* tell Ginny and Lenny about the play. *Little Shop* was one thing, but this fiasco was quite another! Fortunately, I was able to be selective in the news I gave them as we had a new activity to occupy our evenings: Ginny decided to teach me her favourite card game – Posso – officially described as 'a hypercharged rummy'.

'You start with two threes of a kind,' Ginny explained as we sat at a small round wooden table by the piano. 'And if you pick up the wild card, you can take an *extra* card!'

Ginny was fiercely passionate about Posso, so I had to learn fast. Lenny, sensibly, just remained by the fire, occasionally calling out to the kitchen: 'More wine! I'm getting dehydrated.' Virgie had now retired, so it was her young replacement, Tracy, who saw to the wine. She lived on site full-time and cared for Ginny and Lenny with great dedication.

Ginny explained that in Posso the wild cards were twos and jokers, and these could be substituted for any card you liked. It was all about getting those wild cards because they helped a helluva lot! And if a player wished to pick up a card which had just been discarded by their opponent they could ask, '*Posso?*' ('May I?') to which their partner courteously answered, '*Sì*'.

The first few times we played I was all over the place – which in turn both frustrated Ginny and equally suited her fine, as she liked to win. When it didn't go her way, a look of panic crossed her face, her eyes blazed with horror and she'd grasp the cards for dear life cursing, 'Oh *shit!*'

If I made the slightest incorrect move Ginny informed me in no uncertain terms. But she wasn't averse to bending the rules herself – at which point she conjured up all the tricks in her book of coquettish Southern charm.

'Sweetheart,' she said, staring into my eyes and smiling, 'I didn't *mean* to discard that, so… why don't I just take it back…?' And whilst maintaining complete eye contact, her fingers subtly crept forward and took whatever they wanted from the centre pile.

'Mississippi card shark!' Lenny called out from the comfort of his chair.

Gradually our Posso matches became suitably competitive – or at least on the surface as, being a gentleman, I sometimes let her win. The only interruptions would be Lenny playing his harmonica, or Tracy placing the latest bunch of yellow roses in the middle of the dinner table. Posso came to occupy more of our time – the elderly couple now didn't venture out quite as much. It was a shame, as many of my friends wished to meet them – although I had one friend whom I wasn't entirely sure I wanted anywhere near them…

'Martin – you've *got* to introduce me to Ginny and Lenny,' fluttered Max. 'There's so few great stars left – and I have to meet them before it's too late!'

My inexperienced heart wasn't yet ready to move on. So, against my better judgement, Max and I went to the National Film Theatre (BFI Southbank) to watch classic films on the big screen.

Max and Ryan were now officially a couple – yet Max

chose to spend the evening of Valentine's Day with me at BFI watching *The Red Shoes*. I should have said no, but maybe deep down I wanted to pretend that Thursford hadn't happened, and that it was a proper Valentine's date. Not my greatest decision.

But the more I saw of Max, the more I came to distrust his general motives… and when I met up with Seymour and told him about the misadventures of Thursford, his jaw hit the floor – a lot of what I said sounded all too familiar. Therefore, when Max kept asking to me to introduce him to Ginny and Lenny, I was sensible enough to listen to the alarm bells ringing in my head saying NO!

It took a long time – a good way into the year – but eventually I was able to say, hand on heart, that I was over Max. And quite possibly it was the thought of him potentially meeting Ginny and Lenny which clinched this. No – just no. I couldn't allow it. He didn't deserve to meet them. Or Fenella. Or Alan. Or any of my treasured friends. I finally said to Ed and Guy, '*What* was I thinking?' I was growing up.

Around July, the offers came out for Thursford 2012. It had crossed my mind that if Max, Ryan and I were back together in the same dressing room, it would make for an interesting time. However, neither Max nor Ryan was offered the contract.

Months later, one night during the rehearsal period, a text message arrived from a mutual friend informing me that Max and Ryan had broken up. Back in London, after the dust settled, I met up with Ryan. We had a lovely day out and our friendship was restored. Ever since, I have only ever wished Ryan well.

Max dropped off the radar for a while, but at the start of 2013 he suddenly re-emerged and came to see a show I was in. He asked to meet for lunch the next day. 'We've got things to discuss,' he told me. 'Good things!' I let curiosity get the better of me.

'I've met this amazing guy,' he began. 'He's from New York – and he's invited me to go out and stay with him! I want to meet as many people in New York as I can, so can you introduce me to your friends in America? I want to meet Steve Ross and Annie Wakefield and Mary Rodgers and…'

It beat all world records for running, jumping or standing gall. I said to Ed and Guy afterwards, 'What did he expect me to say to all my American friends? "This is the cunt who broke my heart – you should have lunch with him!"?'

I politely but firmly declined. He was getting no introductions from me. At that point Max said he had to dash as he was meeting someone else… and left before I'd finished my main course. All I could do was burst out laughing.

I have not come across Max again since. But every time I watch the final scene in *All About Eve* and hear the immortal line with which Bette Davis puts down Anne Baxter, I think of him.

CHAPTER TWENTY-ONE

'She certainly did surprising things!'

Iolanthe

It was 17 February 2012 – Ginny's ninety-eighth birthday, and a year to the day since I'd met her. Ginny had been looking forward to her birthday for months, and I was to learn that her annual parties were elaborate affairs. This year it was at Bocca di Lupo, the Soho restaurant owned by her grandson, celebrated chef Jacob Kenedy. Ginny and Lenny sat at the head of the table beneath a recent portrait of Ginny holding a film still of herself with Gary Cooper in *Unconquered*.

Ginny's daughter Haidee Becker greeted me warmly – she was an artist whose paintings had been exhibited on both sides of the Atlantic. Her father John (Ginny's second husband) had been an art gallery owner in New York – presenting, amongst others, Picasso to an audience unaccustomed, at that time, with the avant-garde. Years later, poet laureate Ted Hughes actively endorsed Haidee's work, and she received much attention for her portraits of Mark Rylance and the cast of West End play *Jerusalem*.

Also present was Ginny's half-brother Jay from America. Several years after Ginny's mother died, her father had married again. When Jay was born, Ginny insisted he have nothing but the best. His gratitude was evident, and Jay regaled everyone with a special memory:

'When Ginny was living in Rome in the fifties, I was in school and came over on vacation. Ginny said we were going to a party and she'd got a date for me. We parked outside a house, and Ginny said to knock on the door and my date would answer. It was Audrey Hepburn!'

Every time I'd visited Ginny and Lenny for dinner, new stories emerged from the lives of one or the other, although Rome was a subject we had never properly discussed. But during the birthday meal, Ginny's neighbour asked me: 'You know Fellini based the character in *La Dolce Vita* on Ginny?'

After Ginny's recovery from tuberculosis, she and John Becker travelled across Europe, finally settling in Rome, becoming leading socialites during the city's post-war renaissance. The family took an apartment (where, John Cheever wrote, 'the roses grow up to the bedroom balcony') in Palazzo Caetani, home to Prince and Princess Caetani, whose ancestry dated back to Ancient Rome. The prince, who still lived there, had known Brahms, whom he claimed was a 'funny little man… smoked a cigar before breakfast'. The prince's cousin was T.S. Eliot, who would often visit, and the walls of the palace were adorned with murals by Guicciardini and Poussin.

Ginny excelled as a society hostess. Having studied puppetry in her youth at a Washington finishing school, the Beckers established a marionette theatre in their apartment – Ginny directing and creating the marionettes, whilst John provided the scripts.

The glamour and allure of post-war Rome was at its height, and the Becker salons became a mecca for artistes and intellectuals. Old friends such as Hume Cronyn and Jessica Tandy joined eclectic figures – the likes of Alice B. Toklas, Alexander Calder, Lady Diana Cooper, Aaron Copland, Karen Blixen, W.H. Auden, Robert Graves... and Federico Fellini.

The master of Italian cinema was in the process of creating *La Dolce Vita* – destined for classic status. The roles of American ex-patriots Mr and Mrs Steiner were inspired by Ginny and John (although Mr Steiner was also partly based on Italian writer Cesare Pavese). To portray a Becker-style salon in the movie, Fellini duplicated the interior of Ginny and John's residence and invited their regular guests to appear as themselves in the scene. Iris Tree, the bohemian actress, poet and model received featured screen time, speaking in both English and Italian, reciting her poetry.

The paintings on the wall of the Steiner apartment are Ginny's creations – for by this time she had also established herself as an acclaimed artist, painting in the naïve style. In the Steiner scene there is a doll-like painting to the right of Marcello Mastroianni's head as he listens to a recording of birdsong – the portrait is of Haidee. She and her brother were the inspirations for the two Steiner children who observe the exotic assortment of guests from their bedroom doorway, as Haidee and Cam had done throughout their Italian childhoods.

Fellini asked Ginny to play the role of Mrs Steiner and even offered to feature the marionettes. Wary of the director's intentions and satirical eye, the Beckers declined the offer. For the rest of her life Ginny never confirmed whether she had seen the film.

After moving from Rome to Vienna, the Becker marriage was dissolved, and Ginny performed with her marionettes on cruise ships. Just for the sheer fun of it, she came to London and trained as a plumber at night school, and eventually, thanks to the burglar, met Lenny.

'I want music!' Ginny suddenly announced – which was my cue to sing. I'd rewritten the song 'Chitty Chitty Bang Bang' as 'Ginny Ginny Campbell' – with references to DeMille, her Broadway career and the sailing boats which she and Lenny had once navigated.

I was accepted at large by Ginny's family and friends. This had been a birthday party to cherish. More than ever, I had been included and shared in the love of a truly happy birthday.

When I next visited the flat, I asked Ginny more about her marionettes and the finishing school in Washington.

'Oh, my dear – it was a very interesting, off-beat school. Twenty-eight students – all girls. We had an hour of deportment every morning – and we learned how to pour tea and wear the right kind of dresses to the right kind of places.' This was, indeed, a school from a world gone by. 'And at that point I wanted to be a dancer – so I took drama to supplement the dancing. The school saw to it that we always had an outlet. For the dancing I was given a job in the ballet of the opera house. And for the acting – because it was an all-girls school, with no boys to do plays – I elected to study marionettes.' And then with a twinkle in her eye she asked, 'Would you like to see a show?'

'Of course!' I replied, assuming we'd be watching film footage. To my surprise, Lenny rose from his chair, took Ginny's hand and, holding tight, led her across the room. He started helping her scale eleven stairs, one at a time, very gently, climbing towards a small upstairs area.

I was both fascinated and terrified – it had never crossed my mind to ask what was in the small space above – but there was no railing or bannister, and by her own admission Ginny couldn't 'do' stairs. Ginny's smile was outwardly confident and poised, but I followed immediately behind with my arms extended, ready to leap into action!

Ginny revealed a beautiful floor-to-ceiling marionette theatre, complete with stage and proscenium arch, above which was written 'Teatro Delle Quattro Stagioni' – Theatre of Four Seasons. The curtains were now faded, and the theatre had seen better days, but it was nevertheless an impressive and unexpected sight. Next thing I knew Ginny had opened what looked like a cupboard door but which led to a walk-in backstage area.

'Now,' she said through the darkness, lifting dusty marionettes from where they hung on wooden beams, 'these I made.' There was even a puppet she'd created as a self-portrait, with an uncanny likeness.

Lenny and I were Ginny's private audience for *The Princess and The Moon*, a regular piece from Ginny's repertoire. Granted, it was abridged, there was no soundtrack and sometimes there were long pauses between characters' entrances… but nevertheless the magic of what had once been in Rome was evident. It was also, to my knowledge, possibly the last time Ginny and her marionettes ever performed.

I bought a DVD of *La Dolce Vita*. The Steiner sequence

gave fascinating insight into Ginny's Italian world; the discussions of life, culture and poetry at her salons sublime. It was an era of history which, like her Southern upbringing, was now but an historic memory. The paintings on the Steiner walls were unmistakably Ginny's – and from then on, I paid more attention to her paintings displayed in the lounge and hallway in Chelsea.

On certain nights I was joined there by Sarah Simmons, a friend of Ginny's for almost forty years. Ginny and Lenny's private world was now small and select – partly because they entertained only whom they wished; partly because they had now outlived their contemporaries. When Sarah and I came over for dinner and Posso, it was humbling to know that our hostess had once been known as the greatest of them all.

CHAPTER TWENTY-TWO

'Oh, the man who can
rule a theatrical crew,
Each member a genius
(and some of them two),
And manage to humour
them, little and great...'

The Grand Duke

Back during *Perchance to Dream* I'd considered that maybe I could direct a show. I'd just turned twenty-five – the age at which Orson Welles directed *Citizen Kane* – and what was good enough for him was good enough for me. I decided to make my professional directorial debut.

An opportunity arose at the Finborough Theatre in Earl's Court, a small but highly regarded venue from which several shows had transferred into the West End. The Finborough often programmed rare revivals of British musicals – works which had not been produced professionally in London for at least twenty-five years.

To prove a worthwhile effort, I would need to cast ambitiously with a piece unusual enough to guarantee a sell-out. I decided to play to my great strength – Gilbert and Sullivan.

At Buxton in 2011 I'd played a supporting role in *Utopia Limited*, the penultimate G&S opera. Having been revived only twice before in over a hundred years, this rare *Utopia* staging had caused a frenzy of excitement, selling out in a flash.

However, *The Grand Duke*, the last of the Savoy operas, had never been professionally revived; the only G&S piece ever thus neglected. When it opened in 1896 the show was not a financial success, and Gilbert and Sullivan, whose collaboration had always been prickly, were no longer on good terms. The D'Oyly Carte Opera Company swept *The Grand Duke* under the carpet, where it remained overlooked ever after.

If a curiosity like *Utopia* could sell out Buxton Opera House, I was certain that *Grand Duke* could fill the tiny Finborough Theatre – but was the piece any good? To my delight I found it was an absolute gem – if handled properly. Sullivan's score was superior to *Utopia*, and although several sections required pruning, only one number required cutting entirely – a madrigal, 'Strange the Views Some People Hold', which stopped the action dead.

As for Gilbert's book, with judicious editing and an affectionate blue pencil, a very clever and funny piece began to emerge. It seemed to me that Gilbert had been looking to the future – the comedy was reminiscent of *Carry On* and *Monty Python* – and therefore right up my street.

The bonkers plot of *The Grand Duke* revolves around a company of egomaniacal actors in a European grand duchy named Pfennig-Halbfennig. Amidst their rehearsals for *Troilus and Cressida*, the thespians are plotting a coup to overthrow the country's miserly leader, Grand

Duke Rudolph, and install themselves as leaders of the realm. With a convoluted scheme – involving sausage rolls and a pack of playing cards – this is achieved, and once in power they decide to 'upraise the dead old days of Athens in her glory' wearing their *Troilus and Cressida* costumes about the royal court.

As the curtain rises on Act Two, the company cavorts in Ancient Greek togas, singing about 'lesbian wine'; multiple marriages occur (to the same hapless hero); the Prince of Monte Carlo arrives with a chorus of supernumeraries (dressed in even stranger costumes than the togas); and a brazen baroness consumes a very satisfying amount of Pommery '74. This show had Martin Milnes written all over it!

Having seen (and been in) some very bad productions of the Savoy operas, I felt that G&S directors should learn the rules before they break them. That way, any unusual decisions they made would be entirely justified. Several directors I'd worked with didn't trust the text (a mistake); others didn't even understand it – dumbing it down and cutting important lines.

Bravely, I decided that after a lifetime's devotion to G&S – as both amateur and professional – I'd learned the rules. So, I approached *The Grand Duke* with fresh eyes, embracing its craziness but obeying Mr Gilbert's diktat to 'treat a thoroughly farcical subject in a thoroughly serious manner'.

The first G&S stalwart I approached was my great friend Bruce Graham, who immediately agreed to play the Notary. We met for dinner at the Garrick Club prior to rehearsals and paid homage to Mr Gilbert's writing desk, on which he'd written *The Grand Duke*. As I raised the wooden lid and caressed the historic ink stains, Bruce whispered: 'He may have written 'Strange the Views Some People Hold' with that ink – and *you're* not even doing it – thank God!'

From then on, casting was easy. Go-to 'patter man' Richard Suart played the title role, and Charlotte Page was Julia – a tremendously difficult but brilliant part, re-quiring a flawless German accent. In the hands of a lesser actress this could have proved dangerous, but Charlie did more than just steal the show – to quote one review she 'bundled it up, tucked it under her arm and took it home with her'.

Somehow, I found the chutzpah to approach John Owen Edwards and asked him to be our musical director. To my utter amazement he said yes. The former MD of the D'Oyly Carte Opera Company agreed to work with a first-time 25-year-old director for a fee less than pea-nuts... as indeed had all the astonishing cast. But this wasn't down to any great anticipation of my artistic abil-ities. This was where choosing *The Grand Duke* had paid off, big time...

I knew that all zealous G&S professionals wanted to achieve that rare distinction of having performed in every single Savoy opera. Up to 2011, many had appeared in all but two – *Utopia Limited* and *The Grand Duke*. Now that Buxton had just done *Utopia*, they only had *Grand Duke* left to complete the set. The plan worked. And our limited run sold out before rehearsals began, so we added extra matinees.

During rehearsals I was tremendously grateful to my cast – they could easily have attempted walking all over this impertinent young upstart who thought he could direct (and had only given them an absurd two-week rehearsal period). However, every single one of them was totally respectful. They listened to my ideas, and if they were good, they took them. If my ideas could be improved upon, they tactfully suggested other things. These actors had been in the West End, in some cases, since before I was born – so I knew that if they had something to suggest, I'd be a fool not to listen. The entire piece benefited as a result.

The actors also enjoyed being inventive creating their characters – something unheard of in G&S. Traditionally, both audiences and performers had stringent ideas about how all the roles in the regular repertoire should be played. But neither cast nor audience had ever seen *Grand Duke* – it offered a fresh slate.

I tried to be as courteous and polite as possible – I'd seen too many potentially excellent shows ruined by the egos of directors. And I knew from personal experience what the actors *said* about these directors out of earshot, so I was determined not to let that happen to me! Moreover, I was bloody lucky to have them all there, and I knew it.

My team gently guided me, giving me the belief that I could pull this off. John Owen Edwards treated me as an equal, and I learned a great deal from actor Stefan Bednarczyk. His interpretation of Ludwig (possibly the longest and most complicated role in G&S) was both intelligent and hilarious. The show would not have been the same without his considerable talents.

And yet it was a happy mix – in the supporting roles I had a dynamic cast of younger performers. The heart and soul of *The Grand Duke* was the Theatrical Troupe – whom

I cast as individual characters rather than a faceless chorus. The Troupe – Ciara O'Connor, Tammy Davies, Matthew James Willis, Stiofan O'Doherty and Mark Lawson – really held the show together. And after all the personal support which Mark had given me since Thursford 2010, I was beyond thrilled when J.O.E. selected him.

Stiofan O'Doherty was a real find… neither J.O.E. or I had worked with him before, but the moment this outstanding lyric baritone walked into the room (looking like a catwalk model because, that's what, in fact, he was) we knew he was something special. But I didn't realise that he was destined to become my best and greatest friend…

* * *

The Finborough Theatre has one tiny dressing room. We had a cast of nineteen, most of whom wore two costumes, and the costume rail was already bulging with outfits from the play with which *Grand Duke* performed in rep. I devised a system whereby the senior principals had the main dressing room, whilst the poor old Theatrical Troupe changed in the theatre manager's office! Meanwhile, Grand Duke Rudolph's chamberlains (an entirely separate chorus, including Guy Mott) had to wait downstairs in the bar until the show began… and whilst the Theatrical Troupe was on stage, the Chamberlains took over the office! That just left the interval for the entire company to clamber all over each other – climbing into Ancient Greek togas in a claustrophobe's worst nightmare.

I couldn't believe I'd submitted the great and good of the G&S world to these primitive conditions… but somehow, they seemed to be having a great time! During the height of dress-rehearsal chaos, I found Curtis Dabek (whose career began in the sixties as a Black and White Minstrel) pinned against a wall in full costume, unable to move amidst the carnage. He had every right to be hopping mad but said to me: 'I just have to tell you, Martin, how much I'm enjoying this show!'

Opening night – I'd been cool as a cucumber for weeks and done everything in my power to make this production work. Now the audience was filing in – and expectation was high. Suddenly my nerve cracked, but there was no escape – I was sandwiched inside the back row of a sold-out house.

'Who the *hell* thought it was a good idea to put on *The Grand Duke*?' I asked my associate director, Brendan, in a panic. 'Get me out of here!' Brendan – my invaluable aid, who helped my work look better than it was – just took my hand and smiled.

The show began… the audience laughed in all the right places, and then some. 'They're smiling!!!!!' I wrote in my notepad in the darkness. During the interval, the die-hard G&S anoraks, whose disapproval could be vitriolic, gave the official thumbs up, and as the company sang the Act Two finale, I felt happy that I hadn't let anyone down – J.O.E., the cast, Brendan… and yes, Mr Gilbert and Sir Arthur too.

Somehow all the elements came together. Nineteen actors, two pianists and two pianos on a stage the size of a postage stamp made magic and completely reinvigorated a work which had been dismissed for 116 years.

But the critics were sniffy. With some rare exceptions,

critics are predisposed to dislike Gilbert and Sullivan. It's incorrectly viewed as too lightweight by 'serious' musicians, and sadly, too many bad productions over the years have prejudiced too many critics – not all of whom, I've found, can tell the difference between a bad production and a bad piece.

Michael Billington in *The Guardian* was kinder than others, writing, 'one can only salute the heroic dedication of director Martin Milnes and his nineteen-strong cast', highlighting the excellent contributions of J.O.E. and the 'faultless' Bruce Graham. But my work certainly didn't satisfy others; a theatrical newspaper suggested I should have taken 'liberties' with the material to make *The Grand Duke* 'more palatable to a modern audience'. But something happened which, to me, demonstrated otherwise. Tammy Davies of the Theatrical Troupe was a young G&S veteran who'd performed at Buxton many times. Her nan loyally came to see all Tammy's G&S shows… but admitted to not having understood the storyline of a single one. But at the Finborough, Tammy approached me and said: 'My nan's just told me that she understood the *entire* plot of this show!'

It was one of my proudest moments – especially considering the plot of *Grand Duke* is so convoluted! It proved that you needn't take liberties with G&S. By all means, be inventive, but if you stay true to Gilbert and tell the story clearly, by saying the words exactly *as he wrote them* (as our cast did), you cannot go wrong. Gilbert was a master craftsman, and in every G&S piece, the director and actors will find that Gilbert's already done the hard work for them. Gilbert sets up the bowling pins and you knock 'em over, and it works.

But if *The Grand Duke* didn't appeal to critics, it most definitely pleased those whose opinions mattered most – the audience. At each performance queues of people waited on the off chance of return tickets becoming available.

One lady who booked her seat in plenty of time was Fenella. I was thrilled when she went on record as saying the production was 'smashing… wonderfully cast… a joy from start to finish'. Many of the company wanted to meet her, including Stiofan.

'I had quite a long conversation with her,' he reported afterwards, 'but I can't remember a word she said because I was just so fascinated by her eyelash – it was sticking to her eyebrow, and she had no idea!'

I was absolutely thrilled to find a personal hero of mine roaring his ribs out on the front row – Gyles Brandreth, one of the greatest living English wits (also a TV presenter, author, actor, royal biographer, theatrical producer, former Conservative whip, Lord of the Treasury and Honorary President of the Association of British Scrabble Players). 'My *boy*!' he boomed during the interval when I introduced myself. 'I'm buying *you* a *drink*!'

However, I wanted the approval of one final person – and if *he* was satisfied, then it meant we'd all done our job properly. This was Mike Leigh, the Oscar-nominated and BAFTA-winning writer and director.

Leigh's Oscar winning film *Topsy-Turvy* tells the story behind the creation of *The Mikado*. The film is testament to the director's lifelong devotion to G&S, having grown up watching D'Oyly Carte tours as a child. Mike Leigh was not only a director I held in the greatest respect, but he was also a G&S authority of whose knowledge I could only stand in awe. When I originally decided upon *The Grand Duke*, I wanted to find a way to invite Mike Leigh. But the Finborough informed me that he'd already booked tickets. And it turned out he was coming the same night as Ginny and Lenny... which also happened to be the night I ended up playing the Notary.

When Bruce Graham accepted *Grand Duke*, we agreed he could be released for one evening to fulfil an engagement at the Albert Hall. So that night, I played the Notary myself (as more of an eager young lawyer out to prove himself, whereas Bruce was the wizened voice of experience).

But that evening I did have a slight problem... Ginny couldn't manage stairs, and to reach the auditorium, patrons had to walk up a winding flight from the theatre bar.

'Darling,' I said to Guy. 'You're nice and strong... how would you like to carry a 98-year-old movie star upstairs to see the show?'

The Ginny and Lenny 'party', headed by Haidee and Sarah, arrived in plenty of time... I met them downstairs and introduced Ginny to Guy. Loving the attentions of a handsome young man, Ginny was in her element, flirting coquettishly. By 7.25 p.m. the bar had cleared, but as the last stragglers made their way up, Ginny approached the doorway and saw the stairs.

'Oh, *God!*'

Before she had time to think, Guy swooped her up in his arms (much the way Gary Cooper had in *Unconquered*) and safely escorted Ginny to her seat... into which, much to the astonishment of the audience, and her delight, he placed her directly!

Afterwards Mike Leigh told me, 'There was a lady in front of me. She was carried into her seat! She must have been at least a hundred years old.'

'Close,' I replied. 'She's ninety-eight and appeared in movies for Lubitsch and DeMille.'

He then signed my copy of the *Grand Duke* vocal score: 'To Martin – Wonderful! Thank you so much! Well done – you've proved it works!'

The rest of the run was a joy. Happy audience members even described the production as 'historic'. Bruce Graham certainly made history: *Grand Duke* not only completed his 'set' of the entire canon, but he also achieved the unique distinction of playing two different roles in *The Grand Duke* on the same day. Our Prince of Monte Carlo had an emergency one matinee, missing the performance. As I already knew the Notary role, I went on again and Bruce played the Prince of Monte Carlo – performing a flawless 'Roulette Song'.

In the weeks after the show I was thrilled to receive continued correspondence from Mike Leigh. If I may, dear reader, I would like to be completely egomaniacal and tell you what he wrote about *The Grand Duke*. I hope it will encourage others to explore Gilbert and Sullivan's remarkable final work:

Sparkling musically, and performed with great wit and enthusiasm, Martin Milnes' hilarious production of The Grand Duke *is like a breath of fresh air. It totally destroys the myth, once and for all, that Gilbert and Sullivan's last opera is a damp squib not worth reviving. On the contrary, the piece is a neglected classic.*

The story continued. English National Opera approached Mike about directing a G&S piece – and having seen our Finborough production he wanted to do *The Grand Duke*. ENO's management, however, preferred the idea of *Pirates* – and without bias I can say that Mike Leigh's *Pirates* revival remains my favourite because he stayed true to the text. A young audience – mostly, it seemed, discovering the piece for the first time – had a terrific evening, full of laughs and genuine dramatic tension. (For reference, the critics didn't like *this* G&S revival much either. But it sold out and subsequently had to be revived yet again!)

Mike even kindly mentioned *The Grand Duke* in a pre-show talk at the Coliseum, and wrote in his *Pirates* programme notes that '*The Grand Duke*... proved, under the direction of Martin Milnes at the Finborough Theatre, to be as hilarious as it is a musical feast.'

Once again, the approval of someone from an older generation was opening doors and making a difference. And the generosity shown to me by J.O.E., Bruce, Charlie Page and all the other senior members of the cast was inspiring. I made a silent promise that in future years, if I was able to help or inspire someone else in turn at the start of their career, I would remember the kindness of all these people and repay them by helping another.

I was deeply proud of *The Grand Duke* – but I needed a break. Most people age twenty-five, when they go off on holiday, head to the beach with their friends. And that was precisely my plan. My friends were off to Italy, and I'd been invited to join them...

CHAPTER TWENTY-THREE

'Diamonds, Hearts and Clubs and Spades'

The Grand Duke

As the sun blazed down, Ginny sat regally beneath a yellow umbrella in a deckchair. Even on the beach she looked like a movie star – with a large-brimmed hat and huge pair of sunglasses, reminiscent of Bette Davis. Lenny sat next to her drinking wine (what else?).

Sperlonga, the coastal retreat between Rome and Naples, had been part of Ginny's life for sixty years. When she and John Becker bought the apartment, Sperlonga had yet to be discovered by tourists. Now it was a different story. Alfred and Rhoda had driven us down the hill to the beach, but it was a slow, careful journey out of the car across the sand.

'Signora Becker!' the lifeguards cried – even after all these years, Ginny was known locally by her former name; the 'BECKER' nameplate hanging above the front door of the apartment had never been removed.

'Okay, honey, let's go!' said Alfred as we gently approached the water. Ginny walked into the sea with the help of the Zimmer frame... but, once in the water, she cast off and swam with the youthful zeal of a woman half a century younger! My favourite sight of the entire holiday was the abandoned Zimmer frame, with the waves gently lapping around its legs, looking forlorn, whilst its owner backstroked away at top speed.

Alfred and Rhoda stayed nearby – the slightest current or breeze might whip Ginny out to sea. She was tiny and light, and the waves could be powerful. If wind levels were high, a beach trip was impossible.

Ginny and I swam together – she was faster than I was! Before we left, I took a selfie in the sea with both her and Lenny. I was thrilled to be there, having had an eventful journey…

'Hi, Adrian!' I'd texted from Gatwick. 'Just confirming that my plane will arrive at Fiumicino in two hours' time. Looking forward to meeting you. See you soon! Martin.'

Not speaking a word of Italian – and Sperlonga being two long train rides from the airport – I was glad that someone had been sent to collect me. Adrian was an octogenarian screenwriter who for twenty years had worked in Rome for Sophia Loren and Carlo Ponti. He and two other American ex-pat friends, Alfred and Rhoda, had upped sticks and moved in with Ginny and Lenny for the duration of their Sperlongan sojourn. I'd bring down the average age of the villa's occupants, along with an Italian cook named Francesca.

I'd met Alfred and Rhoda when they'd visited London but had no idea what Adrian looked like. Upon arrival in Rome I saw a tall white-haired man holding a placard, with my name scrawled.

'Adrian!' I said, extending my hand. 'A pleasure to meet you! I'm Martin!'

'Ohhh.' He smiled vaguely. 'Good! You're here!'

'I hope you haven't been waiting too long.'

'Oh,' he replied nonchalantly. 'Four hours.'

It turned out that Adrian was a little fuzzy. He hadn't looked at his phone, nor read my email – sent the previous week – with my arrival time. He'd just turned up at the airport and patiently stood all afternoon.

We got a train out to the railway terminal in Rome. Adrian then started walking up Platform 12, but even with my non-existent Italian I could tell from the departure boards that the train to Sperlonga left from Platform 13. Being young, British and polite I didn't like to say anything, but as he clambered onto the train I asked:

'Don't we need Platform 13? This is twelve.'

'Is it?'

'Ohhh!' Alfred cried as we walked into the apartment. 'Ya got here!' And then he yelled over his shoulder, 'They got here!'

'Ohhhhh, they got here?' I heard Ginny declare from somewhere in the villa.

'*Where* the hell have ya been?' Alfred asked Adrian, rolling his eyes.

'What took so long?' enquired Rhoda, walking in from the kitchen.

'What d'ya think?' muttered Alfred. 'They sent *Adrian* to get him.'

'They sent *Adrian* to get you?' Rhoda asked, raising an eyebrow. In Hollywood terms, Rhoda was a Thelma Ritter-type. Her wisecracks, knowing looks and disbelieving asides could have been scripted for Birdie in *All About Eve*. Even the face she pulled as Adrian sank into his chair screamed 'Ohhh, brother!'

Alfred, on the other hand, was a dynamo. Acting as General Factotum of the apartment, his authority, energy and booming voice kept everything shipshape. His iron fist was hidden beneath a velvet glove of love and affection for his hosts – although at times he threw down the gauntlet, refusing to make concessions for Ginny's age. Alfred wouldn't take no for an answer, which was good as it kept her active, vital and engaged.

'Where is he?' a familiar voice called. 'He's here?'

'Go on in,' said Alfred. 'She's been asking for you all night!'

I walked through the main room and onto the balcony.

'Ahhhh!' Ginny cried, throwing her arms in the air. 'Sweetheart!'

'Hello, my friend!' said Lenny, extending his hand.

'Darling, have some wine…'

'Have *this* one,' Alfred hurriedly whispered. 'We dilute theirs!'

We sat around a table groaning with food. Even though it was dark Ginny wore sunglasses. Lenny told me he'd been enjoying himself 'idling'.

'Tomorrow, we swim!' Ginny said and smiled. 'But now,' she announced, 'I think we ought to go to bed.'

'It's 10 p.m.,' said Rhoda. 'I think that's a good idea.'

'Darling,' Ginny coaxed, eyeing Lenny's glass. 'Please finish this!'

Fearing procrastination, Rhoda urged, 'He doesn't *have* to drink it, Ginny!'

'I do!' Lenny chirped, his eyes sparkling.

'He doesn't have to drink it?' Ginny asked, a little squiffy. 'Then how does it disappear?'

'Down my throat!' And they both giggled like school-children. Alfred and Rhoda helped Ginny inside.

'Come on, sweetie,' she called. 'Finish your drink.'

'All in good time, my dear!'

Lenny and I remained on the balcony, listening to the waves. Content in each other's company, we enjoyed the tranquillity of the Italian evening. Knowing Ginny and Lenny had already proved a life-changing experience. Accepting me into their private world in London was the highest compliment I'd even been paid. But to be with them at home in Sperlonga was the ultimate honour. And when they'd invited me to join them in Italy, Ginny and Lenny had insisted on paying my air fare. They really did want to spend time with me. The pain and rejection I'd once felt – and not all that long ago – was now but a dim memory.

The next day, back in the car, we attempted to leave the beach. But Adrian, squashed in the back between Lenny and me, was cause for concern.

'Seatbelt!' Alfred hissed from the front. '*Seat-belt!*'

'Pizza?' Adrian asked.

Alfred lowered his eyes and asked me, sotto voce: 'Can you believe this? Can you believe…?' And then he roared, 'SEATBELT!'

'Oh, boy!' Ginny declared back at the apartment. 'And now we nap.' It was time to siesta – but it was my first day in Italy, and I wanted to look around.

'Well, I guess it's true what they say!' Alfred exclaimed. 'Mad dogs and Englishmen…'

The ruins of Emperor Tiberius's villa were a stone's throw from the apartment. Beside the beach was the Emperor's cave, where Lenny told me the Roman nobility had once enjoyed seven-course banquets. Back inland, purple bougainvillea lined the streets, and I had the village entirely to myself.

It was the calm before the storm. At 4 p.m. precisely, everyone gathered on the balcony for Posso. Over the last few months Ginny's tuition had ensured that I could hold my own against a single opponent. Now I was thrown in at the deep end. Alfred and Rhoda – who were experts – were playing too. Four players meant five packs of cards. The stakes were high.

As in London, Lenny had the good sense to sit aside with his wine. Sometimes he'd observe the heated game with a sly grin on his face. Other times he gazed out to sea, looking far into the distance – his thoughts taking him goodness knows where.

Adrian, meanwhile, was excused from play, and sometimes went on errands to buy supplies. Francesca kept everyone's glasses full, emerging onto the balcony with a smile as big as her personality.

'I want I speak English!' she declared. 'I speak only English while I work here!' And indeed, she mostly did, except whenever her dog rang to hear Francesca's voice. She missed her canine friend so much that she'd arranged with her mother, every few days, to let it bark at her down the receiver.

As the game began, the birds were screaming like mad, and I was nervous. Not only had I never played Posso with multiple partners, but Alfred was even more competitive than Ginny! I hoped for the best and prayed for wild cards. Ginny started beating the table like a tom-tom.

'That's for good luck!' she declared, repeating the percussive action at regular intervals. To my amazement

– and Ginny's too – I started off well, finding my two threes of a kind straight away.

'King, king, king!' I said and smiled, placing them down.

'Oh, God!' Ginny wailed in disbelief. 'No!'

'Queen, queen, wild card!' I added.

'Hey, we're rolling along,' said Alfred. 'Now discard one!'

'Three of diamonds,' I said, triumphantly tossing it onto the table.

'For heaven's sake!' Ginny complained.

'Posso?' Rhoda leapt in.

Alfred winked. 'Attaboy.'

'Hold your hand up!' Ginny ordered Alfred. 'I can see your cards! *Everybody's* doing it!'

Half an hour later things were getting heated. Alfred Posso'd a card that Ginny wanted for herself but hadn't picked up in time. And having previously claimed that she *could* see everybody's cards, now she claimed that she couldn't.

'*Please* understand,' Ginny implored – every inch the actress – 'that it's *very hard* for me to *see it*!'

'You can see the cards right there!'

'You could at least *tell* me what they are…'

'No! I'm *not* gonna treat you like an old lady! I'm just not gonna do it…'

'Alright,' Ginny sulked.

'I'm discarding an eight of spades…' said Rhoda.

'I just think that would be terrible!' Alfred overlapped to Ginny.

'Okay,' she sighed. 'It's your play!'

'It's *your* play!' Alfred corrected her. 'So *watch it* next time!'

Oblivious to everything, Lenny suddenly decided to

sing: '*Did you ever catch your bosom in the mangle? / What a tangle! / What a tangle!*'

As in London, Ginny permitted herself all the time in the world to analyse her own hand.

'Virginia, it's your turn!' Rhoda nudged.

'I know!' she barked. 'I'm looking at it!'

But whenever I took too long, I was told briskly: 'Come on!'

'*We* wait on *you*, sweetie,' Rhoda reminded her. 'Let him do it.'

Towards the end of the game Ginny was in the lead. But when Rhoda won the final hand, Ginny insisted there'd been a mistake and that *she* was the rightful winner.

'Excuse me!' she growled, banging her fist. 'It was a Posso!'

'Horseshit,' declared Alfred. 'Horseshit! I don't believe it!'

'It is *not* horseshit!'

'It's horseshit!'

'Can you believe this?' Rhoda asked me. '*Grown people?*'

'But you're silly!' Ginny insisted.

'*You're* silly!' cried Alfred.

'I can remember when she didn't speak to me for a week!' Rhoda whispered.

'I had the wild card!'

'I didn't *mean* to win…'

'I *might* have won it!'

'But ya didn't!'

Lenny just sat and sipped his wine. Finally, the last hand was analysed in painstaking detail to convince Ginny that Rhoda was the rightful winner.

'If you were going to win,' Alfred explained, 'you would have removed the wild card and put it down on the bottom.'

'And then moved the wild card to another position,' Rhoda confirmed. There was a pause.

'Oh!'

The penny finally dropped. Alfred threw his hands in the air. Having stayed silent, I was now rendered hysterical.

'Oh my *God*!' Ginny wailed, contrite.

'If you'd moved the wild card then you woulda *had* it! But don't listen to Alfred. Just scream! And I'll scream back at ya...'

'Well, thank you for telling me! I never thought of that!'

'Virginia – you'd have had us all by the balls.' There was a pause.

'But if I'd *had* a wild card, I wouldn't have had to worry about it...'

'I'm not gonna go there again,' Alfred declared. 'No, no, no!' And he made his way inside as Rhoda gathered the empty wine glasses. Ginny turned her pleas in my direction.

'Darling,' she simpered, 'I had everything except one card – because all the wild cards I had were *used*! But if I'd had an extra wild card, I could have *won*!'

'I think on Sundays we shouldn't play cards,' Rhoda sighed. 'It's the Lord's Day!'

* * *

One morning it was too windy for Ginny to swim, so we watched her scenes from *Unconquered*. Ginny sat close to the television, observing herself and Gary Cooper with professional objectivity. Her best-known scene is when Ginny gives Paulette Goddard a bath in a rain barrel.

'Ginny!' Rhoda smiled, as Ginny's younger self scrubbed Goddard's back. 'I want you to give *me* a bath!'

Other times local acquaintances dropped by, such as Maria Clara, the self-appointed Queen of Sperlonga. She'd heard whispers about 'a singer from London' staying with Signora Becker and duly called round in order that I, the visitor, could pay homage. Maria Clara spoke little English, but we nodded at each other, and I smiled as if being inspected on parade.

Afternoons, without exception, were dedicated to Posso.

'Let's do something intellectual,' Rhoda vainly suggested. 'Like read Shakespeare!' But Ginny was already dealing. 'Relax, honey,' Rhoda advised. 'Your blood pressure's going up!'

The evenings were full of laughter, wine (albeit diluted) and song... Ginny liked to show me off to her friends and told me, 'You know all the songs of my youth, and you sing them so beautifully!'

The arguments of Posso were forgotten as we sat on the balcony enjoying fine food and each other's company. There was forty years of history between these friends, so their unhesitating acceptance of me within their circle was a privilege I did not underestimate.

'Here's to us!' Ginny cried, raising her glass. 'Happy days!'

'Happy days!' repeated Lenny.

Ginny always retired around ten. When coaxed to turn in, Lenny good-naturedly complained, 'I'm surrounded by traitors!'

Alfred told me stories about the apartment in its heyday and the sparkling 'puppets and pasta' parties with the marionettes. These were, to quote Lenny, 'times long gone'.

'La dolce vita is over, baby,' Alfred sadly admitted. 'Rome in the sixties – you wouldn't believe. It's not the same now.'

Meanwhile, Alfred kept an affectionate eye on Adrian, who was growing increasingly vague. One day Adrian had to go to Rome but lost his wallet en route, causing much confusion.

'Adrian's a bigger problem than *they* are,' Rhoda sighed, glancing towards Ginny and Lenny's darkened bedroom.

But there is humour in all things, and one day Posso became so stressful that Alfred, Rhoda and I went for a proper – undiluted – drink in the town. When we returned, Ginny had the cards ready to go: 'Shall we finish the last hand?'

I similarly descended into hysterics mid-game, when, out of the blue, Lenny leaned over and announced something bizarre: 'I once nearly started World War Three!' He went on to explain, 'It was during the Cold War, after the Berlin Airlift. I was stationed in West Germany. I was bored to tears, doing night-time patrol – nothing happening at all. A brilliant moonlit night. And that evening I happened to have my aerobatics team with me, and I decided they needed some night-flying experience. So, I took up seventy-two planes, all flying close together. But as far as the Russians were concerned, looking on their radar, they thought that one *huge* new aeroplane had appeared. Panic broke out!'

Ginny giggled. 'They didn't realise it was Lenny with all of his planes! They thought it was one *huge* plane! And they got frightened!'

'Ten o'clock in the morning, I was summoned by my commander. "What were you up to last night?" he said. "Nothing. I was doing my patrol," I replied. "Yes. And what were you up to?" he asked. "Well, I thought the aerobatic team needed a little night experience." And he *roared* with laughter: "Ho! Ho! Ho!" And that was that.'

The next afternoon Posso took place indoors as it was slightly cold. The start of the game was delayed by a search of the villa for Lenny's wallet, which he usually kept in his jacket pocket but claimed he'd misplaced. It eventually turned up in his jacket pocket.

'You boob!' Alfred gently scolded.

Lenny blushed. 'I'm getting careless with money.'

The game began and the intensity was palpable. Lenny looked out through the window and then asked, 'You see that dark line on the horizon?'

'I do,' I replied.

'That's air pollution from Naples. And you can see it from Norway. Coming back from a raid on Berlin one night, I flew out and found myself as far as Naples. It was a winter's day, and there was a great trail of smoke. You only get that on a very cold day. Otherwise it goes up.'

'Queen of spades,' said Alfred, eyes on his cards. But Lenny was in the mood to reminisce.

'During the war we used to have a wonderful cook from Canada. He was the only cook who was officially credited with shooting down the German Focke-Wulf 190 Fighter!'

'Three of hearts!' I announced, discarding but keeping my focus on Lenny.

'Shot it down with a submachine gun! Ha ha!'

'Did he?' asked Alfred, concentrating on the hand.

'He hid in this foxhole. The Germans flew past at low level. The German pilot looked down, saw him and then he did *that*,' Lenny demonstrated, raising two fingers. 'And that's the last thing he did! The cook climbed out of the foxhole and shot him down!'

And then... chaos ensued. The sewers in the streets outside began to explode. The air filled with the animated cries of the locals and the stench of something unspeakable. Alfred and Rhoda hurriedly ran out with Francesca to find the whole village in chaos and excrement flowing along the pavements. Downstairs, the cellar began to flood with filthy bilge. Alfred took charge of the rescue operation and returned to keep us informed.

'We had to turn off the water – and then turn it on and turn it off. The whole toilet is blocked up and it's running out into the street!'

This warranted a temporary hiatus to Posso. However, the timing couldn't have been better... Lenny, completely unprompted, continued to share his memories.

'I had some very interesting experiences during World War Two, which I shouldn't have had!' He chuckled. 'I was always doing things I shouldn't have been doing. Ordinary service life was so bloody boring! And in those days, you never knew whether you were going to see the next day. So you didn't take much care about anything except having a good time. And doing a good job.'

'What sort of things did you do which you shouldn't have done?'

'Oh! Instead of going home on leave I joined the French underground.'

'Really? Where was this?'

'On the Franco–German border, near Alsace-Lorraine. I nearly lost my life through not smoking!' And he painted a vivid picture…

'I'm being smuggled through the German lines dressed as a French woodcutter. We have all the right papers – forged in Baker Street, London. We're walking down the middle of the street – and suddenly we're surrounded by all these German armed guards! But they think we're friends, so chat happily to us on our way through.

'Then one of them handed round a pack of Gitanes cigarettes – which are the strongest cigarettes ever made – and I thought I'd better have one so as not to arouse suspicion. But I didn't realise the effect these cigarettes had on a non-smoker. About three minutes later, I felt beads of sweat breaking out on my brow! I kicked my friend and said, "Get me out." He told the Germans I had a weak stomach. So he took me away – and I was sick! Round my neck, of course, I had my dog tags. I'd have been shot straight away if they'd known.'

Against the improbable background of the exploding sewers, Lenny continued to elaborate.

'Another thing I shouldn't have done – just for fun – I took off at midnight on a moonlit night – and climbed up to 25,000 feet. The whole of Europe was spread out in front of me, from Spain to Norway. So I rolled on my back, turned the engine off and glided down. Absolute silence except the *whoosh* of the wind. I rolled back and then hoped the engine would start again… which it did. It created a sensation of absolute loneliness. Quite an eerie sensation, actually.'

There was a pause.

'One commander I particularly liked was General Eisenhower.' He smiled. '*Absolute* great guy! I knew him very well. A very clever man. He knew what was *really* going on at the sharp end. I met him through the Second Allied Tac of the Allied Air Forces Central Europe. I was in charge of fighter operations. Somehow, he got hold of my name, and he invited me up to his headquarters. He kicked all his staff out, put his feet up and started asking me questions. He very quickly found that I didn't exaggerate, and that when he asked me a question, I'd just answer it. And if I didn't know the answer I'd say, "Well, I don't know, but I know somebody who does!"' Then Lenny folded his arms and with a practical note in his voice said, 'I've never talked about it. Even Ginny didn't know about that for a long time!'

'No, sweetie.' She smiled. 'I didn't.'

'After I left the Air Force, I was working for Computing Devices of Canada and I took several meetings in Washington. Ike used to go to the National Presbyterian Church on Nebraska Avenue. One Sunday I was taking my morning walk, and I heard him yell, "*HELLO, LENNY!*"' and he laughed warmly.

'Ike was a great man. During the war he kept twelve different nations, who were meant to be fighting the Germans, from fighting each other! The Americans didn't like the French, the French didn't like the Americans… sometimes I disliked both of them!' He chuckled. 'The Americans had some very aggressive generals. The sort who thought they could do anything. They were wrong. But they made a *huge* contribution to the war. We'd probably have been forced into stalemate without them. Anyway – times long gone.'

The sound of highly strung Italian voices continued to float up from the street.

'It's a big mess!' Rhoda announced, walking in.

'What?' asked Ginny.

'All the shit downstairs! They're trying to wash it out. They still haven't figured out where the leak is, and it's running all the way down the steps. Francesca's down there sweeping the garbage away – she's marvellous! She's worth her weight in gold!' And with that she disappeared again. Another moment of silence.

'I knew General Montgomery very well,' Lenny continued. 'Didn't like him. And he didn't like *me*. But he had to work with me, because my metier was close support to all his foreign troops. I did respect him. We just didn't like each other.' And then he growled, 'He was an *arrogant* S.O.B.'

'And how about de Gaulle?' I asked, remembering that Lenny had mentioned him once before.

'I didn't particularly like him either, but I did admire him. He was a bully. But I was unbullyable! So we got on fine! Unfortunately, he disliked the Americans – and that probably added maybe six months to the war. But I never got mixed up in politics.'

Alfred re-emerged, looking exhausted.

'It hasn't ended yet!' he groaned. 'They had to shut everything off.' And as Rhoda re-entered, he told us, 'You are allowed to take a shower. You can use the water if it's clean. But you *cannot* poo-poo and you cannot pee-pee.'

'Well, how long is that going to go on?' Ginny asked, a little disturbed.

' 'Til tomorrow morning.'

'*What?*'

'Tomorrow morning.'

'I can't pee-pee or poo-poo until then?'

'You can go out the window,' Alfred told her, straight-faced. 'We're in Italy!' And he collapsed into a chair. 'Tomorrow morning they're gonna come and open up the street!'

'What do you mean "open up the street"?' asked Ginny, alarmed. Alfred animatedly imitated the sound of a digger.

'Open up – take it out – and see where the tube is broke!'

'Every day something happens,' Rhoda sighed. 'Never a dull moment. Yesterday: Adrian. Today: the toilet. Tomorrow... ?' And looking at me, she asked, 'Are you gonna tell your friends all this? No one would believe it!'

* * *

On my final night – the cellar and streets having been cleared – we headed out to a local restaurant in the town. Alfred ordered all kinds of elaborate items. I stared suspiciously at a rather exotic-looking seafood dish... not my favourite cuisine.

'Martin,' he stated frankly, 'you look as if that plate is goin' to bite ya!'

Francesca asked me to sing, so I put my arm around Ginny and serenaded her again with the 'Ginny Ginny Campbell' number. It brought the restaurant to a standstill and Ginny couldn't have been happier.

When we got back to the apartment, Lenny once more remained on the balcony whilst Alfred and Rhoda escorted Ginny to her room. As we sat in silence, hearing only the waves breaking on the shore, I took stock of everything which had happened, and the remarkable circumstances over the last eighteen months which had led to this moment.

I was at peace.

'Lenny,' I said, turning to my friend. 'Thank you for everything you did during the war.'

He smiled, touched, and then finished his glass.

CHAPTER TWENTY-FOUR

'A complicated gentleman
allow me to present'

Utopia Limited

After the final performance of *The Grand Duke* I was
pleased to find that G&S star Simon Butteriss had enjoyed the show.

'My dear!' he cried. 'You've managed to make a silk
handbag out of a sow's ear! Are you directing again? What
are you thinking of next?'

'Well,' I replied, 'this has worked well, so I'd like to
maybe consider another British musical which has been
neglected for a while.'

Simon looked at me, the cogs turning in his head. 'You
should do *Valmouth*. That's perfect for you! I could put you
in touch with Sandy Wilson – and if you asked Fenella to
do it, I'm sure she'd say yes.'

It was an offer I couldn't refuse; I'd adored *Valmouth*
for years – it was the epitome of a cult show. Premiered
in 1958, *Valmouth* was one of the most unusual, delicate
and eccentric musicals ever written. Book, music and
lyrics were by Sandy Wilson, fresh from his international
success of *The Boy Friend*. *Valmouth* made a star out of

Fenella: she'd been on the brink of giving up the industry altogether, but at the age of twenty-nine secured the role of a lifetime – elderly nymphomaniac Lady Parvula de Panzoust. It brought her lasting fame, but also typecast her for life as a man-hungry seductive vamp. It was an image she was never able to shake.

Valmouth had been revived just once – at Chichester in 1982, with Fenella recreating her original role and Simon as one of the juvenile leads. J.O.E. was musical director. The piece had lain untouched ever since, meaning there was now an entire generation which hadn't seen it, and yet another generation (in Simon's words) of 'old queens simpering about the 1982 production' who'd surely leap at the chance to see *Valmouth* again.

In Sandy Wilson's musical, Valmouth is a mythical Edwardian spa town, the waters of which revitalise the elderly with their aphrodisiac qualities. The plot, such as it is, revolves around the exuberant black masseuse Mrs Yajnavalkya. She observes the outrageous shenanigans of ageing religious fanatic Mrs Hurstpierpoint, who assumes spiked garters and sprigs of holly in her underwear to mortify the flesh.

Lady Parvula, meanwhile, is determined to bed the local virile young shepherd boy. Sister Ecclesia – a nun doomed to a vow of silence, having been overly chatty – is permitted to speak just once a year on her Talking Day. A Roman Catholic cardinal dances a tango before his excommunication for the sin of christening a dog named Clapsy, and eventually a fire from Heaven brings an unearthly retribution, and the town is destroyed in an apocalyptic tempest.

This show appealed to me on every level – and Fenella was now more age-appropriate than ever to portray the aged siren Lady Parvula. It would make theatrical history for the same actress to return to her original role after fifty-five years! However, Fenella was now eighty-five, so I was aware it may prove a major risk. But I decided to be optimistic and ask whether she might be interested in playing Lady Parvula just once more – if Mr Wilson granted me the rights.

'Well, I should say I *would!*' she exclaimed down the phone. It strengthened my case in the carefully worded letter I wrote to Sandy Wilson.

I was doing a short G&S gig in Norwich when I received a voicemail: 'Hello, Martin, it's Sandy Wilson. I received your very charming letter. Please do give me a call.'

I'd been advised that Sandy had recently been quite ill, so when I spoke to the 88-year-old composer I was particularly reverential.

'I warn you,' he told me in a thin but determined voice, 'my permission is not easily granted.'

'Mr Wilson,' I replied, 'if I was lucky enough to be granted permission to direct your incredible piece then I assure you that I'd want to do everything properly – or not at all.' I was invited to his Gloucester Road apartment the following week.

I immediately let Simon know. He was pleased but advised treating Mr Wilson carefully. I was warned that, on occasion, 'Sandy can be very tricky.'

I rang Fenella.

'Well, dahling, that's wonderful! But do be careful – because, you know, Sandy can be very tricky.'

I texted John Owen Edwards. He replied: 'We should talk. Sandy can be very tricky.'

I rang Nanny Jean, who then called LA and spoke to Sandy's close friend Annie Wakefield. Jean then rang me back.

'I've got a message for you from Annie, darling.'

'What's that?'

'She said to tell you that Sandy can be very tricky.'

I delicately enquired into the nature of Mr Wilson's trickiness and was advised that due to his unwavering passion for all his musicals – and his desire to see them staged exactly to his specifications – he'd often been known to behave fiercely.

The explanation was traced back to the original Broadway production of *The Boy Friend* in 1954 when the American producers, Cy Feuer and Ernie Martin, ignored Sandy's diktat that the piece should be played with subtlety and elegant charm. Feuer and Martin were adamant that subtlety wasn't for Broadway.

Having brought the London director Vida Hope over to New York, Cy Feuer fired her and took over direction of the show himself. Suddenly, *The Boy Friend* became brash, exaggerated and obvious; the delicate orchestrations altered to a big, brassy Broadway sound. When Sandy challenged Feuer and Martin, they literally threw him out – bodily – onto the sidewalk and forbade him to enter the theatre; a Pinkerton detective was posted at the stage door, barring his entry. Sandy ultimately detested the Broadway *Boy Friend* – but American audiences responded in a big way, and it made a star out of Julie Andrews.

Therefore, whenever a director staged his musicals appropriately, Sandy Wilson's praise was unstinting, and he couldn't have been more generous. But when Sandy felt that his work had been misrepresented, his reaction was vitriolic. Ken Russell's bastardisation of the *Boy Friend* movie, with which Sandy had no connection, was a sticky subject!

I was informed that in more recent years Mr Wilson had thrown an extremely famous director out of his apartment for merely suggesting that in his proposed revival of *The Boy Friend* the Perfect Young Ladies might enter in a motor car. During *Valmouth* at Chichester, Sandy had apparently taken his extremely protective nature to yet another level.

'And,' J.O.E. told me, 'the show had the cast to start World War Three!'

'Fenella and Bertice Reading hated each other,' Simon remembered. 'After her number with Fenella, Bertice stormed off saying, "If she does dat one mo' time I's gonna take out my twat and play wid it!"'

Simon discharged his scene as best he could, then rushed to Fenella's dressing room to find out what she'd done.

'Dahling,' Fenella explained, very matter-of-fact, 'she was screaming in my ear in that rabbinical voice of hers – so I took a brown bread sandwich out of my handbag and put half in each ear. It's the only way.'

Director John Dexter notoriously treated his actors with acerbic disdain.

'Fenella Fielding, you smelly tart!' he yelled during a rehearsal. 'I see you chose not to sit down when I told you!'

'But, dahling,' she replied. 'I was nowhere near the chair.'

Chichester's management ensured that matters took a further turn for the bizarre.

'We rehearsed in a lunatic asylum,' J.O.E. continued. 'And during lunch Fenella got lost. The staff found her wandering around and thought she was an escaped inmate. They took her away and locked her up!'

But the extraordinary anecdotes of *Valmouth* stretched back to 1958. Sandy had been approached to write a vehicle specifically for Bertice Reading (who, like Fenella, later recreated her role at Chichester). He found the perfect role for her in Mrs Yajnavalkya from Ronald Firbank's 1919 novel.

'Have you read it?' J.O.E. asked me. 'It's impenetrable!' I found he was correct – as in all Firbank, there's no conventional plot, but acres of wildly camp improbable dialogue. Sandy borrowed reams of it, including Lady Parvula's declaration of lust for the shepherd boy: 'I want to spank the white walls of his cottage!'

Every inch of the rehearsal process had been overseen by Sandy – his complete creative control ensured by sinking his personal fortune from *The Boy Friend* into the budget. Choreographer Harry Naughton was Sandy's current amour, but underwhelmed by Naughton's work, Sandy grabbed him by the scruff of the neck and, in front of the entire company, threatened, 'If you ruin my show, I'm going to kill you!'

Sandy, for reasons best known to himself, became besotted by the sound of a Hammond organ, and decided to orchestrate his score entirely around this quirky instrument. He arrived at rehearsals with the organ, beyond excited and oblivious to the appalling sound. No one dared speak until Fenella piped up, half-heartedly: 'Oh. How lovely.'

Bertice Reading arrived on the back of a motorbike, clad in leather from head to toe. She took off her helmet to reveal a head of shockingly distorted silver hair – the effects of an aborted dye job. Her entrance was in revolt against several weeks in hiding from creditors, which caused her to miss the start of rehearsals. Out of artistic necessity, Reading was finally bailed out by *Valmouth*'s producer – a very young Michael Codron.

'She fell in love with Michael, you know,' Fenella confided. 'Or at least *said* that she had. She told me about it on the train to Liverpool, where we tried out. But Michael is gay, so I told Bertice, "I think you'd be much better employed learning your lines."'

The show previewed in Liverpool to general audience bewilderment. Backstage Fenella wailed, 'It's playing like Eugene O'Neill, and we haven't even reached Act Two!'

However, back in London at the Lyric Hammersmith *Valmouth* was a critical and commercial smash – particularly amongst the gay and religious communities. Legions of monks and nuns returned time and again to see Fenella emerge from a Catholic chapel covered in chicken feathers after her attempted molestation of the shepherd boy, carrying fowl. Critic Harold Hobson in *The Sunday Times* declared: '*Valmouth* is caviar; but enticing, but the best.'

The strictly censored London stage had never seen interracial lust, thinly veiled homosexuality and such daringly provocative views of churchmen – all presented with abandoned amorality! Patsy Rowlands, who played a simple village girl, even wanked off a fish; she lay on her back with the huge fish between her feet whilst singing a weary love song about the man she adored from afar…

Valmouth transferred to the West End's Saville Theatre (now the Odeon Covent Garden), but without Bertice Reading. Her replacement was Cleo Laine – whose husband John Dankworth refused, perhaps not unreasonably, to let his wife sing with a Hammond organ, resulting in an enormous feud with Sandy and the re-orchestration of the Mrs Yaj numbers.

The show was an unexpected West End success, which surprised the Saville management, who'd been hoping to squeeze in *Valmouth* as a limited run prior to the pre-booked London premiere of *Candide*. Sandy's musical closed after 102 performances, much to the sorrow of its cult audience.

As for Sandy himself, he achieved immortality of a certain kind thanks to BBC radio programme *Round the Horne*. The characters of Julian and Sandy, played by Hugh Paddick and Kenneth Williams, were inspired by the mild-mannered Julian Slade and waspish Sandy Wilson. Much to Sandy's chagrin, the public continually mixed up the composers of *Salad Days* and *The Boy Friend*, often crediting each man's show to the other.

The Boy Friend gave Sandy lifelong financial security (Prince Charles apparently once met Sandy in a line-up and cheekily commented, 'Your *Boy Friend* must be keeping you very comfortably!' which did not amuse Sandy in the slightest), but it was *Valmouth* which remained his favourite piece – so much so that his country house in Somerset shared the same name. In fact, such was Sandy's pride and confidence in *Valmouth* that he publicly declared the songs were the finest he'd ever composed: 'They are better than the whole score of *My Fair Lady*.'

Knowing all this, only a fool or an extremely brave individual would possibly have considered reviving *Valmouth*. I wasn't sure which of the two I was – but nevertheless, I was off to Gloucester Road...

I was welcomed by Sandy's long-time partner Chak, who showed me into the front room. It was crammed from wall to ceiling with Sandy's memorabilia, including a large cut-out of Polly Browne (the lead character from *The Boy Friend*) standing in the fireplace. Sandy himself, although physically frail, looked regal but dwarfed in a large throne-like chair, which I had to walk across the room in order to reach.

'Good afternoon, Mr Wilson,' I said, extending my hand.

'I've spoken to Simon and Fenella about you,' he opened abruptly. 'Fenella said you directed her. What was that for?'

I explained about the sitcom. He asked how I knew Simon, and I told Mr Wilson that both he and Fenella had recommended we speak about *Valmouth* having seen my *Grand Duke* at the Finborough.

'I hope you're not thinking of doing *Valmouth* at the Finborough!' he declared. 'It's a West End show. Where in the West End are you thinking of staging it?'

This took me aback. There was no way I'd get *Valmouth* straight into the West End! The chances of that, as a one-time director with a very obscure piece, and during a recession, were nil. But Mr Wilson was looking expectant, so I plucked the name of a West End theatre out of thin air.

'Well, I've always rather liked the Comedy Theatre.'

Sandy's face lit up. 'I love the Comedy Theatre! I directed the first revival of *The Boy Friend* there.' Fate was on my side. He began to relax, and I asked him questions about *Valmouth*, subtly putting across that I knew the show inside out. He smiled and reached for a pile of pristine 1958 glossy production shots, all of which featured Tony Walton's extraordinarily beautiful sets and costumes.

'Who would you cast as the ladies?' he asked me. 'They shouldn't be singers. They must be actresses who can put over a song.' I mentioned a couple of names which he discreetly mulled over.

I told him that I had an ideal young man to play the shepherd boy – Stiofan O'Doherty. His stunning looks, acting ability and dulcet tones were perfect for the role. Sandy seemed interested but non-committal. However, he was more than happy to approve Fenella recreating Lady Parvula.

'She wasn't first choice originally, though,' he claimed. 'I asked Vivien Leigh, but she turned me down. Then I wanted Judy Campbell, who said' – and here he affected a clipped British accent – '"Oh, darling, I'd simply *love* to, but I've *promised* to take the gells to the Hebrides!"' I laughed appropriately.

'Vida,' he continued – referring to director Vida Hope – 'never wanted Fenella. But I'd known Fenella since she was nineteen. We met doing a revue in Edinburgh at the Festival, and ten years later when I thought about her for Parvula I knew she could do it. It was what she was like at parties when she'd had a glass of wine.'

We chatted further and then he announced, 'I need to pee. Because I'm old. Come with me.' I had a tour of his memorabilia en route to the bathroom. I was shown framed *Valmouth* costume designs and photographs from all the different early *Boy Friend* productions throughout the musical's long and difficult journey to the West End.

'This,' he said, picking up a frame, 'was when we did it in Swiss Cottage. All the original cast were able to do it except two…'

'Yes!' I said, smiling. 'Annie couldn't get out of her panto contract, could she?'

Mr Wilson looked impressed. After returning from the bathroom, he resumed his regal pose in the chair.

'Right. Let's get down to business. I would very much like you to go ahead with this. And I'd very much like to work with you *on* it. My contract states that I have absolute approval of *everything* – and I warn you now, that isn't easy to get.'

And there was another catch – he wanted *Valmouth* in the West End. He categorically did *not* want a small-scale production in any way, shape or form. He then gave me the details of his agent and instructed me to arrange a meeting. Before leaving, I asked him to sign a 1958 *Valmouth* programme which I'd brought along from my collection. I then extended my hand.

'Mr Wilson, thank you so much. I'll report back as soon as I can.'

Before releasing my hand, he looked up at me – and for the first time appeared somewhat more vulnerable. 'I want to see *Valmouth* again before I die,' he told me sincerely. 'Don't take too long.'

* * *

It was a Herculean task. And frustratingly I had smaller theatres and production companies snapping my arm off. I had meetings with producers interested in a limited run at a mid-scale theatre, which might well have worked with ambitious casting and a sensible budget.

Despite these offers Sandy remained adamant – an open-ended West End run for *Valmouth* or nothing. But in the twenty-first century, 'caviar' didn't sell to tourists interested in *Mamma Mia!* and *Jersey Boys*. Added to that, I was a further risk. As a director I had no West End track record, and no matter how successful *Grand Duke* had been, that wouldn't convince anyone to back this show.

One producer I knew – another renaissance man – offered a compromise. He was willing to put on a one-night West End gala of *Valmouth*, cast to the hilt, in honour of Sandy's ninetieth birthday in 2014. It seemed the perfect solution: a West End house, and a very short-term but high-prestige engagement attracting a glittering cast and press interest.

Unfortunately, Sandy wasn't interested in that either. He didn't want a gala. He wanted a full run. Production budgets in the 2010s were astronomical compared with 1958. In a last-ditch attempt, I wrote to Sir Michael Codron, producer of the original *Valmouth*, asking for advice. He'd always retained an affection for the show and rang personally to invite me to lunch.

Sir Michael, now eighty-two, had only just retired from full-time producing. He was something of a theatrical legend, having commenced his career in the 1950s,

bringing to the stage original productions by Harold
Pinter, Alan Ayckbourn, Joe Orton, Alan Bennett and
Tom Stoppard. Over the course of a thrillingly jolly lunch
this charming and elegant gentleman, with a twinkle
in his eye, regaled me with some wonderful anecdotes
– which I lapped up – confirming that Bertice Reading
had indeed made vain advances.

But when it came to *Valmouth* in the twenty-first century, even the great Sir Michael was stumped.

'*I* wouldn't know how to produce *Valmouth* in the West
End in this day and age!' he declared. 'But I think the timing's right. I always thought we were ahead of our time in
'58. When they did it in Chichester the timing somehow
wasn't quite right then either – and Bertice was sick on
press night, so it never came into town as all the producers
saw the understudy, who hadn't rehearsed. The production
wasn't at its best that evening. But I think the timing may
be right for *Valmouth* now.'

'What can I do about it though?'

'Well, what you ideally need is some eccentric million-
aire who loves *Valmouth* to fund it for you. And that's
Sandy. He did back in '58, of course…' But then he sighed,
'Although I doubt he will now.'

Indeed, Sandy would not and did not. He reached his
ninetieth birthday but passed away a few months later –
his wish to see *Valmouth* again sadly unfulfilled. Fenella
kindly informed me of Sandy's demise as soon as she
heard.

Sandy requested no funeral or memorial service and
donated his body to medical science. His agent informed
me that Sandy's estate was bound to serve the late

composer's wishes, especially where his beloved *Valmouth* was concerned. So, at the time of writing, there has been no revival of *Valmouth*.

I often wonder what might have been had a production – in some form – taken place. What would Sandy have been like in the rehearsal room? Actually, I can probably imagine that… and so could J.O.E. His former Sandy experience was such that when I asked whether he might like to revisit the piece he told me, 'My dear, if I never go anywhere near *Valmouth* again, it will be too soon!'

And could Fenella have pulled off Lady Parvula? If she had it would have been endlessly sensational. But I know in my heart that there would have been enormous problems – Lady Parvula is a very lengthy role – and it would have been a major undertaking involving personal risk for both Fenella and the production. So perhaps, all things considered, things turned out for the best.

But no experience is ever wasted – I got to meet Sandy Wilson, which was a tremendous honour. Not to mention Sir Michael Codron and numerous others, all of whom generously shared memories of a musical which, with the passing of time, fades from living memory but remains unique.

In this industry, sometimes great things happen, and much-cherished projects come to fruition – and other times they simply don't. But no one can take away from me that ideal production of *Valmouth* which I frequently play in my head. Fenella spanking the white walls of Stiofan's cottage and emerging from the chapel covered in his chicken feathers would have been completely sublime – and the thought will always make me smile.

CHAPTER TWENTY-FIVE

'There can be no harm in revelling in the past'

The Gondoliers

'And just one last thing,' said the producer. 'This show does feature a number of – shall we say – rather senior ladies. And there's not much room backstage, so we're looking for young people who can be very sympathetic to older actresses…'

'Don't worry,' I said. 'I'm having lunch today with a 98-year-old who worked with Lubitsch and DeMille.'

I was offered the job. The show was *Gay's the Word*, Ivor Novello's musical comedy about an actress who opens a drama school. The cast featured a procession of illustrious names from the past including Elizabeth Seal – who, under the direction of Peter Brook, had won the 1961 Tony Award for *Irma la Douce*. Already a celebrated dancer, Seal had been guided by Brook to international success in the musical's demanding all-round title role. Meanwhile, veteran actress Eileen Page had spent years with the RSC, but after appearing in plays with Olivier, Rex Harrison, Anthony Hopkins and Paul Scofield reinvented herself as a West End musical star.

A group of young performers played the students of the ramshackle drama school. And from this glorious eccentric production, opening in February 2013, I developed lasting treasured friendships with veterans and contemporaries which taught me a great deal.

By this time, thanks to my friends – young and old – my demons of the past had been banished. I was enjoying a period of tranquillity, content within myself – and inseparable from a wonderful best friend – Stiofan. The catwalk model had thrown himself into my eccentric lifestyle. When he wasn't being the face of leading fashion brands, Stiofan found himself in Buxton – his god-like grace worshipped by anorak admirers in the Festival Bar.

And I hadn't been lacking for romantic companionship. To paraphrase my old friend Mrs Patrick Campbell, I found myself satisfyingly between the hurly-burly of the chaise lounge and the deep, deep peace of the double bed.

Thursford 2012 had been my favourite-ever season – I'd left the drama to other people and just enjoyed being part of a wonderful show. In my spare time I'd organised a naked calendar photoshoot in Fantasy Land. Ginny and Lenny had been much tickled by the end product, and Ginny had traced her finger around the outline of my friend Ted's bum, commenting, 'Oh, that's *marvellous!*'

I saw Nanny Jean whenever I could. Would that she'd lived in London – *Gay's the Word* was right up her street!

We rehearsed at the Club for Acts and Actors in Covent Garden, where old-time variety bills adorned every wall. During rehearsal breaks, Eileen and actor Frank Barrie recited Shakespeare, just for the fun of it. Elizabeth Seal – who had vitality-plus and could still do the splits, months from turning eighty – reminisced about impresario Binkie Beaumont and bumping into 'Larry and Vivien' on holiday in Spain. As well as the Oliviers, Charlie Chaplin came backstage to see her during *The Pajama Game* – the show which made Elizabeth a star at the age of twenty-two.

We played at the miniature Jermyn Street Theatre for a blissfully happy and dotty month. The dressing rooms were located down a precarious flight of stairs from stage level – so one of our many grande dames ended up sitting on the lid of the disabled loo by the wings for the entire duration of Act One!

During the interval, Elizabeth – who blossomed in youthful company – kindly shared her memories with me and two other youngsters, James Bentham and Daniel Cane.

'During *Irma*,' she told us, 'Groucho Marx came to see me in my dressing room. As he left, he said, "Well, my dear, I mustn't keep you" – and then he turned back with those eyebrows of his and added, "Much as I'd like to!"'

Everyone had visited Elizabeth backstage – from Princess Margaret and Anthony Eden to Montgomery Clift and Frank Sinatra. Cole Porter had been her ardent admirer. And I loved that James and Daniel were as eager as I to hear about Elizabeth's past...

'I was in the chorus of *The Glorious Days* starring Anna Neagle,' Elizabeth confided. 'She was especially kind to me, and when I asked her why, she said, "Because, Elizabeth, no one ever looked after *me* when I was in the chorus."'

This revival of *Gay's the Word* brought Elizabeth full circle. She'd made her professional debut in the same musical in 1950, age seventeen, and met Ivor Novello at rehearsals. The show's producer was Jack Hulbert, who took a chance on the inexperienced teenager, casting her as a dancer in the show, which starred his wife, Cicely Courtneidge.

A scene in the original production entailed 'Gay Daventry' (Courtneidge) coaching a young girl on the balcony scene from *Romeo and Juliet*. One night, Elizabeth had to unexpectedly understudy the girl, and when instructed by Courtneidge to throw herself around the balcony, Elizabeth's nervous enthusiasm drew enormous laughs.

'During the interval I was summoned to Miss Courtneidge's dressing room. "Elizabeth," she said slowly. "*Who* is the star of this show?" And I replied, "*You* are, Miss Courtneidge." She said, "Precisely. And *don't – ever – forget it!* The laughs in that scene are *mine!*"' By 1958, with Elizabeth the West End star of *Irma la Douce*, Miss Courtneidge had long forgiven her and personally delivered a basket of African violets to the stage door.

Legendary American producer David Merrick intended to premiere *Irma* on Broadway in 1959. Elizabeth had a two-year contract for the London production – and many major stars were eager to play her role in New York…

'But after Merrick saw the show, he came backstage and told me, "I'm going to wait for next season – you are my Irma."' She won the Tony Award over Julie Andrews, Carol Channing and Nancy Walker.

Soon after our Jermyn Street run, Elizabeth moved to a new house. The first time I visited, I asked where she kept her Tony. It was wrapped inside multiple plastic shopping bags, stuffed in a drawer upstairs. There was no pretension with Elizabeth Seal!

Wild Card

* * *

During the run I had an audition for a male soprano role in an opera and sang Novello's 'Glamorous Night', originally written for his muse, opera star Mary Ellis. Eileen Page, now eighty-seven, overheard me rehearsing and took me to one side: 'I saw Novello and Mary Ellis on stage at Drury Lane – in *The Dancing Years*. It was the last matinee before they closed Drury Lane for the duration of the war. I was thirteen!'

Eileen never left Jermyn Street – or any other theatre – unless she was wearing a hat. This tradition and respect for the theatre had been instilled in her at RADA, where she'd trained in 1942 'with Johnny Clarke before he became Bryan Forbes'.

During *Gay's the Word*, Eileen was terribly ill with a chest infection. However, this trouper of an actress, a professional for over seventy years, arrived at work promptly every day without complaint of her ailments. Concerned, I'd escorted her to Piccadilly Circus Tube, but she just said, 'One goes on, doesn't one?' She didn't miss a show.

Two years later I directed Eileen and Daniel Cane in a rehearsed reading of J.M. Barrie's play *Rosalind*. Eileen's role was originated in 1914 by Dame Irene Vanbrugh, who'd had parts written for her by Shaw, Maugham and Coward. During a Q&A afterwards, I asked Eileen to tell the audience about her direct link with her predecessor: 'At RADA, Dame Irene taught me how to place flowers in a vase on stage. I was terrified, but she picked me out and instructed me in front of my whole class. Years later, I played the mother in *Hay Fever* and the director told me,

"Eileen, I've *never* seen anyone place flowers in a vase on stage the way you do!"'

These were happy days. Elizabeth and Eileen were living history, and passed on to James, Daniel and me the batons of knowledge and professionalism which in turn had been passed to them by the greats. Lasting bonds were formed, and afterwards everyone supported each other's shows...

* * *

A year later, the producer of *Gay's the Word*, Richard Stirling, wrote a one-woman play for actress Liz Robertson. In answer to Lloyd Webber's musical *Stephen Ward*, Richard penned *Valerie Hobson* (aka Mrs John Profumo).

James Bentham and I attended with Elizabeth – Stephen Ward had been a friend of her late husband, Michael. In fact, Ward's sketch of Michael now hung on Elizabeth's living-room wall! We bumped into another veteran actress, Anne Rogers, the original West End Polly from *The Boy Friend*. I'd first met Anne when she came to see *Gay's the Word*. She'd tap-danced across the stage after the show – just because she could.

At a reception afterwards, Richard Stirling approached us and said: 'There's someone here whom I'd very much like you to meet – and that is Christine Keeler!' We looked across the room. There stood a horribly dirty and unattractive-looking old crone.

Anne Rogers – now in her eighties – grabbed my arm and hissed in my ear: 'My *God*, darling! If *that's* what having too much sex does to you then *I'm* giving it up immediately!'

There was a sense of awe and reverence in the room, and Keeler seemed to be enjoying herself. She talked about her birthday party at Cliveden and gossiped about Mandy Rice-Davies as she posed for photographs. I turned to speak to Elizabeth – and found that she'd vanished. James pointed towards the photographers. In an instant, both Elizabeth and Anne had materialised either side of Keeler and Liz Robertson, whilst delighted cameramen snapped happily away.

As she left, I dived in to pass Keeler her coat, which she'd placed on a chair.

'Thank you,' she said with a satisfied smile.

'Well, come on, tell us!' said Anne. 'What did you think of the show?'

'I liked it.' Keeler slowly nodded. 'Of course, in the trial Stephen Ward was made a complete scapegoat, you know…'

Anne and I listened attentively whilst Keeler elaborated. A few minutes later she departed and slipped back into the obscurity of the street outside.

I emailed Richard to congratulate him on a splendid play – and he replied with a revelatory surprise. He'd sent the photographs of Keeler and Robertson to various papers – and it appeared that the Christine Keeler who'd attended his reception was definitely *not* the real Christine Keeler! The papers had compared the image of Richard's Keeler to recent images of the reclusive Keeler taken by their own photographers.

Richard was astounded. The invitation was definitely sent to Keeler's correct address – but she'd clearly decided to pass her invite card on to a friend, who'd then turned up and impersonated her. The impostor fooled everyone.

* * *

Nanny Jean invited me to Birmingham to meet 'the children'. I knew who she meant, of course, but one of Jean's neighbours didn't. Anticipating meeting 'children', he was confused to be greeted by a room full of pensioners...

These 'children' were from the original cast of *The Sound of Music*. Barbara Brown created the role of Liesl, and two years into the run had married her Rolf, George Rutland. Fiona Dickson was Barbara's understudy and had also met her husband, Roy Castle, around the same time.

George drove us to the pub for lunch. Sandwiched on the back seat between the two Liesls they sang to me in unison, '*To write on...*', when, at Jean's request, I sang Rolf's verse of 'You Are Sixteen'. Later we played the cast recording LP. In the show, Maria and Liesl sing a reprise of 'You Are Sixteen' in the second act. As they listened, Jean's eyes filled with tears as she held Barbara's hand and whispered, 'I'm back there with you on stage!'

The quartet howled with laughter telling me about Silvia Beamish (Sister Berthe) who got sacked for leaving the theatre in her nun's habit and ordering a pint in the pub. Nanny Jean remembered her friend Elaine Stritch's 'great spaghetti', and also Stritch's astounded reaction when Jean brought Broadway producer Cy Feuer back to her mews cottage in Knightsbridge: 'I didn't know you were bringing such a big wheel!'

After Jean's hamburger with Richard Rodgers she went to see *Camelot*, and whilst catching up with Julie Andrews, there was a knock on the dressing-room door. Richard Burton walked in.

'Richard, this is Jean,' Andrews informed him. 'She's going to play Maria in *The Sound of Music.*' Burton looked Nanny Jean up and down, and answered: 'Jean's pretty enough to play *anything!*'

* * *

A short while later, I was asked to write Russell Grant's narration for an Ivor Novello tribute show. Prior to his fame as an author and broadcaster, he'd been a successful actor, and toured with Nanny Jean in Novello's *King's Rhapsody*. Russ was one of the most genuine people I'd ever met, and I was thrilled when he agreed to appear in my next directorial venture.

But it turned out to be a project of colliding worlds that would live in infamy…

CHAPTER TWENTY-SIX

'A nice dilemma we have here'

Trial by Jury

July to September 2013 was a period of complete and utter madness, tearing all around the country in five different shows. My logistical problems were enhanced by return trips for production meetings: Gyles Brandreth had asked me to direct the London premiere of his play *Now We Are Sixty*.

Despite the influx of work, my bank balance wasn't rosy, and I just couldn't afford to pay obscene London rent whilst I was away. Yet, I did need somewhere to hang my hat. A friend in Willesden Green offered a solution.

'Why don't you stay in the Fridge Room?'

'What's that?'

'Well, it's the spare room in the house where I live: £50 a week.'

'Why is it called the Fridge Room?'

'Because the room's got a fridge in it.'

'You mean it's the utility?'

'Well, yeah.'

The Fridge Room came complete with its own mouse, scampering around in the pitch black. One evening I turned on the light and found it sitting on my clothes placed over the chair (I had nowhere to hang my own things). Then it scurried away… into the fridge.

'I think you should know,' I alerted the house owner, 'that there's a mouse in your fridge.'

'Oh yeah,' she said casually. 'I know about that.'

'Well… don't you want to try and catch it?'

'Oh, but I'd feel really bad! I can't kill it! I'm just going to let it do its thing.'

From then on, I ate out. But at least my next project was sure to be exciting and career advantageous…

Now We Are Sixty had premiered at the Cambridge Arts Theatre in 1986, commemorating sixty years of A.A. Milne's stories about Winnie-the-Pooh. Gyles Brandreth's witty script celebrated Milne's life and literary works, complete with 1920s songs by H. Fraser-Simson and others specifically penned for *Now We Are Sixty* by Julian Slade.

In Cambridge, the 'bums on seats' name was fifteen-year-old boy soprano Aled Jones. When he appeared in the second act as Christopher Robin singing 'Vespers' (*'Hush, hush, whisper who dares…'*) the elderly audience – who'd read the Pooh stories as children – wept buckets. The West End beckoned – then Aled's voice broke. The money vanished, and it all fell through.

Gyles proposed I direct the show's belated London premiere. Having been impressed by *The Grand Duke* he awarded me carte blanche: 'I leave the script entirely in your hands – reinvent it as you see fit!'

And a certain amount of reinvention was necessary. In 2013 we couldn't rely on childhood nostalgia: no one I encountered had ever read Winnie-the-Pooh. They only knew the Disney cartoon; the name A.A. Milne drew blanks. Even Gyles had to admit that the show's original target audience had diminished: 'A.A. Milne is dead, Christopher Robin Milne is dead, Julian Slade is dead, and I'm not feeling too good myself!'

In the original show, the darker side of Milne's relationship with his son had been completely overlooked – and with good reason. Christopher Robin Milne had then been very much alive, and a friend of Gyles Brandreth (who proudly claimed to have shaken the hand that shook the paw of the real Winnie-the-Pooh). With Gyles' blessing I added new material heading into deeper territory, and found Christopher Robin in the form of Steffan Wayne, the ten-year-old son of my long-time friend and singing teacher Elen.

Milne was portrayed by Olivier nominee Andrew C. Wadsworth, with Charlotte Page, of *Grand Duke* fame, the natural choice to play his wife. Russell Grant played a variety of comical character roles, and I offered the juvenile lead to James Bentham.

Another Olivier nominee – Susie Caulcutt – designed the show, creating miracles on a less-than-shoestring budget. I learned a great deal from Susie, and the integrity of the show was increased tenfold by her involvement.

But *Now We Are Sixty* was no easy ride. There were major problems from the outset – both on artistic and managerial levels...

Many lines of dialogue kept referencing the word 'Pooh' – which caused more than a few undesirable sniggers in rehearsal. Somehow, Andrew C. Wadsworth kept a straight face whilst singing the immortal phrase '*Wherever I am there's always Pooh*'. Charlotte Page protested, 'The audience can't see the "h" on the end of the word!' and, not unreasonably, asked to cut her lines about '*Poohing in the sun…*'

Because this was a limited run scheduled around the cast's other commitments, *Now We Are Sixty* could only play on Sundays and Mondays – just six performances in all. Few London theatres catered to this schedule, and our first-choice venue was unavailable. Therefore, we tried somewhere else. Artistically, the space was perfect in terms of playing area, and the ideally sized house offered profitable capacity.

I kept reminding myself about these plus points when contract negotiations with the venue became fraught, stressful and horrific. In addition, the theatre management seemed at loggerheads with the management of the bar – unhelpfully the two enterprises were separate businesses and they didn't always pull together. In time this would lead to catastrophic disaster for *Now We Are Sixty*.

As a Sunday/Monday production, we had to adapt and play 'on top' of the set of the show being performed during weekdays – which in this instance was a Wild West musical. Designer Susie was convinced there'd be an immovable cactus standing centre stage. It didn't quite come to that, but Susie remarkably transformed a desert outpost into something quintessentially English.

Back in the rehearsal room, ongoing problems were caused by a member of the technical team – the only person sourced by third parties. It was a valuable lesson. Ever since *Now We Are Sixty* no one has ever come onboard with my shows whom I have not personally approved.

Tech and dress rehearsals were a nightmare. The theatre had forbidden our lighting designer to touch the lighting desk (apparently for reasons of insurance and safety). Therefore, the theatre provided us with their own employee to plot all the lighting cues into the desk *during* our tech... but it turned out he'd never laid eyes on this model of lighting desk. He didn't know anything about *Now We Are Sixty*; nor did English appear to be his first language.

But somehow the magic of theatre prevailed, and it all came together. Gyles was thrilled, the cast was fantastic and a full house gave its thorough approval. *Grand Duke* had been a walk in the park compared to *Now We Are Sixty* – but in many ways I was equally as proud. It had been, all round, a very tough nut to crack.

After the opening shows I relished the next five days off. Now I could relax – we'd opened and were a success! *The Lady* magazine, no less, informed its readership that *Now We Are Sixty* 'has so much going for it I was rather surprised the run is so short... it is something of a lost gem... a light-hearted musical that still sends the audience home thinking'. Russ was interviewed on ITV's *Alan Titchmarsh Show* about the production – and sales were strong. What could possibly go wrong now?

Over the days off, I enjoyed volunteering for the Battle of Britain Memorial Trust. The Few gathered at the RAF Club prior to a short Saturday service at the Battle of Britain Monument on Embankment. Now in their mid-nineties, the veterans were still in first-class spirits with enviable mental agility.

On the Saturday evening, Patrick and Janet Tootal took us volunteers to Westminster Abbey to stand in for the veterans at a rehearsal for the next morning's thanksgiving service. We had the Abbey entirely to ourselves – and processing up the aisle to a drumbeat from the rafters was beyond thrilling!

But then Sunday happened. And on every level, it was a cataclysmic Sunday…

Swarms of cyclists had invaded the city for the annual 'Boris Bike' ride – roads were closed, and traffic was in uproar. The normally swift journey from Piccadilly to Westminster proved a nightmare – and the clock was ticking. Not only did the veterans need to rehearse their walk up the aisle, but straight afterwards they had a private commemoration in the Abbey's tiny RAF Chapel. This included the all-important laying of a wreath, by The Few, on the grave of Lord Dowding.

Supervising the veterans on and off the coach, into their rehearsal, and then up to the wreath laying in double time was a delicate operation. The RAF Chapel lies at the furthest corner of the Abbey, accessible only by a flight of centuries-old stone steps. A wheelchair-bound veteran insisted on draping himself over the iron bannister and hauling himself up under his own steam. It looked like a terrifying action reversal of Joan Crawford battling the stairs in *Whatever Happened to Baby Jane?* Next – another long walk with the veterans to the Dean of Westminster's house for coffee, before at last finding our seats in the Abbey. And the day had only just begun!

During the congregational hymns I noticed that my voice was tired. *Still*, I thought, *It doesn't matter. I can just enjoy myself tonight and watch the show – I don't need to actually* do *anything!*

Then – a reception at Church House with the Prince of Wales before finally returning to the coach. But the diversions took us all over Central London and we *walked* the final distance back to the Club. Sweating and exhausted, I wolfed down lunch with Squadron Leader Tony Iveson (who after the Battle of Britain had flown the mission which destroyed German battleship *Tirpitz*) before dashing across town to the show.

At the theatre all was tranquil and serene. Everyone was present, everything was harmonious, and I settled myself for a nice easy evening.

And then…

'Martin – can I have a word?'

It was James Bentham. 'I feel awful!' he whimpered in a quivering voice. 'I just don't know what's happened! I've got these horrible pains in my stomach!'

This was bizarre. Only moments beforehand, James had been right as rain – and now he was keeling over, physically deteriorating. He then curled up in a ball in the middle of the floor, physically shaking and crying out in excruciating pain.

Meanwhile, my dad arrived to watch the show and couldn't help but notice that an ambulance had pulled up outside. Two paramedics rushed backstage.

'Is everything alright?' Dad asked one of the cast.

'Well… er… not really. I think Martin's going to have to go on tonight…'

It was now 7 p.m. Curtain up was 7.30 p.m. And my juvenile lead was being carted away on a stretcher writhing in agony. There were no understudies – the audience was arriving – and I was indeed going to have to play James' role myself.

'You're loving this, actually, Martin, darling, aren't you?' asked Russ, bringing much-needed light relief to the proceedings. Anyone would think he knew me well…

James was six foot two. I was five foot ten, so James' costume – a smart period suit – wasn't going to fit me. But miraculously I was still wearing my own smart suit from Westminster Abbey! I was even wearing a 1930s wristwatch – a present from Nanny Jean some years ago. Unwittingly, I'd arrived at the theatre dressed for the role!

The next two hours passed in a blur. Afterwards, I went into meltdown. Susie – who knew all about the Fridge Room – realised I was in no fit state to catch the Tube home and took mercy, generously putting me up. I slept for most of the next day!

The following afternoon James was discharged from hospital but was still too weak to perform. The test results eventually confirmed he had coeliac disease; this attack had followed a series of unexplained illnesses. Coeliac necessitated major changes in James' life, all of which he dealt with brilliantly; after *Now We Are Sixty* he switched career, becoming a senior management figure for a worldwide fashion brand. My second performance as the reporter passed – thank God – uneventfully.

James returned for the final day – a Sunday with both a matinee and evening show. As proud as I was of *Now We Are Sixty*, I wasn't going to miss all its associated drama. But at least, after everything that had happened, there couldn't possibly be anything more the fates could throw my way.

* * *

It was a beautiful, sunny Sunday – and unusually hot for the time of year. The matinee was a super show with a lovely audience, including my wonderful Stiofan. As the audience filed out, I smiled content in the knowledge that we had a full house that night. In a matter of hours, the eventful, stressful and yet somehow triumphant London premiere of *Now We Are Sixty* would be completely done and dusted.

I'd wanted to get an archive video, so a friend had put me in touch with someone whose camerawork I'd seen and thought excellent. After the matinee this chap arrived to set up his gear in the auditorium. His camera was poised, and everything was in order – so I didn't think anything of it when he went and sat in the bar.

In the meantime, Ginny and Lenny arrived with Haidee and Sarah. Stiofan and I helped Ginny out of the car and walked her into the theatre, where a front-row bench had been reserved next to the aisle.

Ginny and Lenny were safely settled as the auditorium began to fill, crammed to capacity. I noticed that it was getting rather hot – the result of many bodies crushed together, coupled with the unusually hot weather. There was no air conditioning, so I immediately ordered every door possible to be opened. Our cameraman then emerged from the bar. My heart sank. Let's just say this gentleman seemed to have had a jolly time since ordering his first pint two hours previously.

The show began – and all went well. The room was hot but bearable. During the interval I checked on Ginny and Lenny. They were eating ice creams and having a super time. Lenny had apparently become misty-eyed during the Act One finale, underscored by 'Pack up Your Troubles in Your Old Kit Bag'. Ginny looked forward to hearing Steffan sing 'Vespers': 'I want to see the little boy!'

The second act began – with good pacing, and good laughs. We reached my favourite comedy sequence, in which A.A. Milne demonstrates to a young author how a playwright approaches his craft. This involved Russ entering dressed as Hamlet – interpreting 'to be or not to be' in various different ways – segueing into a send-up of a Noël Coward drawing-room comedy.

The Hamlet section was going down a storm. But then... I heard a chilling sound... a clearly audible thud... as something... or someone... fell to the ground. Next thing I knew Haidee had sprung to her feet.

'Is there a doctor in the house?'

I tore out of the auditorium and told the bar staff to call an ambulance immediately.

'Is it Lenny?' I asked a friend. But with my heart pounding, I already knew the answer.

The houselights were up but the audience remained seated, talking animatedly. I rushed down the aisle to where Lenny lay flat on his back on the auditorium floor. This was a disaster. On every single level.

No, Lenny! No! a voice screamed in my head. *Not like this!* Please *not like this*! I was petrified. There was no dignity here. This was unworthy of a D-Day hero. *Please, Lenny*! I internally pleaded. *No!*

But Lenny's jovial blue eyes were staring up at me. He even waved. Momentarily stunned, I finally asked, looking down: 'Hello, Lenny! Are you alright?'

'Fine!' he chirped, smiling. James Bentham's sister – a doctor – was in the audience and had been attending to Lenny since the moment he'd collapsed.

'I think he's just overheated,' she explained. 'But we need to wait for the ambulance crew to check him over.' Ginny, meanwhile, sat fretfully on the bench, holding Haidee's hand.

'What are you doing down there?' she asked, agitated. 'Get up, Lenny!'

Later I discovered the full story. Lenny's stubbornness had got the better of him. Despite the hot weather, he'd insisted on wearing a sweater beneath his blazer – which try as Haidee and Sarah might, they'd been unable to convince him to remove. The high temperature made Lenny feel faint – and sitting on the end of a bench, he'd fallen sideways, straight off. Things could have been worse had it not been for a man on the row behind, who cushioned Lenny's head in his hands in time to break the fall.

The audience filed out into the bar – which by now was packed with boozy revellers. The ambulance crew (arriving at the theatre for the second time within a week) looked Lenny over, strapped him up in a chair and – whilst Lenny sang cheerful ditties – made their way out through the crowd. A pathway was cleared, and I followed behind with Ginny.

'Your place is with your cast,' Sarah advised me as we reached the door. 'We'll handle it from here!'

As the audience returned, I realised the entire godawful incident must have been captured on the archive film. I looked around but couldn't see the cameraman.

'He's gone,' said the lighting man. 'He wasn't entirely compos mentis – and seemed to think the show was over.'

Brilliant.

Andrew C. Wadsworth – the model of professionalism – made a short upbeat speech thanking the audience for their patience and understanding: 'I'm told that as the gentleman left the building, he was singing!' There was warm laughter and applause. The audience was on our side. Andrew, James and Russ resumed from a couple of pages prior to Lenny's collapse, and then sailed straight into the Coward sequence.

At the back of the house I was having extremely conflicted emotions. I was relieved the show was up and running – but worried sick about Lenny, not to mention Ginny who must have been terrified. I knew that everything had been under control as they left the theatre… but what was happening now? Was Lenny still okay? If he relapsed and something happened, I'd never forgive myself. Never. I'd be wracked with guilt.

And then, back in show mode, I realised something else. We'd lost about twenty-five minutes between Lenny keeling over and the act resuming… and at 9.30 p.m. sharp, in the bar directly behind the auditorium, a six-piece amplified jazz band was going to blast off the roof.

This was a regular weekend occurrence – but as *Now We Are Sixty* always came down by 9.15 p.m. it had never been an issue. However, the bar was under separate management to the theatre, and the theatre claimed to have no control over the bar's live music.

As the audience guffawed during the Coward pastiche, the colour drained from my face. By the time we reached

9.30 p.m. there'd still be ten minutes left of the show. And they were the most tender, poignant and beautiful moments of the entire play! *Now We Are Sixty* wrapped itself up in a finale leaving the audience reaching for handkerchiefs.

I found the theatre front-of-house manager. I found the bar manager. I found the band leader. I explained. I pleaded. I implored. Nothing doing. 9.30 p.m. was the time at which the band was contracted to start performing.

'Just ten minutes later – please!'

No chance.

As the show continued – and Steffan beautifully sang 'Vespers' – I had a sinking feeling in my stomach. I felt like I was trapped in a Hitchcock scene of suspense. Whilst everybody sat around oblivious, enjoying the show, I was the only person who knew exactly what would happen at zero hour.

Then – 9.30 p.m. Andrew was on the cusp of delivering the momentous key lines of the play – and suddenly the walls shook with the amplified blast of blaring jazz and swing. I wanted to crawl into a deep, dark hole, never to emerge again.

How could they *do* this? Ten minutes' wait would have made no difference to the band. But to us it made *all* the difference. Months of blood, sweat and literal tears had gone into this show... and in these final few minutes, just when matters couldn't have got any worse, suddenly they had. On stage, Andrew and Steffan handled it admirably. The audience was clearly in sympathy with our plight – at the end their applause was heartfelt.

Suddenly, everything was happening at once. I had to see the cast – I had to see the crew – I had to call Haidee

– I had to supervise the get-out. Haidee informed me they were on their way home. Lenny was fine. So was Ginny. It had been a simple case of fainting from the heat. I was completely choked up, fighting back tears of both relief and dread at the prospect of what *might* have happened.

Downstairs it was a travesty. The theatre management had surpassed themselves. Two get-outs and a get-in were happening simultaneously. The Wild West musical had ended its run the previous evening. But because *Now We Are Sixty* played on top of its set, they hadn't been able to strike anything until after our final performance. Therefore, they'd been told to arrive after our last show and do their get-out alongside ours.

In addition, the next show – opening at the theatre in the days ahead – had been told to arrive now with *their* set and costumes to move *into* the venue. And all three shows were now trying to move *everything* – props, set, costumes, the lot – either in or out of the auditorium through the jam-packed bar, fighting against the boozy revellers, whilst jazz played at ear-splitting decibels.

I observed the carnage with horror, but one of the *Now We Are Sixty* producers grabbed me and said to just get the hell out – and go to the post-show reception we'd laid on for the cast (which, thank God, had been pre-booked elsewhere in quiet, civilised wine bar).

I arrived to find Su Pollard – energetic star of TV sitcom *Hi-de-Hi!* – holding court, making an extremely exuberant speech praising the cast. James poured me a drink and asked if I was okay. I wasn't entirely sure how to answer. Later, I stumbled outside into a taxi, loaded with gifts from the cast, plus an enormous *Now We Are*

Sixty billboard. I eventually collapsed back into the Fridge Room… and was greeted by my roommate, the mouse.

First thing next morning, Ginny and Lenny's carer Tracy assured me they were both fine. Lenny was in good spirits, but clearly very embarrassed. However, all that mattered was that my friends were safe and well. And apparently as the ambulance drove them to the hospital, Ginny had complained: 'But I wanted to see the little boy!'

I emailed the cast and crew, thanking them once again. Then I emailed the theatre… and *that* email I can assure you, dear reader, was written in a somewhat different tone! For a very long time after that horrific evening I found it extremely difficult to reflect on what might have been a worst-case scenario.

I had a week or so before leaving London for Thursford and saw as much of Ginny and Lenny as possible. Every moment became ever-more precious. Ginny would become a centenarian in a few months' time, and Lenny would turn ninety-four whilst I was away. To me they'd both appeared indestructible. But seeing Lenny helpless was a brutal reminder that these two remarkable beings were human and extremely fragile. Knowing them had touched my soul and ensured that for the rest of my days I was destined to be a happier and better person. So, for whatever time we had left, I was fully prepared to bring Ginny and Lenny whatever happiness I could in return.

Now We Are Sixty had been the most difficult theatrical undertaking of my life. This ill-fated production had been thwarted at every twist and turn. But from now on, *nothing* in my career could possibly faze me. Artistically, however, we'd been a great success. The show made money and Gyles felt that we'd more than done justice to his piece. In fact, even before the run had ended, he'd approached me about collaborating on another project.

In the meantime, I moved out of the Fridge Room – never, thank God, to see it, or the mouse, ever again. I was off, for the ninth time, to my spiritual home of North Norfolk. And the fates weren't through with me yet.

CHAPTER TWENTY-SEVEN

'I am still here'

Patience

Thursford was changing. In 2005 the most taxing chore-ography required of the singers was a box step. By 2013 the boys were doing lifts with the dancing girls and kick-ing their legs up to their ears. The *Christmas Spectacular* had evolved down a contemporary musical-theatre route – and within the show I was used much less.

After *Now We Are Sixty*, I thought I'd relish a not-so-busy Thursford. Within a week I was climbing the walls. It wasn't only Thursford which had changed. I had too.

I no longer wanted to dance with a Fat Santa. I wanted to *tell* someone to dance with a Fat Santa. Or better yet, artistically devise the show and *decide* that someone should dance with a Fat Santa.

Therefore, when the opportunity arose to produce a one-off show for an event in Fantasy Land, I leapt at it. I needed to write, direct and create again. When casting, I called upon Thursford's finest, including *Grand Duke* stalwart Tammy, and my great 'Hail Poetry' friend Rob!

Thursford had a new assistant musical director. His name was Dominic Ferris. Like me, he was a showman of the old school, and his keen sense of the ridiculous matched mine – he loved my raffles!

Rehearsing the Fantasy Land show, Dom and I each discovered that the other possessed skill sets not show-cased by the *Christmas Spectacular*. Dom turned out to be the most gifted pianist I'd ever met. A musician of the highest calibre.

'For the finale,' I told him. 'I'd like to do the "Supercalifragilistic" West End arrangement. I'll bring in the music tomorrow.'

'Oh, don't bother,' he replied and played the whole thing by ear, then and there. Then he asked, 'Can I sing some-thing?' I was surprised – and a little concerned – *could* he sing? It turned out that he could – and damn well.

The Fantasy Land revue featured comedy, rock, show tunes, tap dancing, falsetto and an elaborately staged per-formance of 'The Marrow Song'. Dom and I became great friends – and decided we should work together more often.

* * *

In January 2014, I had a problem – nowhere to live – and I wasn't going back to the Fridge Room! Ginny and Lenny were eager to see me. I told them I'd be round as soon as I could, but first I needed to find a place in London.

Haidee made an incredibly kind suggestion – why didn't I stay with Ginny and Lenny? There was a spare room, and with Tracy to look after them I'd be there purely for company. My comings and goings would pro-vide stimulation – and Ginny and I could play Posso. Now I had the best of all worlds – a wonderful London base and the opportunity to see Ginny and Lenny every day. When I arrived, Ginny played hostess extraordinaire.

'Sweetie! Let me show you your room!'

'You'll find Marilyn Monroe in there waiting for you,' said Lenny.

'Marvellous!' I laughed. 'I don't think I'll say no to that!'

'Good!' Lenny chirped, his eyes sparkling. '*I* didn't!'

Life at the flat was gradually slowing down. Over the last twelve months Ginny had suffered a series of mini-strokes. After each TIA she'd been cloudy for a couple of days but always seemed to bounce back… and couldn't get to the card table quickly enough. But each mini-stroke took its toll, affecting her memory. There'd be no more evenings of anecdotes now. And sadly, there could be no more trips to Sperlonga.

Life began revolving exclusively around the Chelsea apartment. *Deal or No Deal* on Channel 4 became a ritual, with Ginny screaming at the television.

'Deal! *Deal*!' she'd plead imploringly. Then she'd get pissed off and bark, '*Deal* for Chrissake!'

Lenny's health was better than Ginny's – but Lenny was a gentleman. Therefore, if Ginny stayed put, so did he. After dinner, Ginny liked Lenny to retire with her – and Lenny complied without procrastination.

That wasn't to say he didn't still enjoy his wine. Lenny could be a sly dog. When Tracy and her husband Bobot returned briefly to the Philippines for a more than well-earned holiday, Tracy was covered by a girl named Liane. One night, whilst Liane was in the bathroom look-ing after Ginny, Lenny leapt out of his chair, dashed up the hallway and – thinking the new girl wouldn't notice

– raided an unopened wine box! I'd never seen him move so fast! Eyes wide, the picture of complete innocence, he just looked at me and said: 'Whatever it was, I didn't do it!'

On 17 February 2014, Ginny turned one hundred. She looked a million dollars, dressed in gold; a hat with a butterfly and peacock feather adorning her head. This was the most important birthday party to which I had ever been invited – but as I looked at Ginny and reflected on her extraordinary century, it struck me that *all* birthdays are a celebration of life. And I'd learned about life from a lady who knew how to live.

Alfred accompanied me as I sang 'This is the Moment' from her Lubitsch movie *That Lady in Ermine*. Looking down at Ginny from the stairs leading to the marionette theatre, I finished with her favourite, 'Night and Day'. She might not have recalled the names of certain party guests – but with her eyes closed and tiny delicate hand protected within Lenny's loving clasp, Ginny sang along word perfect: '*Till you let me spend my life making love to you day and night…*'

'If you do,' Lenny said, chortling, 'you'll end up in hospital!'

* * *

At the flat I was immersed in a gentle serenity. But my social life had a pulsating drive. I'd been catching up on things I'd missed as a late developer. James Bentham introduced me to Soho nightlife, taking me to G-A-Y Late, and Heaven beneath the arches of Charing Cross.

At first, I was a rabbit in the headlights – but thanks to James' comforting presence and assurance I began to revel in something I never thought I'd enjoy. This was a far cry from the Martin who didn't know where Old Compton Street was! Soon I had no qualms about heading to Heaven alone. At 4 a.m. I'd creep back into the flat, past Ginny and Lenny's room, and still be up for breakfast at 9.30 a.m. But as far as Ginny was concerned, I'd been in bed, like her, since 10 p.m.

'Did you have a nice long sleep?' she'd ask, smiling, and I'd tell her – through stifled yawns – that I'd slept like a log. Lenny was far more clued up. Once, when Ginny was getting ready for bed, he looked up and asked, knowingly, 'Are you off partying?'

But sometimes out partying, in a passionate clinch, things became difficult to explain.

'So,' declared the gorgeous guy. 'Are we going back to yours or mine?'

'We can't *possibly* go back to mine!' I squealed. 'My flat-mate's a hundred years old!'

* * *

I was having my hair cut in Covent Garden when a copy of *Esquire* magazine was placed in front of me. Leafing through, I suddenly did a double take – silent-movie star Anita Page was staring up at me. Astounded that Anita Page should be in *Esquire* I turned back – and read agog.

It was an interview with twin brothers – Austin and Howard Mutti-Mewse – who'd just released a book entitled *I Used to Be in Pictures*. Now in their forties, the brothers had been writing to old Hollywood stars from the age of twelve, starting with Lillian Gish. Subsequently they met and befriended everyone still alive. Frank Sinatra invited them to his barbeque; Hedy Lamarr and Marlene Dietrich would phone up at all hours; Bette Davis claimed the twins had 'turned on Old Hollywood'. The only star who eluded them was Garbo… although they did meet her stand-in, who was just as reclusive and always ate 'alone'.

I bought their book and couldn't put it down. I've *got* to meet these guys! I decided. They're basically *me*! I tracked them down on Facebook and explained I was a 28-year-old movie buff living with a hundred-year-old movie star. The Mutti-Mewses and I clicked instantly.

Both the twins' lives and mine had been touched by the generosity and friendship of an ageing generation, and our lifestyles were not dissimilar. As a young man, Austin, too, had lived with a movie star, Mildred Shay, who'd played Joan Crawford's French maid in *The Women*.

The brothers invited me to a garden party in Chelsea where they introduced me to their friends Peggy Cummins and Princess George Galitzine. This was beyond exciting – Peggy Cummins was one of the last surviving 'above-the-title' stars of 1940s Hollywood. Her leading men included David Niven, Ronald Colman, Victor Mature and Edward G. Robinson; she'd dated Cary Grant, Howard Hughes and John F. Kennedy. But Cummins' legacy was *Gun Crazy*, a cult film noir in which she played a pistol-wielding femme fatale. It had ensured her cinematic immortality.

Princess Galitzine was born Jean Dawnay. After working in espionage at Bletchley Park, she became Christian Dior's top supermodel and the best friend of Terence Rattigan. Also an actress, she married into Imperial Russian royalty.

The charity garden party glittered. Peggy Cummins was

instantly recognisable, her voice and hair unchanged from the movies. Upon discovering I was an actor she cried, 'I must come and see you in something!' and signed her photo on the covers of my vintage *Picture Post* magazines. One of them, from 1947, showed Peggy and Rex Harrison filming on location.

'The bracelet!' she declared, pointing to a gold bracelet on her wrist in the photo. I then noticed that Peggy was wearing the same bracelet that afternoon. 'Beatrice Lillie gave it to me,' she said casually. 'She had it on and I complimented it, so she tore it off and gave it to me. I wore it in all my films!'

Peggy didn't stay too long – she wanted to get home and watch the tennis – she said she'd call. But neither of us anticipated that our first meeting that day would change my life in ways yet unknown to either of us.

Princess Galitzine was virtually blind, but still every inch a glamour girl. She was charmed that a young man wished to talk to her and said, 'Call me Jean!' The Princess told me to ring and arrange a date to come around to her apartment in Eaton Square, where she was the longest-standing resident.

I arrived at 4 p.m. Not wishing to outstay my welcome, I anticipated leaving at around 6 p.m. I stayed until 10 p.m. Jean was a delight, and despite her visual impairments cooked us a stew for supper. I'd bought her a DVD of her only film, *Wonderful Things!*, a 1958 Frankie Vaughan musical. We watched the whole movie together, accompanied by her live commentary. She told me about her discussions with Rattigan whilst he was writing *Separate Tables* – she'd been the inspiration behind the character of

Anne Shankland (played by Rita Hayworth in the film). And there was more, as she reminisced about her various careers…

'Leo Marks at Bletchley called me "one of his very best". I'm convinced he hypnotised us, because I can't remember a thing about what we did!

'Grace Kelly and I were friends from her modelling days, and when she married Rainier, she invited me to the wedding. My boyfriend at the time didn't want me to go. He was jealous, convinced I'd meet someone glamorous at the wedding and marry them! So, stupidly, I turned down the invitation. But the next day I joined Grace for cocktails on Rainier's yacht. We had to wind down the shades as the press were in little boats alongside, trying to get pictures.'

Before I left, she signed a photograph – 'To Martin, thank you for a lovely day, Love Jean' – and giggled as she said, 'We're best friends now, aren't we?'

Alas, Jean became ill soon afterwards. I never saw her again, although we spoke on the phone several times. She was pleased that I'd found a copy online of her 1956 bestseller *Model Girl*, but annoyed it was only £30. 'It's a collector's item! It should be at least £80!' Austin and I both tried calling again… but the Princess had become foggy, and she sadly passed away.

* * *

The day after meeting Peggy and Jean at the garden party, I received a bombshell email. I had not been offered a contract for Thursford 2014. After nine years of service this was very upsetting – but did not, however, come as a total surprise.

I'd seen the way the wind was blowing. Nevertheless, I was hurt. To be dropped felt like a savage decision.

I'd grown up in that building – literally. In every corner there was a memory. The seminal events of my young existence had revolved around that show. Thursford had become a way of life.

But did I really want to stay? After all, I'd learned that when the party was over, there was no point vainly clinging on. I had to agree with my tenor friend Ed (who'd been dropped the year before) when he said, 'Mr Milnes! This is the best thing that could have happened to you!'

I was touched by the outcry – cast, crew, management and staff all got in touch. George and Betty were more upset than I was! I even had a phone call from John Cushing – who said some remarkable things I'll never forget. And I made sure that Colin Window knew I was genuinely grateful for everything he'd done for me, both personally and professionally.

The Thursford rejection signposted the end of an era. I'd said I didn't want to dance with the Fat Santa – so here was the chance to reinvent myself. But for the first time in my career, the waters felt strangely uncharted...

* * *

Dominic Ferris had turned down Thursford 2014 to work on his own creative projects – and now I came onboard. We discussed collaborating officially, producing our own shows. I was there when he received a phone call which, on the surface, appeared trivial, but in the grand scheme proved pivotal. Dom knew the owner of a drama school in Chichester. The sixth form was doing *Side by Side by Sondheim* in three weeks' time, but the musical director had suddenly dropped out. Could Dom come immediately? Dom admitted he wasn't very familiar with Sondheim. I, on the other hand, knew the entire Sondheim canon. Dom told the school, 'I'll only come if Martin comes too.'

The sixth form consisted of two boys and seven girls aged between sixteen and eighteen. They were far too young for Sondheim's songs of ambivalence and mid-life crisis – but for the school, *Side by Side* was a happily economical show, requiring only a bare stage and two benches!

One afternoon, our attention turned to 'I'm Still Here' – my favourite song from my favourite musical, *Follies* – I explained to the cast how this song was a hymn of survival. The character in *Follies* is an ageing actress who's lived through every ordeal life can throw at her – the highs, the lows – but she's emerged triumphantly. Having experienced all that, nothing can faze her now. She's going on. She's here.

There was no way seventeen-year-olds could relate to all this. They hadn't lived long enough. So, at Dom's urging, I told them about my friends…

I told them I lived with a hundred-year-old movie star who pre-dated World War One by six months and remembered a time before cars. She'd lived through, and seen, everything from Model T Fords to social media. And was here.

I told them about Nanny Jean. People instantly associated Maria with Julie Andrews, Mary Martin, and even reality-show winners… but why didn't they instantly recall Jean Bayless? She was here.

I told them about Peggy's worldwide humiliation, age

nineteen. Whisked to Hollywood, in a blaze of publicity, to play the most sought-after movie role of the year – and then sacked, accused universally of being 'not sexy enough'. And Fenella, swindled out of her life savings by an unscrupulous agent. After decades as a star she ended up on the dole. But Peggy and Fenella overcame all this with humour and dignity. And were here.

I told them about Eileen Page, widowed at twenty-six, her RAF pilot husband lost in the English Channel. With only a small pension to support her two infant children, Eileen's only option was to give up the theatre – her life. She was helped by her father, who, just as he'd done for over forty years, stood outside Baker Street station selling newspapers. Eileen was now eighty-nine and had never remarried. She'd survived. She was here.

And I told them about Lenny – who'd seen his friends blown to bits. And the Battle of Britain veterans, who in 1940 had never known if they'd live to see the next day.

But look who was here – *they* were still here.

By the time I'd finished, the students were in tears. I passed my phone around so they could see photos of my friends. They saw Ginny on her hundredth birthday, her eyes shining, smiling proudly straight into the camera. They saw The Few – modest, majestic, noble.

Now the students understood 'I'm Still Here'. Their performance of the song was transformed.

My friends were a constant inspiration to me. Now I saw that their lives and stories could make a difference to others. I had a duty to keep their legacies burning bright. It wasn't so much that my generation *should* know about them. They *needed* to know about them.

CHAPTER TWENTY-EIGHT

'We show ourselves to loud applause'

Utopia Limited

I'd been doing *Falsetto* shows at The Pheasantry for two producers, Richard and Doug. They offered me a return date on 1 April 2015, so I asked Dom if he fancied joining forces as a duo. He thought it sounded fun. For the Act One finale we wanted a showstopper – and created a mash-up medley. It featured everything from Kate Bush to *La Traviata*; 'The Holy City' to Disney. We totted up the total number of songs, and the running time: '20 Songs in 4 Minutes'.

There was no way Ginny and Lenny would be able to come. So, the day before the show, I took Dom round to the flat and we gave them a 'mini concert'. The first-ever performance by Dominic Ferris and Martin Milnes was a private production for Virginia Campbell and Leonard Lambert.

Ginny had just passed her 101st birthday. That party had been perhaps the loveliest of all – Ginny had blown out the candle on her cake with a single energetic puff. But the mini-strokes continued. My darling Ginny had begun to fade.

However – when we performed, something remarkable happened – Ginny blossomed with the music, giggling and gasping as she watched Dom's hands fly across the piano keys. Afterwards she talked lucidly for the first time in months. I watched, astounded, as she looked up and said, 'This is the greatest thing I've ever seen in my life! And you know, I've had a long life – on Broadway – and in Hollywood!'

We had an illustrious crowd for our debut show – Peggy Cummins, Austin Mutti-Mewse, Elizabeth Seal, Eileen Page and Gyles Brandreth were just a few of the friends who showed their support. I was thrilled Peggy was there. I'd done something personal that night inspired by her, and in honour of Nanny Jean. I loved that in every film Peggy made, she'd worn the bracelet given to her by Beatrice Lillie. So, I'd decided to do something similar. Nanny Jean had given me a gold signet ring. It had a buckle design, encrusted with garnets. I wore the ring that night in my debut show with Dom – and continue to wear it in every show to this day.

Dom and I seemed to be on to something. We'd created our own piano and vocal arrangements for every number – and they seemed to be exciting the audience. Then we got to '20 Songs in 4 Minutes' – and the audience appeared to go berserk. Mash-up medleys seemed to be the way forward…

Producers Richard and Doug, in association with The Stephen Sondheim Society, were preparing a major event – Sondheim's eighty-fifth birthday gala at Theatre Royal, Drury Lane.

'We need to be in this!' I told Dom. I emailed Richard and Doug asking whether they might like a bespoke

Sondheim mash-up for their gala. They emailed straight back: 'Consider yourselves booked.'

Had Dom not become familiar with Sondheim's work through *Side by Side,* he later told me that he might have been in two minds about accepting this challenge – considering the importance of the occasion, we *had* to get the medley right. It could make us or break us. We locked ourselves away – and emerged with '33 Sondheim Numbers in 5 Minutes'. The medley was far more technical than its predecessor – at one point there were three songs happening simultaneously (one in the piano accompaniment whilst two others were sung).

I had a beautiful falsetto excerpt from the *Follies* number 'One More Kiss'. This made me think about Eileen Page, who, years ago, had performed 'One More Kiss' in a gala performance of *Follies* at Drury Lane. As she received a grand ovation after her solo – standing on the same stage from which in 1939 she had seen Ivor Novello and Mary Ellis – Eileen told herself, *I'll have this moment for the rest of my life.*

Afterwards, Stephen Sondheim approached Eileen and told her, 'Tonight you were perfect. You stood and took the applause which was rightfully yours. Thank you.'

Eileen booked to see Dom and me in the Sondheim gala at Drury Lane on Sunday 25 October. I hoped to do Sondheim, Novello, Mary Ellis and Eileen Page proud.

* * *

In the six months since our mini-concert, Ginny had grown weaker. In my heart, I knew that she probably didn't have long. The week of the Sondheim gala, Dom came around again and we performed for her and Lenny one last time.

It was an extremely emotional half hour. Haidee and Sarah were there too, and Ginny's grandson, Jacob. Ginny bloomed again listening to the music – but this time her reactions were diminished. And afterwards she could not speak as lucidly.

I had a lump in my throat as I looked down at her from the staircase, singing the lullaby 'Hushabye Mountain'. By the time we reached the grand finale, 'New York, New York', everyone was choked up. I knelt beside Ginny in her wheelchair, holding her hands, and sang directly to her. Ginny's adoring gaze beamed straight into my eyes.

We all knew this was a farewell concert. Sarah was crying unashamedly. I managed to hold out until I went to my bedroom to retrieve Dom's coat – at which point I burst into tears.

* * *

The gala was directed by Olivier Award-winner Bill Deamer, under the musical direction of maestro Gareth Valentine. We demonstrated the medley to them a few days before the show and wondered if they might want to tweak it. They left it exactly as it was.

I dropped by to see Alan Curtis in Chiswick. Having directed many shows, he asked me at which point in the gala programme we appeared.

'Second in the second half,' I replied. Alan was jubilant.

'Don't you realise,' he cried, 'that's the strongest slot in the whole show? Your director *really* knows what he's doing! That's where I always used to put my best comics! The audience has come back after the interval – they get settled, and then – bang! You've got 'em!'

The night before the gala, Peggy Cummins left a voicemail: 'I'm wishing you all the luck and everything I can think of!'

On Sunday 25 October I had breakfast with Lenny. Ginny wasn't up yet – but I did get to see her just before I left. She was sitting with Tracy on the edge of her bed, in her purple dressing gown. Ginny remembered that something important was happening for me today – and beamed, wishing me luck.

Alan Curtis rang the stage door and asked them to send a message up to our dressing room: 'This is it!'

As the second act began, Dom and I stood in the wings on opposite sides, ready to make our entrance down the steps. I touched my ring from Nanny Jean – and just like Eileen, on that same stage, told myself, *I'll have this moment for the rest of my life.*

'Ladies and gentlemen,' came the announcement. 'Martin Milnes and Dominic Ferris.'

Dom and I stepped out into the light and walked down the stairs to centre stage.

* * *

Back in the dressing room, whilst Act Two continued, I rang Nanny Jean.

'How did it go?'

'We stopped the show.'

CHAPTER TWENTY-NINE

'Light of my life, farewell!'

HMS Pinafore

The start of 2016 heralded a busy year. Dom and I were offered a residency at London's St James Theatre – performing a new show approximately every two months, building an excellent momentum and audience base.

We branded ourselves officially as Ferris & Milnes, and released a music video of the Sondheim medley, filmed at Steinway Hall. In the meantime, a live recording from the gala found its way to Stephen Sondheim – who sent us a remarkably kind email giving the mash-up his approval.

But whilst everything took off with Ferris & Milnes, Ginny was slowing down – although, of course, we still played Posso. Sometimes I'd barely walked through the door before she cried, 'Ah! Sweetheart! Good! You're here! Now! Two threes of a kind…'

I sometimes made sure she got the wild cards. It made her happy. But things were liable to get confused. Dealing the first hand, she looked up at me, perplexed: 'Sweetheart! There's something wrong with these cards – they're all either red or black!' Another time, Lenny broke his own rule and came to join us at the table. But Ginny was playing Posso whilst Lenny seemed to be playing something entirely different…

She still asked me to sing. Having been thrashed at Posso I was about to leave for a rehearsal, wrapped up in my coat and scarf. Sad that I was leaving, Ginny looked up and asked, 'Are we going to have a song?' So, I gave her a Cole Porter number right then and there in the lounge.

And the flat was never without yellow roses. They'd become my calling card. The colour was bright and vibrant, like Ginny herself; even when her eyesight weakened, I knew she could still clearly see the flowers in bloom. And the yellow rose, as Sarah had pointed out to me, represented friendship.

At the end of January, the night before the first St James Ferris & Milnes show, Ginny had another TIA. No one quite knew whether her 102nd birthday party on 17 February would go ahead, but Alfred and Rhoda flew in from Italy anyway. Her son Cam would be arriving too, so I stayed elsewhere whilst the apartment housed guests from overseas.

On the fifteenth I'd arranged lunch at the flat with Alfred and Rhoda. Alfred informed me that during the night Ginny had suffered another, more serious, stroke. Ginny lay asleep in her room. Her tiny head poked out from under the duvet. She didn't know I was there. I blew her a kiss and told her I loved her… and quietly closed the bedroom door.

Early in the morning on 17 February I received a text from Haidee saying that Ginny was very ill, and the party was cancelled. But not long after 11 a.m. she called me…

Ginny died on her birthday. For Ginny it had been all about her birthday. No sooner had one birthday passed than she was planning the guest list for next year's party. It was too much of a coincidence that she'd departed on her birthday. I think Ginny knew exactly what she was doing. She'd been holding on, determined to make 102.

She had also been in my life for an exact five-year period – to the day. Those five years changed me forever.

Sarah and I spent the evening in each other's company. We each needed to be with someone who loved Ginny. In the days afterwards I called on Lenny. Sometimes he was happy to talk. Other times he sat quietly, his eyes glistening with tears.

* * *

A Louisiana jazz band walked ahead of the hearse as Ginny arrived. They played a gentle arrangement of 'Swing Low, Sweet Chariot', with the banjo strumming in true Southern style. During the service, Haidee placed a beautiful hand-made replica of the marionette theatre on Ginny's coffin. Sarah spoke warmly about the years in Sperlonga, and Jacob recalled how as a child he'd been left overnight in Ginny's care – Haidee had returned flabber-gasted to find Jacob very much awake, lighting Ginny's cigarette at the disco she'd thrown for him! And, only three days before Ginny passed away, she'd beaten Jacob at Posso.

I addressed the gathering of friends and family wear-ing a yellow rose in my lapel… and felt it appropriate to provide music. I'd rewritten the lyrics of 'Thanks for the

Memory'. The references ranged from her movies to 'puppets and pasta' and even the prunes she ate for breakfast. There was a wake back at the apartment. Lenny sat in his usual chair – very quietly.

Neither Sarah nor I said much as we drove away from the flat. I felt a weird mixture of emotions – relief that it had all gone well, coupled with the inevitable grief of saying goodbye and, of course, ongoing concern for Lenny.

But I also felt a strange sensation of 'so what now?'. I'd lost a titanic figure in my life. And although at 102 her passing could hardly be described as unexpected, my instinct was that life would undergo a shift. It must be the same for many who care about the elderly – the status quo is maintained for as long as possible, providing stability for all. And then, all of a sudden, there is a release, and everything moves on. The change isn't necessarily good, nor is it necessarily bad – but whatever it is, it's different, and for the first time in what might have seemed an eternity, the immediate future is strangely unknown.

I collected my thoughts as I gazed out of the car window. London went about its business as usual. Cyclists whizzed past. Crowds huddled in coffee shops. Drivers sat impatiently in queues, demanding to speed away. The world continued to turn, but for the first time in 102 years Ginny wasn't in it.

I thought about the half-decade in which her presence had influenced and shaped my life. Vignettes flashed through my mind – Ginny whisked into the Finborough auditorium in Guy's arms, playing cards together the night of the Great War centenary as candles flickered and the madness of Sperlonga. My world would not fall apart – but it would be forever missing something wonderful.

Back at Sarah's, I changed out of my smart clothing into more casual attire. But I still had my yellow rose in my lapel. It had survived through the long morning, although it wouldn't last much longer. But there was no way I could just throw this final 'Ginny' rose into the rubbish – and the idea of keeping hold of it, seeing the petals gradually wilt away, didn't appeal to me at all.

And then I knew what to do.

I left Sarah's apartment block, which looked out over the Thames, and walked away from the flats upstream a short distance, where I found myself entirely alone. There was a gentle breeze and I smiled seeing a few small boats moored nearby – appropriate as Ginny had always loved her boating.

Finally, I released the torrent of emotion I'd been holding within all day, having channelled Ginny's super-human strength to get through my song. I'd cried before, of course, over the week since her passing, but I knew that this was now finally it – the last goodbye.

I took the rose from my jacket, held it tight and said a few private words of farewell to my dear, unique friend. I thanked her for the enormous privilege of being permitted to enter her world. I thanked her for everything she'd taught me, for I would treasure it for the rest of my life. Her eternal optimism, her dignity, her style, her wit, her fire. Ginny had experienced life to the full – and shown me how to embrace it.

Living under the same roof had brought me closer to this incredible lady at an age experienced by few. Even towards the end, when days were difficult, she greeted each morning with a smile and burst of joy, inspiring me with her strength and resilience. She'd imparted to me a lifetime's wisdom and experience... not necessarily through what she said, but sometimes just through her very presence and being.

Above all she'd offered me the kind of friendship that I had once, during my childhood, thought I would never know. Growing up I had been snubbed, laughed at and excluded by my peers. But Ginny, who'd lived her life among the greats because she herself had been one of them, welcomed me as her equal. And that had changed my life.

'As long as I live,' I whispered through my tears, 'I will never cease to try and pass on everything you taught me.'

As I leaned on the railings over the river, I thought that anyone who'd spent time with Ginny couldn't help but absorb her magic... and then I realised that, if this was indeed the case, Ginny would always be with everyone who knew her. And if I was able to fulfil my promise and pass on her wisdom to others in turn, then Ginny's imperishable magic could touch people for generations to come – and the world would be a brighter place.

I sang the last few lines of 'Night and Day'... and then I threw the rose over the railings and into the river. A brisk breeze had whipped up the current, and Ginny's beautiful bright yellow rose sailed off down the Thames in a gallant and stately fashion.

The waters of the river were dark and black – but there on the surface, sailing nobly into the distance, was Ginny's rose, the dazzling yellow of the petals magnificently illuminating the waves as it journeyed downstream. I smiled and then laughed… it was sailing right past Sarah's flat, as if Ginny was drifting by to say one last farewell to her too.

The whole episode seemed fitting in so many ways because Ginny had always been that dazzling ray of brightness and colour amidst the dark waters of life. She'd always been sailing off somewhere – literally and figuratively – to discover new adventures in a fresh part of the world, and always with that same confidence and assurance with which the rose travelled down the river.

In Ginny I observed a rare feat – she was happy within herself. It may not have always been that way, for life is a well-travelled road of laughter and tears. But having lived through all this, the older generations have acquired greater wisdom.

Living symbiotically enriches the existence of both young and old. Each generation will be inspired. Youth will be guided and advised. Elders will be rejuvenated, made to feel wanted, and escape that most crippling of emotions – the profound, debilitating sting of loneliness.

As loved ones grow older it's never easy watching them fade – but I've observed that at this stage of life, the elderly crave love and company more than ever before. The most special way to say thank you to our elders, I feel, is to be their friend – however difficult at times this may prove. For one day, we too, God willing, shall know how they feel. And, like the Tin Man's heart, a life should be judged not by how much one has loved, but by how much one is loved by others.

When I was a guest at Ginny's birthday parties, I rejoiced in her resilience, pride and courage. Celebrating my own birthdays, I was humbled to know that she revelled in being part of my world. Every person's birthday, no matter their age, should be a toast to their very existence, to what has passed and, moreover, to what is yet to come.

Thanks to my friendships, I too, like Ginny, am happy within myself. I've not only asked for the moon – I've had the stars.

* * *

If this was a Hollywood movie of Ginny's era, this moment would have been the final scene. A swelling musical score would have built to a dramatic climax over a last long shot of the rose sailing away into the sunset, with the words 'THE END' emblazoned across the screen.

But this wasn't a Hollywood movie – and nor was it 'the end'. It was a new beginning. And it was time for me to live up to Ginny's belief in who I was and all that I had to do.

I turned and walked towards the main road. Smiling, I blew a kiss to the skies using the farewell with which Ginny had always bid her friends goodbye: 'Ciao!'

CHAPTER THIRTY

'And it's greatly to his credit
That he is an Englishman!'

HMS Pinafore

'I'd worked it all out very carefully,' Lenny explained. 'I had a bag of oranges and maybe nine bottles of lemonade, and some doughnuts, two pages from my school atlas, and my Boy Scout compass. Everything you need to go to Africa!' He looked at me philosophically. 'I never got there. I got as far as Llandudno! I was out there for three nights and four days. When the coastguard found me, I was a very tired, frightened, unhappy little boy.'

At eight years old, inspired by H. Rider Haggard's adventure novel *She*, Lenny set off for Africa from Birkenhead in a boat he'd made from an orange box. It was the first of many close escapes in a life story which might have been too fantastic to believe – had it not all been true.

He still occupied his chair by the fire, but Ginny's position opposite, on the sofa, lay achingly empty. It wasn't always necessary to make conversation. Lenny appreciated company and was happy that someone was there – but he was content just to doze, resting in the warmth.

While Ginny was housebound, Lenny stayed by her side. Now that she'd gone, family and friends encouraged him to venture out; his son and daughter took him on day trips visiting relatives down south.

Closer to home, Bobot and I suggested walks to the Coopers Arms on Flood Street... but when we got there, without saying a word, Lenny's thoughts drifted, and his eyes began to glisten – yet he valiantly maintained his English stiff upper lip. When we got back home, he was satisfied to return to his chair.

But sometimes, recalling former adventures made him smile. And if the stories were repeated a couple of times it didn't matter – they were damn good stories; well told and worth hearing.

'A Focke-Wulf 190 was chasing me, and I couldn't shake him off. He had a better aircraft – but I was a better pilot. What do I do? Flying low level – only about thirty or forty feet – I see these power cables in front of us. I flew under them. He hit them. Bang! Dead.'

And newspaper reports from the time corroborated perhaps the luckiest escape of all: 'My squadron had to find the mobile launching sites for V-2s. I'm circling at 10,000 feet, I look down, and I see a "mushroom" developing on the ground – the rocket's about to launch. Suddenly it shoots up – passing right between me and my wingman! I had the closest view of the V-2 of any man on the Allied side! I had reporters asking what the V-2 looked like. I told them it was very pretty!'

For his services and bravery, Lenny was awarded the Distinguished Flying Cross and the Air Force Cross. Finally, in October 2015, prior to his ninety-sixth birthday, he was awarded the Légion d'honneur for his services during the liberation of France.

There'd always been something new to learn about Lenny. During lunch with Yuri Gagarin they were observed from another table. 'KGB,' Gagarin told Lenny. 'They're going to kill me.' Not long after, Gagarin was dead in an air crash never satisfactorily explained.

He'd flown reconnaissance missions, photographing the Ruhr Valley prior to the Dam Busters raid. There were stories about staying with Barnes Wallis. Whilst serving in West Africa, Lenny kept a pet elephant named Colfax. When he returned after an absence of several years, Colfax remembered and came over to greet him.

On the social side, he'd enjoyed encounters with Édith Piaf: 'She had a deep, almost masculine voice. Very tiny. And an absolute sweetie. I ran around with her for about a year. I was at NATO Headquarters in Paris then.'

And sometimes he reflected on events from 1940…

'About seventy-odd years ago I got caught up in a thing called the retreat of Dunkirk. My survival, I owe to my Boy Scout training. Make the best of a situation! Don't obey the rules – just do something! Do something! *Do something!*' He smiled. 'That was our Scout Mistress – Miss Francis. An incredible lady. She taught me climbing – she climbed Snowdon with me twice! I wonder whatever happened to her… And I learned to navigate by the stars.'

At the age of nineteen, Lenny was serving in France as a driver in the Royal Army Service Corps. The Maginot Line collapsed amidst scenes of utter devastation – and Lenny was abandoned by his commanding officer.

'He wanted to get away! He said to me, "Will you drive

me down to Le Havre?" I said "No!" He replied, "If you don't, I'll have you court martialled!" And I said, "Good for you." He was running away – deserting us! I tore him apart.'

Lenny was told to head for the coast – and with five comrades covered 120 miles on foot. Wreckage littered the road, but they found an abandoned truck, which Lenny started up. The open road was crowded with carts and refugees, but as German planes rained bombs and machine-gun fire on terrified civilians, he spotted two nuns cowering in a ditch with a group of small children. Lenny piled them onto the truck and drove them to safety. One of the nuns was wearing a little wooden crucifix – she hung it around Lenny's neck and prayed tearfully for his survival.

Lenny and his friends found themselves just north of Dunkirk – but the evacuation was over, and now the town was under German command. Lenny and his number two, Harry Merrick, found and launched a small boat. It had two holes which the young men tried to bung up with cork – but the Germans attacked, and they were sunk. 'Harry couldn't swim properly. I swam five miles with him holding on to my shoulder.'

On the beach, the Nazis were looking for Allied survivors. 'The Luftwaffe knew we were on the loose and tried to track down where we were on the ground. Back on shore, the Germans had seen us and were running towards us with machine guns. Luckily I'd got hand grenades which persuaded them to leave us for a while!'

Lenny and Harry had no option other than to hide beneath dead bodies piled up on the beach. It was every man for himself: 'I killed a German officer and took his revolver and ammunition.' Then another German appeared and attacked Lenny with his bayonet, leaving a scar on his wrist – which Lenny showed me many times. 'The man who did it was dead two seconds later…

'I was very tired and couldn't think straight. I'd had nothing proper to eat for about four days – but thanks to my Boy Scout training I'd learned to live off the land. I went into a field and found half-ripe turnips – and made for one of those. Had a disastrous effect on the bowels!'

Lenny and Harry found a wooden dinghy. With pieces of wood for paddles they pushed off… and this time got out to sea. A Little Ship, searching for stragglers, picked them up. Two men in the Little Ship were already dead, but a badly damaged Destroyer lowered a net to take the living and deceased onboard. 'I'd been wounded and lost a lot of blood. The last couple of days are still a haze to me. But we got back.'

'Harry Merrick lost his nerve. Really. And there was nothing he could do about it. He was, as it were, a passenger for the rest of the journey. Later, I got in touch with people in high places and had him invalided out of the forces. But he only lived about five years and died of a heart attack. Poor Harry.'

For the next three months Lenny was in hospital with septicaemia from his wound, sickness and boils through drinking polluted water, and suffered the effects of starvation, exhaustion and exposure.

His family eventually received news that he was alive and had been sent to Sticklepath in Devon, where he convalesced under the care of a Mrs Baron – who became known as 'Aunty B'. She remained a friend for life.

'The Air Force whisked me out of the army while I was still in hospital. Next thing I knew I was training in Canada.'

Lenny reclaimed the beaches of France as a Squadron Leader on D-Day. Later, he encountered the army officer who'd abandoned him, who was now a major – the equivalent rank of a Squadron Leader.

'He came and tapped me on the shoulder and said, "Lambert!" I said, "*Squadron Leader* Lambert to you," and I turned my back on him. Would *not* speak to him.'

Lenny gave the nun's wooden crucifix to his sister Joyce, who kept it as a family heirloom. The nun's prayers for Lenny's safety were answered. Instead of perishing on the beaches of France in 1940, he died peacefully in London seventy-six years later, on 6 September 2016.

In the weeks leading up to Lenny's passing, he was suffering the effects of acute leukaemia. It was no longer possible for him to stay at the flat and he was moved into a home. I visited whenever I could.

Although Lenny was now very frail, his eyes retained their spark, and his sense of humour prevailed – even if it was lost on the staff. The last time I saw my friend, a carer entered whilst we were chatting. He usually ordered lunch from a tray, so she enquired what Lenny had chosen.

'What would you like in your room, Mr Lambert?'

'Marilyn Monroe!'

'Sorry?' the lady asked.

'Never mind,' he said, smiling and shaking his head.

When Haidee informed me of the news, I was at the RAF Club about to escort the veterans to a tea party at Clarence House. It was an annual event in the diary of the Prince of Wales and the Duchess of Cornwall – their personal thank you to The Few.

I felt there was no more fitting place I could be. The Prince and the Duchess always took a genuine interest in The Few. I know they would have saluted Lenny too.

When I left the Chelsea flat on my very last morning, I wandered through the rooms to say my final goodbyes. I had passed here a happy, happy time. The apartment had once rung out with laughter and song. Now it was silent. But I couldn't leave it that way. I walked over to the old music box from the Parisian railway station. For the last time I turned the antique handle – and everything spluttered achingly into life. The six mechanical dancing girls twirled and jumped, and a merry, tinny tune filled the apartment. I took one last look and then closed the front door. On the landing outside, as the lift descended, I could still hear the music playing.

Ginny's ashes had been interred at her family home in Louisiana. Lenny, a quintessential Englishman, was laid to rest in London. His obituary in *The Daily Telegraph* recorded that when Lenny was awarded the DFC, the citation commented on his keenness and courage of the highest order, concluding, 'He is an outstanding operational pilot.'

That was my friend. And I couldn't be prouder to have known him.

CHAPTER THIRTY-ONE

'… and so it fell to my lot To take and bind the promising boy apprentice to…'

The Pirates of Penzance

'Hello, Peggy!'

'No, this is Annie Laurie Starr.'

I beamed from ear to ear. The star of my favourite movie had just phoned me – in character.

'Hello, Laurie!' I yelped in an American accent. 'This is Bart!'

The first time I saw *Gun Crazy* – before I knew Peggy – I'd been knocked out. It was startling, contemporary and relevant – yet filmed on a shoestring budget in 1949. Overlooked upon its 1950 release, *Gun Crazy* was later rediscovered, hailed as classic and selected for preservation in the United States National Film Registry. Martin Scorsese and Quentin Tarantino considered it a seminal work. In fact, when Tarantino finally met Peggy, he'd fallen prostrate at her feet.

As pistol-wielding Annie Laurie Starr, critics claimed that British Peggy gave 'the most ferocious female performance in American cinema'. It was her best role – light years from the fluff which usually came her way: 'I was always cast as somebody's girlfriend or somebody's daughter.' Grateful producers knew that she elevated weaker material, but *Gun Crazy* proved, in the words of Hedda Hopper, that Peggy Cummins was a 'firecracker gal'.

At eighty-eight, she had the looks and energy of someone decades younger. She lived for the moment and drove meals on wheels to contemporaries less fortunate than she. When we first met, my interest in Peggy bemused her, and she claimed, 'I'm really not that interested in talking about my career.' Happily, as we became friends, she opened up…

When Peggy and Austin attended the debut Ferris & Milnes show, I sang 'Jealousy' holding a rose; at the end of the number I gave it to her, and back home, she pressed it into her journal. During the interval we crossed paths on the way to the bathroom (no private facilities for performers at this venue, dear reader!). She jumped, excited, and cried, 'Oh! How *wonderful* to meet by the loo! You're sensational!' And in Act Two, no one sang along with 'Those Were the Days' more lustily than Peggy.

Ideally for a tennis devotee, her West London flat overlooked numerous courts. My first visit was during French Open season; a match was in full swing on television.

'I'll go out and make some tea,' said Peggy, walking to the kitchen. 'Tell me what's going on!'

I'd never followed tennis, but about two seconds before she re-emerged with a tea tray the commentator reported, 'And Murray's up two-love.'

'Murray's up two-love!' I announced, informatively, as she walked in.

Peggy was just back from Croatia, where she'd flown by herself to give a talk about 'a film of mine called *Gun Crazy*'... and she'd been keeping a gift for me since before she left. In 2013 Peggy had been guest of honour at the San Francisco Film Noir Festival – where she received a four-minute standing ovation. But Peggy made it clear to the audience that the movie they'd enjoyed was testament to her co-stars and colleagues behind the camera – the people to whom 'you can never say thank you enough'.

A special poster had been designed for the event, featuring an artist's impression of Annie Laurie Starr. Peggy had a limited number of these, and she'd autographed and dedicated one to me. Her own copy, signed by the adoring festival management, hung framed in the hallway... but uncomfortable with the wording 'Peggy Cummins the Legendary Star', she'd sellotaped a piece of cardboard over her billing.

That afternoon we talked about all sorts, including, inevitably, *Gun Crazy*. As we discussed the movie, she sat there wearing the gold bracelet so visible in many key scenes. Then she asked: 'What did you think of the girl in the film?'

For a moment I was confused... but then realised 'the girl' Peggy referred to was herself, or rather Annie Laurie Starr. As we chatted about the character, she kept telling me to eat the cakes she'd laid out. I reminded her about the 'most ferocious female performance' comment and complimented her dramatic range. Peggy discreetly smiled and said: 'Well – considering that I also played Alice in Wonderland...'

At Austin and Howard's next garden party, Peggy met

Hazel Ascot. Hazel had been a 1930s child star in British film musicals, billed as 'Britain's answer to Shirley Temple'. Peggy clasped Hazel's hands and wouldn't let go – she was thrilled to be with a contemporary who remembered the same friends, places and events. There was a trust, admiration and understanding between these survivors from a vanished era.

'It's so sad,' Peggy had said to me before. 'Everyone I knew from that time is now dead!'

Fortunately, if anyone could match Peggy for zest it was Elizabeth Seal – the ladies had lost touch for several decades but were reunited at the Ferris & Milnes show. When Elizabeth and I planned a theatre trip, Peggy asked to join us, claiming: 'I don't go out anywhere!'… so said the lady who'd literally just driven herself back from a weekend in the country and arrived showing no signs of fatigue! At the end of the night, the merry ladies headed down into Piccadilly Circus station, Peggy hanging on to Elizabeth's arm.

If only people knew, I thought as they vanished. *If only they* knew *who these ladies are, walking down to the Tube*!

In September 2015 I invited Peggy to the RAF Club – where I was now a member – to meet The Few. She'd dressed specifically in sky blue, and we lunched with excited Spitfire pilot Geoffrey Wellum – who'd carried Peggy's photograph during the final year of the war. Peggy mentioned that her late brother Harry, whom she'd dearly loved, had been a pilot. He'd once given her an RAF brooch with wings – but across the years Peggy had fallen victim to ten burglaries, and amongst the many items stolen of great sentimental value was the brooch.

At a Battle of Britain event soon after, I found a brooch which looked very similar to what Peggy had described; in December I presented it as her ninetieth birthday gift. She kindly said she was 'overwhelmed' and had worn it to her birthday lunch with family in Winchester.

We were now very firm friends.

After seeing me perform, Peggy kept saying, 'I want you to meet my grandson!' This grandson – named Harry, after her late brother – was considering an acting career, and I told Peggy that I'd be very happy to advise him if he'd ever like to chat.

On 31 January 2016, Peggy invited me to BFI for a special screening of one of her films. Considered lost for decades, a print had recently been discovered – and after a restoration, it was now being viewed for the first time in seventy-two years.

Welcome, Mr Washington was cheery wartime propaganda encouraging good relations between British villagers and visiting American GIs. Teenage Peggy wore pigtails and carried bales of hay on her shoulder. Before the screening, Austin and I met Peggy in BFI's green room – and suddenly I had a thought: 'Peggy... is your grandson here?'

After hearing so much about him, I finally met Harry Dunnett.

We hit it off immediately. I gave Harry my card, and that evening he looked up the Sondheim medley on YouTube. The next day we began chatting in earnest – and a beautiful friendship emerged. I found I had the most terrific new chum!

Harry sent me audio recordings of his singing. He

appeared to have an excellent voice and clearly took his studies seriously. Respecting his dedication, I told him I'd always be happy to help and support, and a mentorship gradually evolved.

When Harry played Jean Valjean in a youth theatre production of *Les Misérables*, I travelled to Eastleigh to see my protégé in action. He gave an impressive performance which defied his years – and certainly sang 'Bring Him Home' far better than I had the night Claude-Michel Schönberg played the piano! Then a few weeks later, Peggy, Harry and his parents came to see the new Ferris & Milnes show at the St James.

I'd never been short of cross-generational friendships. But I'd always been the younger party, looking up to someone older. Now the positions were reversed. At last I felt I could give something back, helping someone starting out in their career – just as others had once helped me.

Harry was close to his gran – and one night the three of us had dinner together at the flat. Earlier in the day, Harry texted me saying, 'I have a CRAZY story to tell you later.' That afternoon, Peggy had taken Harry for lunch at Zizzi with a friend of hers, the actress Sylvia Syms. Learning that Harry wanted to perform, Miss Syms passionately advocated her advice.

'Make the rounds of agents' offices!' she projected, booming across the room, 'Tell people who you are!' Peggy went to offer a suggestion. 'Shut up, Peggy!' the dowager bellowed, announcing to the restaurant, 'I'm Sylvia Syms!'

'Sylvia put a £20 note in my hand,' Harry explained, 'and told me to go over the road to buy her some cigarettes...'

'I want ten Mayfair Light!' Miss Syms had instructed. But Harry was a little uncertain.

'Well, I'm only seventeen,' he replied politely. 'And I haven't got any ID. What do I do if they ask me?'

'Tell them they're for *Sylvia Syms*!' came the assertive reply. 'Tell them I'm your auntie!' Then she looked at Peggy. 'Tell them we're *both* your aunties!'

Peggy was enjoying the scene far too much to interfere, so Harry set about his task under the watchful gaze of Miss Syms, who peered across the road into the newsagents.

'I was really nervous,' Harry said, 'because I wasn't sure if the guy in the shop would have heard of Sylvia Syms. So, I said, "Can I have ten Mayfair Light, please?" And he said, "Have you got any ID?" And I said, "Er… they're for my auntie!"' Harry then pointed to where Sylvia Syms was madly gesticulating. Peggy stood next to her stifling the giggles.

'It was so crazy!' Harry remembered. 'I didn't know what to make of it all…'

'That sort of thing happens in my life on a daily basis,' I told him. 'Welcome to my world!'

Peggy never drew attention to her Hollywood years – and was the soul of discretion. Regarding her dates with Cary Grant and J.F.K. she remained completely schtum… but she had a warm affection for co-star Victor Mature and became fluttery at the mention of Gary Cooper. Peggy clearly knew a lot of backstage gossip but respected the memory and privacy of her friends.

Occasionally, however, I glimpsed titillating insights. In a play we attended, one character asked another whether

Cary Grant and Randolph Scott had really been an item. In the seat next to me, Peggy gave a hearty guffaw – but offered no other comment.

I discovered from a throwaway remark that MGM mogul Louis B. Mayer had a soft spot for Peggy: 'He called me "Limey".' She challenged 20th Century Fox studio chief Darryl Zanuck over artistic differences. And in 1946, Howard Hughes promised Peggy that he'd whizz over her house on the maiden flight of his new prototype plane. She'd stood in the garden waiting – but Hughes never arrived. He'd spectacularly crashed the plane, which burst into flames, almost killing him.

Harry told me that Peggy had a story about Charlie Chaplin – and that night at dinner, we persuaded her to tell it. Harry mentioned that he'd recently seen the biopic *Chaplin*, which he'd found 'very inspiring'. So, I casually asked Peggy: 'Did you ever know Chaplin?'

She gently looked up from her quiche Lorraine with a nostalgic but modest smile. 'Oh yes,' she said quietly. 'Well…' And there was a tantalising pause before she decided to continue. 'I used to go to eurhythmics classes every week with Ingrid Bergman and Constance Collier…'

My jaw hit the floor. 'Oh my *God!* You knew Constance Collier?' (A renowned Edwardian actress who in 1906 played Cleopatra to Beerbohm Tree's Mark Antony.)

'Ingrid was very good at eurhythmics. Constance was quite grand – but not domineeringly so. You remember how she was…'

I nodded, remembering her flighty film roles.

'I knew Oona O'Neill,' Peggy continued. 'It was before she and Charlie were married. So, one day, Constance said that after class we should drive up to see her and Charlie. He was being hounded by the press for some reason. I can't remember why...'

I did some mental date-shuffling... 'That must have been after the Joan Barry paternity suit!'

'Oh, *yeah!*' cried Harry, his face lighting up, remembering the scandal from the *Chaplin* film.

'So, Charlie didn't want to be seen by the reporters,' Peggy continued, 'and he hid in the boot of my car while I drove away.'

'Did he fit?' Harry asked.

'Oh yes. He was so physical – he could make his body fit into any shape. We also had a conversation about feet. It was quite a strange thing to talk about – but he was right when he said that they're so important for your stance.'

'Was this while he was still in the boot?' Harry asked, wide-eyed.

There was a momentary pause. 'No. He'd got out by then. How many wives did Chaplin have?'

'Four,' I replied.

'Well, that's not bad.'

'Not compared to Rex Harrison's six!'

A discussion ensued about Rex. In *Escape*, opposite Peggy, he played a convict who breaks out of prison. Chatting about his third wife Kay Kendall sparked a memory: 'You know I was supposed to do *Genevieve?*'

'No! Which part?'

'The Dinah Sheridan part. But I got pregnant. And anyway, she was much better than I would have been. Such a shame though, as it's a classic. But it was meant to be me!'

Peggy still regularly received fan mail from around the world, and she read us a letter from a 44-year-old American man. He was serving a fifty-year jail sentence, having murdered his drug dealer. As a reward for good behaviour, he was permitted to watch the Turner Classic Movies channel, where he'd found *Gun Crazy*, *Night of the Demon* and *Hell Drivers*. Of the latter, he asked, 'Did I hear right that your boss called you a slut?' He wanted to see all Peggy's other films too – but she looked up at me and said, 'I'd better not send him a DVD of *Escape*!' We did, however, look through Peggy's bag of photos to find one which she could sign.

After I'd gone, Harry told Peggy that he and I planned to host the hundredth-anniversary screening of *Gun Crazy* at BFI in 2050.

'That's not for years yet!' she cried… but privately, she seemed tickled.

* * *

Things were taking off for Ferris & Milnes. We played West End LIVE in Trafalgar Square, an annual event attended by thousands of musical-theatre fans. Dom and I performed our mash-up celebrating all the musicals in the West End, and the night before the gig – in line with the mentorship – I invited Harry and his friend to watch us rehearse.

They were both there to support us the next day, and I was pleased to have Stiofan in the press pit taking photos (by now he'd changed careers and was a successful photographer). Backstage, standing against the lions of Nelson's Column, we heard the roar of a massive crowd. Now I knew how the Christians felt before entering the arena! In my heightened state, I told Stiofan, 'Pray for me!' – and then remembered he was an atheist.

The medley went down very well – but if anyone had told me a year prior to this that I'd be rocking out songs from *Motown* in Trafalgar Square, I wouldn't have believed them!

In October, Dom and I flew to New York. In yet another act of inspiring generosity, Steve Ross had opened every door in the city for Ferris & Milnes. His name was an instant entrée to the highest echelons of New York's musical society. Steve also introduced us to Jonathan-Bruce King, with whom we instantly clicked. He became our New York manager.

Broadway veterans bent over backwards to help. Sondra Lee – who created the role of Minnie Fay in *Hello, Dolly!* and played Tiger Lily to Mary Martin's Peter Pan – became an instant champion. Richard Seff, the legendary agent who'd discovered Chita Rivera and represented Kander and Ebb, went out of his way to support.

Stephen Sondheim invited us for drinks, and we discovered a mutual love of movies. Steve's knowledge was encyclopedic – and we discussed the films of Peggy Cummins, particularly *Moss Rose*, in which Peggy almost gets murdered by Ethel Barrymore. The moment Dom and I left, I texted Harry: 'I've just been chatting to Sondheim about Gran!'

Steve also let us in on a secret: 'There is going to be a *new* production of *Company*. With a *female* Bobby!'

Our flight home was the same evening that *Sunday in the Park with George* opened at New York City Center starring

Jake Gyllenhaal. Disappointed that we'd miss the show, Steve kindly arranged for us to watch the dress rehearsal.

The older generation was passing the baton to Dom and me. We intended to run with it and do them proud – and then pass it on ourselves...

* * *

Ferris & Milnes Christmas Cracker played Ambassadors Theatre in the West End. Peggy and Harry were there – as were Fenella, Elizabeth, Eileen, J.O.E., Stiofan, James Bentham and so many others I cared about. The most beautiful gesture of all came from Haidee – who arrived at the stage door with yellow roses.

The show featured an ensemble of BA Musical Theatre students from ArtsEd Schools. Inspired by old-time TV Christmas specials, Act One took place in Martin's Living Room. The students played rapping carol singers who invaded my house. In the process, Dominic and Martin (for we played heightened versions of ourselves) taught the youngsters about the great stars of the past: 'Vitality' from *Gay's the Word* segued into a major production number for the whole company, 'Broadway Rhythm'.

In rehearsals, life reflected art. Two of the students, Alex and Eleanor, asked me for advice about *Private Lives*, their project for acting class. I sent them the timeless recording of Noël Coward and Gertrude Lawrence performing the 'very flat, Norfolk' scene – they were grateful and thrilled to be exposed to something they'd never heard.

Student Tom Hopcroft loved G&S and had played The Pirate King... so in the show, I turned his rapping carol singer into a G&S convert, running off with Martin's enormous tome *The Gilbert and Sullivan Book*. In a rehearsal break, I found Tom quietly sitting in a corner on the floor – actually reading the book!

Harry, meanwhile, continued to work hard. He rehearsed scenes with Gran – although some of what his college acting tutors preached seemed to her somewhat highfalutin.

'So,' Harry told her, 'this is where I have to slow down and think of my inner tempo and the motivation and…'

'Can't you just say the line?' Peggy asked, perplexed. In her films, Peggy's acting was always straightforward, truthful and honest. And no matter how bad the actual written dialogue, she always put across the *meaning* of the line!

In October 2017 Dom and I returned to New York. We premiered a Gershwin mash-up in a concert at the Lincoln Center. A Broadway 'Angel', Jeffrey Lawrence, then arranged a private audition for us with a Broadway producer. At the historic Coffee House Club, we performed our mash-up for him on a piano once played by George Gershwin himself.

'Okay,' the producer nodded. 'Okay!' Then he turned to Jonathan and announced, 'I wanna be part of the process to bring these guys to Broadway.' And just a few hours later, Steve Ross arranged for us to perform for Mel Brooks – who, after watching the medley, ran up and hugged us in front of a large audience.

In November we performed at The Friars Club, followed by a showcase for more Broadway producers. And in December we entertained The Broadway Association (theatre owners and producers) during their Christmas lunch at the legendary Sardi's Restaurant – where in 1955 Nanny Jean had been applauded upon arrival by New York's elite after she'd opened in *The Boy Friend*.

Back home, Peggy was rooting for us and couldn't have been more excited. We spoke on the phone and arranged to meet upon my return, just in time for Christmas.

Two days after Sardi's we had another private producers' showcase. But early that morning, I awoke to a text from Harry asking if he could call…

Peggy had suffered a major stroke. Only the night before she'd been her normal, happy, jolly self, pinching Harry's phone to speak on FaceTime to his friend. The news hit me like a tonne of bricks. At ninety-one, Peggy had shown every sign of going on for years. With Ginny there'd been time to emotionally adjust, as her decline was gradual. But Peggy had still been catching tubes and driving her car, looking towards a vibrant future.

I bawled my eyes out but then pulled myself together – Dom and I had a show to do – and Peggy would expect utter professionalism. I wondered whether I should cut my evocative ballad 'I'll Be Seeing You'… but went ahead and sang it for Peggy; in my blazer pocket I wore the silk handkerchief she'd given me for Christmas.

The showcase was a success. Afterwards I was approached by a producer who offered me a lead role in the workshop of his new Broadway musical. I think Peggy would have been pleased.

Peggy Cummins – a great lady and a great star – quietly slipped away on 29 December 2017, shortly after her ninety-second birthday. Austin, Elizabeth and I travelled to the church where Peggy was laid to rest alongside her husband. Harry read a beautiful tribute. Gran would have been proud.

In September 2018, Harry commenced his studies at the terrific London School of Musical Theatre. I even got to play a small role in his training as a guest lecturer in the history of musical theatre.

Once again, I told the students about the stars whom I'd been privileged to know – and they listened with rapt attention. I spoke about Peggy Cummins – and asked the youngsters to always remember what she'd said about those who've helped you along the way: 'You can never say thank you enough…'

CHAPTER THIRTY-TWO

'Nothing could possibly be more satisfactory!'

The Mikado

My thirty-second birthday at Freedom in Soho was a blast. I'd finally learned to love my birthday as much as Ginny had loved hers! Stiofan kept Prosecco flowing whilst I boogied with my *Christmas Cracker* friends Ollie and Charlie, as well as Simon and Maison, graduates from that same musical theatre course.

Now that they've launched their careers, I make myself available to chat or advise should they wish. Anna Neagle told Elizabeth that when she started out, no one looked after her. At Thursford and in my other early jobs, I fortunately met people who cared. Now I can give back. I know my young friends are grateful, but I tell them, 'You can thank me by doing the same for someone else in the future.'

The staff of the RAF Club know that Mr Milnes always brings guests. It's a convenient and quiet place to chat – and I've found that history works best when it's relatable. I take young friends into the Churchill Bar and point out the portrait of Lord Trenchard, founder of the Royal Air Force. Then I take out my phone and show them a photo of Trenchard with Lenny, just after the Berlin Airlift.

Suddenly, the man in the portrait has become real – and my guest is talking to a friend (me) who knew someone (Lenny) who knew him (Trenchard). Then I show them a photo of Lenny and me at the flat. You're only a few handshakes away from anyone in history.

I also tell them about the Battle of Britain Memorial Trust. It does surprise me how many young people don't know about the Battle of Britain – it seems to be missing from some schools' curriculums. Therefore, the work of BBMT becomes ever more important...

To mark the seventy-fifth anniversary of the Battle of Britain in 2015, the Trust invited Her Majesty the Queen and HRH the Duke of Edinburgh to open The Wing – an interactive learning centre at the National Memorial to the Few in Capel-le-Ferne. In the Scramble Experience, visitors stand amidst a digitally recreated Battle of Britain. For millennials, the Battle is now tangible. The Few said that the Scramble Experience is the most realistic interpretation of the Battle that exists. Patrick and Janet Tootal, plus the trustees and volunteers, do a first-class job.

For the seventy-fifth anniversary, stops were pulled out nationwide – the last major celebrations which a core of veterans were able to attend. It was humbling to escort them down the aisle of Westminster Abbey after that year's thanksgiving service. The crowded Abbey burst into a spontaneous, heartfelt ovation. People wept as The Few walked past. As I write this, I have a framed photograph of six of them above my desk, taken at the Abbey that day.

Wing Commander Paul Farnes is 101 at the time of writing – the last ace from the Battle of Britain. Paul is quite a character. He flew Hurricanes, and in no uncertain terms tells TV reporters he gets 'fed up' when people only talk about Spitfires!

For a royal dinner at RAF Northolt my job was to escort Geoffrey Wellum; after a flypast he galloped towards the Spitfires. He relished the sound of that Merlin engine! I had to get Geoffrey back inside to be received by the Duke of Kent, but he kept saying, 'No, you're not taking me away yet!' What could I do? I let him enjoy his moment.

Geoffrey said, 'The Battle of Britain made me want to put a value on life. I decided that if I survived, I wanted to be allowed to relish it. Now I have a life of deep tranquillity.'

That was true of all The Few... but they still enjoyed a knees-up. Flying Officer Ken Wilkinson reprimanded Prince William for 'flying choppers instead of proper aeroplanes'. When Ken was guest of honour for a concert at Symphony Hall in Birmingham, Nanny Jean and I went with him. Ken's eyesight was very weak, but he heard the applause that erupted when his presence was announced. He was absolutely stunned, especially when I told him, 'They're all standing for you, Ken!' Afterwards, he was inundated by people asking to shake his hand and say thank you.

Back at Nanny Jean's, we put on a Jack Buchanan CD. Ken sang a hearty chorus of 'Everything Stops for Tea' – and later, word perfect, 'The Nightmare Song' from *Iolanthe*. Ken was witty and youthful in spirit – yet harrowing memories of 1940 remained clear. 'I was one of the lucky ones. I saw friends fall out of the sky; aircraft go up in flames... terrible things.'

Remembering The Few puts theatre-career woes into perspective. Whatever happens, I don't lose sleep. I'm hardly going through the experiences of Paul, Geoffrey and Ken. Or indeed Lenny.

Thanks to Austin and Howard I met 1930s child star Hazel Ascot and her husband Peter Banting – a former pathfinder with Bomber Command. Now in his mid-nineties, Peter is a whizz with iPads and the latest Apple technology!

'I must tell you, Martin,' Peter said, 'it was a real privilege to be the generation which lived through the war. There was a unifying spirit and united front. The entire country was a family. Complete strangers cared about each other.'

Would that we'd kept that esprit de corps. And if I'm lucky enough to reach my nineties I hope I'm half as content as Hazel and Peter. Hazel was a champion tap dancer. Her father Duggie ran a dance school on the top two floors of the building which is now Foyles on Charing Cross Road; the family lived in an apartment there. In 1937 director John Baxter dropped by, scouting rehearsal rooms for a proposed film entitled *Music Hall*. He discovered Hazel dancing – and then rewrote the movie as *Talking Feet*, a vehicle for her talents.

In 1943 Hazel was in *Magic Carpet* at what is now the Shaftesbury Theatre. She shared a dressing room with the dazzling Kay Kendall and her knockout elder sister, Kim. Hazel wasn't old enough to join them dancing with serviceman at the Stage Door Canteen – about which Kay teased her mercilessly – but when air raids prevented Hazel from reaching home in Brixton, the Kendall girls sheltered her at their digs on St Martin's Lane. Over seventy years later, Howard reconnected a delighted Hazel with Florida-based Kim Kendall via email!

Up the road from *Magic Carpet*, Peggy played in *Junior Miss* at the Saville Theatre. Doodlebugs whistled over, but on stage she continued regardless. In 2018, working at ArtsEd, I brought Eileen Page in to meet the students. She told them about training at RADA during the Blitz; then I informed the students that next month, Eileen, age ninety-two, was performing her one-woman play about Eleanor of Aquitaine! Eileen doesn't stop. The students should aspire to her work ethic – and they do. They emailed thanking me for bringing Eileen in.

I call it Passing the Baton – and I refer to it in all my drama-school lectures. But this phrase doesn't just refer to knowledge. Generosity – both personal and professional – should be passed on too…

Steve Clark was one half of the black American tap act the Clark Brothers. They spent eight decades on stage, TV and film, including working for Al Capone in his Chicago club. Mobster Frank Costello asked the brothers to open his new venture, the Sands Hotel, when Las Vegas was just 'a one-horse town'. I felt honoured when Steve invited me to spend his ninety-first birthday with him. He encouraged my dreams, passed on his wisdom and reminisced about friends and colleagues – Tallulah Bankhead, Gypsy Rose Lee, Bill 'Bojangles' Robinson and his own cousin, Sammy Davis Jr. I looked up to Steve Clark. His kindness was an inspiration I shall not forget.

Professionally, my recent career has benefited from the invaluable support of Gyles Brandreth and Russell Grant. Each of them, respectively, opened doors with regards to my two current writing projects. Russ's recommendation of my work has led to something extremely exciting. Gyles' mentorship on a separate project has been second-to-none. Thanks to him, I found myself in Leslie Bricusse's penthouse being advised by the Oscar-winning songwriter about my latest piece.

The older generation likes to give back. Stephen Sondheim found time to pick up the phone and welcome two Englishmen to New York: 'If you need any help or advice don't hesitate, just give me a call.' And then there's Steve Ross. He's changed my life in ways I can never repay... but I try, doing for others what he's done for me.

Sometimes opportunities to say thank you arise unexpectedly. Bruce Graham was the first cast member to sign up for both my sitcom pilot and *The Grand Duke*. His involvement convinced others to come onboard – and those projects furthered my career. A few years later, in 2016, Dom and I had a meeting with Bill Deamer about *Christmas Cracker*. Bill – the choreographer for *Follies* at the National Theatre – came to us direct from auditions.

'We're struggling to find a Roscoe,' he told us. 'We can't find anyone with that proper D'Oyly Carte sound.'

'Well, you need Bruce Graham,' I told him. 'He's original D'Oyly Carte and sings up a storm.' They called him in to audition. Bruce's talent did the rest. Every night his rendition of 'Beautiful Girls' blew the roof off the National.

* * *

I've travelled an interesting pathway. But I'd be nowhere without the love and support of two very special people – my parents, Alan and Pauline. As a child I acted along with G&S videos in the lounge, dressed up as Aline in

The Sorcerer. They didn't bat an eyelid. They drove me to rehearsals up to four nights a week for am-dram shows and ensured that I never missed an opportunity. When the drama schools turned me down, not once did they attempt to dissuade me from forging my own way, and even though my profession entails living on a knife-edge, they're yet to ask, 'So when are you going to get a proper job?'

Some kids bring home an endless procession of boyfriends and girlfriends. I've presented Mum and Dad with a steady stream of elderly film stars and war heroes!

There'd be no story to tell if it wasn't for my parents.

My rock has also been Stiofan O'Doherty. Safe to say we've seen each other through rather a lot. How we giggle! He's met almost all my actress friends – he even took Eileen's headshots.

Nanny Jean rarely comes to London, but one time I took her to meet Stiofan at The Yard, a gay bar in Soho. Bag checks are obligatory, but this glamorous octogenarian so dazzled the bouncers they just gaped and let us pass. Pop hits blared in the background. Nanny Jean asked Stiofan, 'Is this music?'

Sadly, Stiofan never met the veteran I think he'd have adored most. Maggie Rennie was last of the original Windmill Theatre girls who 'never clothed' during the war... or, to quote an anonymous wit, 'Never was so much shown by so few to so many.' If you've seen the film *Mrs Henderson Presents*, that was Maggie's era.

The Windmill is now a table-dancing club. Once, I rang her as I walked past: 'I just wanted to say hello as I'm outside the Windmill.'

'What you doin' *outside*?' she demanded. 'Get *inside!*'

These days whenever I pass the Windmill I look up to the roof and blow Maggie a kiss. She used to fire-watch up there, taking turns with theatre manager Vivian Van Damm. When bombs desecrated Great Windmill Street, she searched the rubble looking for their seventeen-year-old apprentice electrician, Peter. He'd been killed outright. If only twenty-first-century party-goers stumbling up Great Windmill Street knew that.

Firebombs hit nearby stables – Maggie and another Windmill girl ran inside and rescued six terrified horses. Triumphant, they took 'our little rodeo' around Piccadilly Circus singing 'I've Got Sixpence', but another explosion scattered the horses. They eventually rounded them up and arrived at Vine Street Police Station. Van Damm received a phone call: 'We've got two of your Windmill girls here.'

'Why?' the boss replied. 'What have they done?'

I'd take 97-year-old Maggie out for lunch – and was propositioned every time. She was a man's woman, and whilst married to actor Michael Rennie had enjoyed quite a time in Hollywood.

'Danny Kaye – 'e was good, darlin' – if you know what I mean. I looked at 'im. 'E looked at me. It didn't take us long to 'ave a drink and get at it!'

Another time: 'Ever 'eard of an actor called Hugh Marlowe? I 'ad an affair with 'im for two years.' (Movie buffs may remember Marlowe as the playwright in *All About Eve.*)

And tantalisingly: 'Marlene Dietrich made me an offer, but I can't remember now if I took it.'

Her best friend was Elizabeth Taylor. Maggie told

Taylor that she'd slept with her ex-husband Michael Wilding. 'Honey!' Taylor cried within earshot of Burton. 'Wasn't he the *best?*' When Maggie fell on hard times, Taylor and Burton put her son through school; years later, Elizabeth paid for Maggie's stairlift. After Taylor died, Maggie wanted to return her friend's kindness. Elizabeth had once given her an exquisite – and very expensive – piece of jewellery. Now in her nineties, Maggie had no need of it. The jewellery paid for another child's education.

'When we arrived in Hollywood,' she told me, 'Tyrone Power and Linda Christian threw us a welcome party…' Maggie's dress reflected austerity Britain; Christian whisked her upstairs and Maggie re-emerged in a gown with a mink-lined bosom. She was very well-endowed, so Maggie's breasts entered the room several seconds before Maggie.

'Christ almighty!' Bogart cried. 'Who's the dame with the mink tits?'

In old age, having a young friend seemed to make a difference. Once the laughter ceased, Maggie asked me quietly, 'Why are you so nice to me?'

'Because I love you,' I replied. And when I showed Maggie a 1938 photo which I'd found of her at the Windmill, her eyes filled with tears. But she couldn't be serious for long.

''Ere!' she yelled at a waiter, waving the photo. 'Do you wanna see a vision of loveliness?'

I told Maggie about Stiofan. She asked if we'd ever been an item – we hadn't. Besides our being best friends, Stiofan had a strong preference for black men; his current boyfriend reflected this trend. Maggie's jaw dropped.

'I've *never*'ad a black cock! Let me ask 'im what it's like!'

She left Stiofan a voicemail in ladylike tones: 'We have not yet met – we *will* one day because there's one thing in my life – rather a long one – I've never had a black you-know-what. I understand your boyfriend's is pretty good. Take care.'

It was the last time I saw her. Maggie passed away before she could quiz Stiofan. But I received a final phone call whilst I was on the Tube: ''Ere, darlin'! Turn on Channel 4! Hugh Marlowe's on the telly!'

How I miss Maggie… and how I miss Fenella. 'England's first lady of the double entendre' passed away in September 2018 – with her eyelashes on! She went out on a high… so popular was her audio memoir *Do You Mind If I Smoke?* that it went into print and became a bestseller. A few months before she died, Fenella learned she'd been awarded the OBE. I emailed my congratulations.

'Oh, honey,' she replied. 'I can't believe it – it's all a dream. Much love, Fenella.' An hour and a half later, she replied again. 'Martin, how lovely of you. Thanks. Wow! Yes, I think wow's more appropriate. Much love, Fenella.' Then three minutes after that came yet another email, with the entire message written in the title bar!

These memories make me happy. It's just a shame that my eventual partner won't have known my late friends – especially Ginny and Lenny.

A piece of my heart will forever belong to a very beautiful soul I met some time ago, just after my last Thursford. He was nothing to do with the theatrical industry. Sadly, it couldn't work out between us for reasons beyond our control. But today he's still very much a part of my life. Our friendship is unshakeable.

Dating in my profession can be very difficult. I've tried the apps – and fallen into the common trap of getting overexcited by promising conversations in digital ether.

'This guy's incredible!' I told Stiofan. 'I think you'd really like him!'

'Well,' he replied, raising an eyebrow. 'I'd say I'll reserve judgement until I've met him. But I think I'll reserve judgement until *you've* met him!'

In other ways, though, technology is brilliant. On Instagram I run an account which celebrates Old Hollywood and musical theatre: birthdays, stories, anniversaries. And now from around the world, the oldest of souls have connected by the most current social media…

There's Eddie Andrews, a young actor based in Kansas City, Missouri, whom I told about Ivor Novello. He listened to 'My Dearest Dear' and is now a Novello acolyte. Like me, Eddie grew up quoting 1930s movie dialogue. We truly understand one another.

Nicholas Inglis in Brisbane is known as 'The Vintage Costume Collector'. He owns hundreds of cinematic treasures ranging from Theda Bara's 1917 beaded bodice to Yul Brynner's cape from *The Ten Commandments*. From Debbie Reynolds, Nick bought a red velvet dress worn by Peggy in the unfinished *Forever Amber*. We have a hoot across our different time zones.

And then there's the remarkable Arthur Clayton Smith in Mexico City. Art proudly claims to be the world's youngest expert on the films of Jeanette MacDonald and Nelson Eddy – quoting entire scenes verbatim. To commemorate the ninetieth anniversary of MGM's *The Broadway Melody*, he put on a tuxedo (onto which he'd sewn a home-made *Broadway Melody* badge) and walked into school singing the title song.

I wish I'd had these friends growing up. I'd have known I wasn't alone. Old souls of the world: take heart! We've been born into a new era to maintain the old standards.

I intend to go through life passing the baton. To quote Mr Gilbert, 'Life's a pudding full of plums.' And I look forward to tomorrow. For as they say in the movies…

'Tomorrow is another day…'

'Where is she now?'

Princess Ida

At the time of writing…

Jean Bayless is still thriving, looking after five grand-daughters, four dogs and a cat named Moses. Photos of Nanny Jean, Martin and Fenella can be spied on a mirror at Roberts Jewellers on Corporation Street, Birmingham. The 'children' from *The Sound of Music* – George, Barbara and Fiona – visit annually.

Elizabeth Seal maintains the archive of her late husband, the photographer Michael Ward, organising exhibitions of his work and overseeing photographic sales. She still performs and regularly visits family in Italy, France and the United States, several of whom are in the entertainment industry. Elizabeth is currently writing a memoir about the many aspects of her remarkable life and career.

Eileen Page won Best Performance by an Actress at the 2019 New York International Radio Festival Awards for her recording of *Eleanor of Aquitaine: Mother of the Pride*.

Martin Milnes

Her one-woman show about Ellen Terry was revived in London just a week before Eileen turned ninety-three.

Steve Ross – 'the crown prince of New York cabaret' – constantly tours the world and gives frequent master-classes to young performers. www.steveross.net

Ann Wakefield resides in Los Angeles, still dancing the Charleston.

Hazel Ascot and Peter Banting enjoy a restful retire-ment not far from Shepperton Studios where Hazel made *Talking Feet* (1937) and *Stepping Toes* (1938). The award-winning documentary short film *Out of the Blue* (2018) explores Hazel and Peter's lives and careers.

Alan Curtis maintains his Chiswick residence where the Palladium panto plaques are displayed with pride.

The films of Peggy Cummins are often screened at the National Film Theatre, BFI Southbank – an organisation whose work she always championed.

Harry Dunnett graduated from London School of Musical Theatre in 2019. Later that year, age twenty-one, he made his professional debut in the West End pro-duction of *Les Misérables* at the newly named Sondheim Theatre on Shaftesbury Avenue. The Sondheim Theatre is next door to the Gielgud Theatre where Martin made his West End debut in 2008, age twenty-one. The Sondheim is also a stone's throw from the Palace Theatre where in

1944 Peggy played the title role in *Alice in Wonderland*. Harry's opening night in *Les Mis* was 18 December – Peggy's birthday! Eighty-one years previously – on her thirteenth birthday – Peggy made her own West End debut in a children's revue entitled *Let's Pretend*. The baton continues to be passed.

Stiofan O'Doherty is one of London's leading portrait photographers. www.samuelblackphotography.co.uk

A screenplay is in development for the film version of *I Used to Be in Pictures*, bringing the fascinating story of Austin and Howard Mutti-Mewse to an even wider audience. www.muttimewse.com

John Owen Edwards' orchestrations for various musicals are used worldwide. He adjudicates at international music festivals.

The Battle of Britain Memorial Trust welcomes visitors all year round at the National Memorial to the Few on the clifftops at Capel-le-Ferne, Folkestone. The Scramble Experience at The Wing educates all ages about the events of 1940. The public is welcome to attend the annual Memorial Day commemoration each July. www.battleofbritainmemorial.org

The Thursford *Christmas Spectacular* is going strong after more than forty years, artistically devised and directed by its founder, John Cushing. Cast Manager Colin Window continues to look after a new generation of singers, dancers and musicians. Min remains at his post backstage. If you haven't seen the show, you are guaranteed a theatrical experience you will never forget. www.thursford.com

George Fay passed away in 2015. Betty lives in a residential home on the North Norfolk coast. The birds are now trained by George and Betty's great friend and former assistant David Sherwood.

Tracy and Bobot live with their daughter Viel in the Philippines where they run their successful business – Beans and Bubbles Laundry Shop.

Sarah Simmons works in London as a freelance voice and dialogue coach.

Jacob Kenedy, the grandson of Virginia Campbell, has created a beautiful tribute to Ginny at Plaquemine Lock, his Louisiana-themed pub-restaurant in Islington (www. plaqlock.com). The pub is named after the Lock which Ginny's mother – Carrie Beth Schwing – opened in 1909. The Lock allowed passage for boats through Bayou Plaquemine onto the Mississippi; the first boat to pass through was the *Carrie B. Schwing*, named in Carrie's honour by the Schwing Lumber & Shingle Company. At Jacob's pub, Haidee Becker has painted a mural depicting Lenny at the helm of the *Carrie B. Schwing* as she sails up the Mississippi. Ginny and Lenny can also be seen in the painting walking towards the entrance of the pub – no doubt to enjoy a glass of wine!

And should diners at the pub wish to play Posso, a card table is available with instructions engraved on the wall. You start with two 'threes of a kind'...

ACKNOWLEDGEMENTS

'With the gratifying feeling that our duty has been done!'

The Gondoliers

I extend my heartfelt thanks to...

My parents, Alan and Pauline Milnes, for always going above and beyond the call of duty.

Diane Shelley, to whom I owe enormous gratitude for her invaluable ongoing support.

Stiofan O'Doherty, for his friendship, hospitality and listening to chapters in development.

Charles Duff, whose constant encouragement has meant so much.

Peter E. Jones, for his greatly appreciated feedback via transatlantic emails.

Tom Perrin of Zuleika, at whose suggestion *Wild Card* was written. Thank you for your belief, guidance and the opportunity to preserve these stories. As Lenny would say – 'The strongest memory is weaker than the palest ink.' Also, to George Tomsett for his assistance throughout.

Austin Mutti-Mewse and Howard Mutti-Mewse, whose friendship helped shape this tale.

Group Captain Patrick Tootal OBE and Mrs Janet Tootal BEM of the Battle of Britain Memorial Trust, as well as the trustees, volunteers and the staff of the Royal Air Force Club.

Gyles Brandreth, for his tireless support.

Penrose Halson, for her greatly appreciated advice.

Samuel Black Photography and Sutherland Rowe Photography.

Overtures, The Bunnett-Muir Musical Theatre Archive Trust.

To the families of my friends: Haidee Becker – with thanks for everything; Richard Campbell Becker, Jacob Kenedy, Rachel Kenedy, Diane Lambert, Timothy and Maya Lambert, Jay and Kari McDowell, and Clive Sinclair. Also, to those close to Ginny and Lenny including the lovely Virgie, Rhoda Billingsly, Tracy Boston-Nacanaynay, Mary Camacho, Adrian Cook, Alfred Di Rocco, Jack and Liz

Lambert, Patrícia Mahoney, Frederick and Constanza Muller, Platino N. Nacanaynay Jr, Sarah Simmons, Piers Talalla, Henry Talalla and Freddie Talalla.

David and Deborah Dunnett, with very special thanks to Harry Dunnett.

Daniel and Jennifer Johnson, Adam Johnson, and the family and many friends of Jean Bayless.

For listening to my stories and passing the baton: Jay Albray, Loren Anderson, Joseph Annetts, Jacob Bailey, Tom Barber, Josh Barnett, Pearce Barron, James Batty, James Buchanan, Josh Clemetson, Ollie Corbett, Russell Dickson, Charlie Ellerton, James Gower-Smith, Gabriel Hampton-Saint, Ben James, Ben Jolly, Lauren Jones, Maison Kelley, Josh Kemp, Freddie King, Chester Lawrence, Tom Lloyd, Kieran Lynch, Grace McInerny, Ben MacSkimming, Marianna Macari-Ferris, James Moore, Nic Myers, Lorenzo Olivera, Simon Oskarsson, Verity Power, Jake Samson, Lily Shires, Amie Shouler, Will Silver, Adam George Smith, Joe Thomas, Chris Vince, Anna Watson, Shane Whitely, Henry Young and the student cast of *Side by Side by Sondheim*.

For the opportunities, guidance and inspiration: David Charles Abell, James Albrecht, Stuart Barr, Poppy Ben David, Julian Bird, Rexton Bunnett, Ian Burford, Simon Butteriss, Kay Carman, Susie Caulcutt, Alison Chapman, Lynne Chapman, Barry Clark, Sheila Clift, Sir Michael Codron, Lesley Cox, Emma de Souza, Bill Deamer, Alison

Duguid, Bert Fink, Bill Halson, Jean Dudley Hardy, Jan Hunt, Bruce Graham, Russell Grant, Matt Hawksworth, John Howells, Adrian Jeckells, Gareth Jones, Mike Leigh, Ruth Leon, Alastair Lindsey-Renton, Alistair McGowan, Gareth McLeod, Neil McPherson, Celia Mackay, Tom Miller, Cynthia Morey, Richard Morris, Peter Mulloy, The New Actors Company, Paul Nicholas, Charlotte Page, Doug Pinchin, Gavin Prime, Mitch Sebastian, The Stephen Sondheim Society, Richard Stirling, Ben Stock, Zita Syme, Melvyn Tarran and Gareth Valentine.

And in New York: Ted Chapin, Michael Colby, Merrie L. Davis, Ella Dawson, Shana Farr, John and Eleanor R. Goldhar, Jeff Harnar, Mary Holloway, John C. Introcaso, Denis Jones, Simon Jones, Jonathan-Bruce King, Jeffrey Lawrence, Sondra Lee, Andrea Marcovicci, Sharon Rich, Neal Rubinstein, Seth Rudetsky, Richard Seff, Malini Singh McDonald, Stephen Sondheim, John J. Todd and Lawrence S. Toppall.

For the Thursford Years: Emily Allen, Patrick Bailey, Arrogant Beaver, Helena Biggs, Anthony Boon, Evelyn Borthwick, Steve Brodie, Nelly at The Bull, Emma Clare, Lesley Clarke, Helen Clough, O.B. and Mandy at The Crawfish Inn, Karen Cull, Mark Cunningham, Barbara Cushing, John Cushing OBE, Sallie Dalzell, Tammy Davies, Ann Day, John Derekson, Chris Goody, Steve Hewlett, Ed and Katherine Hopkins, Wyn Hyland, Phil Kelsall MBE, Derek and Mary Lee, Philip Lee, John Linley, Keith Loads, Linda Martin, June Mears, Patrick Mundy, Ben Newhouse-Smith, Camilla Rockley, Duncan

Sandilands, Mike and Anne Savage, David Sherwood, Jonathan Smith, Michele Thorne, Sarah Vaughan, Mary Visser, Ian Wilson-Pope and Colin Window.

And finally, for their great friendship and support: Eddie Andrews, Jacob Backhouse, Matt Bartlett, James Benn, James Bentham, Anne Binnington, Charlie Booker, Franz Budny, Daniel Cane, Alex Cardall, Tara Cimino, Jon Clayton, Dominic Ferris, Roger Ferris, Max Fulham, Lee Greenaway, Shem Hamilton, Eleanor Hodgkiss, Allie Hollins, Tess Hollins, Tom Hopcroft, Nicholas Inglis, Cheryl Kennedy, Rudi Last, Joanna Lee, Ted McMillan, Glo Macari, Brendan Matthew, Dillon May, Luke Meadows, Lawrence Michalowski, Freda Milnes, Colm Molloy, Hugo Montgomery, Guy and Ruthie Mott, Sue Norgate, George Rae, Robin Rayner, Ed and Emma Saklatvala, Ian Savage, Alex Simpson, Arthur Clayton Smith, Mark and Gemma Stewart, James Stirling, Ros Swetman, Elsie Szuster, Martin Tailby, Ryan Taylor, Wes and Lindsay Thomson, Liam Tiesteel, Kevin Trainor, Rodney Vubya, Eleanor Walsh, Pam Waring, Phil and Elen Môn Wayne, Hannah Wayne, Steffan Wayne, Rob Wilkes, Sandra Wilkinson, Elliott Wooster, Cristian Zaccarini and Ed Zanders.

Martin Milnes is a London based actor, writer and theatre director. As musical theatre duo Ferris & Milnes, he has played Theatre Royal Drury Lane, New York's Lincoln Center, Ambassadors Theatre and at West End LIVE. Martin directed the first professional revival and re-discovery of Gilbert & Sullivan's final work *The Grand Duke* and collaborates regularly with the Battle of Britain Memorial Trust, preserving the legacy of The Few.

Also a lecturer in Musical Theatre and Film History, Martin's Instagram 'Story A Day' about Broadway and Hollywood birthdays, anniversaries and anecdotes can be followed @martinmilnes

www.martinmilnes.com